ULURU–KATA TJUTA
& WATARRKA

ABOUT THE AUTHOR

Dr Anne Kerle is a consultant biologist who lived in Alice Springs for 14 years. After arriving there in 1982, she quickly became enchanted by the remarkable arid country of Central Australia, and fascinated by its ecological processes. Her work is directed towards enhancing our knowledge of the country to manage the land more effectively for conservation, and her research subjects have ranged from possums to ants. She has been a member of the Territory Parks and Wildlife Advisory Council to the Conservation Commission of the Northern Territory. For her, there is no greater delight than camping 'out bush' under the blanket of stars in Central Australia with her husband and two daughters.

ABOUT THE SERIES EDITOR

The Series Editor of the National Park Field Guides, Tony Lee, is a director of Australis, a leading nature-based tour company. He is currently Convenor of Victoria's National Parks Advisory Council and Reference Areas Advisory Committee, and serves on the committee of the Victorian Tourism Operators Association. Formerly Tony was Associate Professor of Zoology at Monash University, where he researched the life histories and social behaviour of marsupials. He has written or co-authored four books including the popular *The Koala, A Natural History*, also published by UNSW Press.

UNSW
PRESS

NATIONAL PARKS FIELD GUIDES

ULURU

KATA TJUTA & WATARRKA

AYERS ROCK/THE OLGAS & KINGS CANYON

NORTHERN TERRITORY

ANNE KERLE

SERIES EDITOR
TONY LEE

A UNSW Press book
Published by
University of New South Wales Press Ltd
UNSW SYDNEY NSW 2052
AUSTRALIA
www.unswpress.edu.au

First published 1995
Reprinted 1998, 2000, 2002, 2005, 2006, 2008, 2011

National Library of Australia
Cataloguing-in-Publication entry:

Kerle, J. Anne (Jean Anne).
    Uluru — Kata Tjuta & Watarrka — Ayers Rock/the Olgas & Kings Canyon, Northern Territory.

    Bibliography.
    Includes index.
    ISBN 0 86840 055 6.

    1. Natural history – Northern Territory.
    2. Aborigines, Australian – Northern Territory.
    3. Uluru National Park (N.T.) – Guidebooks.
    4. Watarrka National Park (N.T.) – Guidebooks.
    I. Title. II. Title: Ayers Rock, the Olgas & Kings Canyon. (Series: National parks field guides).

919.4291

Series design Di Quick
Text layout Karolyn Doherty
Maps DiZign (pp. vi, vii, 81, 137, 138, 165, 171 & 176)
Printer Everbest, China

Previous pages, photographs:
Page i The rock-dwelling fat-tailed antechinus *K.A. Johnson*
Pages ii–iii A marsupial mole leaves its track across a sand dune *M.W. Gillam*

CONTENTS

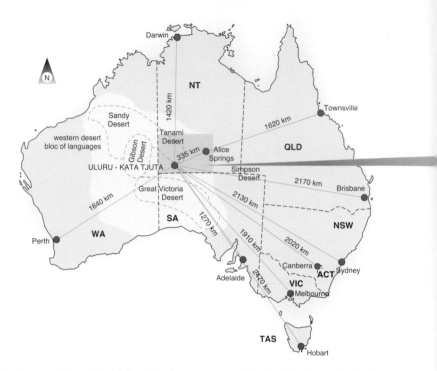

The 'western desert bloc' (above) is the area covered by Aboriginal people who have language and kinship affinities with the Yankunytjatjara, Pitjantjatjara and Luritja people of Central Australia. The alignment of Kata Tjuta, Uluru and Atila (Mount Conner) is evident on the map of central Australia.

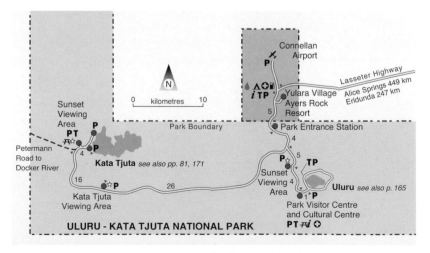

TJUTA AND WATARRKA NATIONAL PARKS

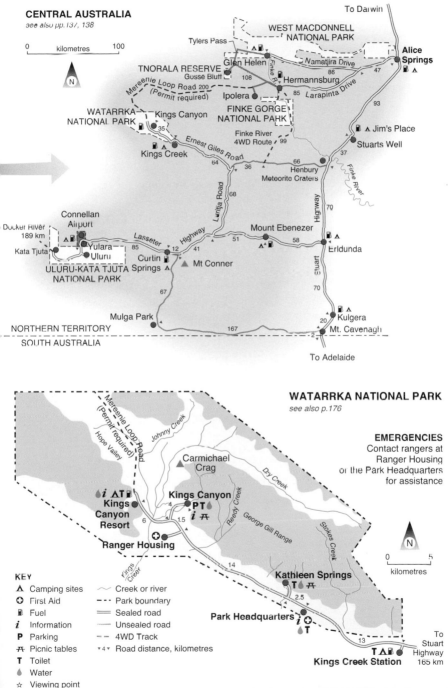

CENTRAL AUSTRALIA
see also pp.137, 138

0 — kilometres — 100

To Darwin

WEST MACDONNELL NATIONAL PARK

Alice Springs

Tylers Pass

Glen Helen
Gosse Bluff
TNORALA RESERVE
Namatjira Drive 86 47
Hermannsburg
108
85 Larapinta Drive
Ipolera
Mereenie Loop Road 200
(Permit required)
FINKE GORGE NATIONAL PARK
93

WATARRKA NATIONAL PARK
Kings Canyon
35
Finke River 4WD Route 99
Jim's Place
Stuarts Well

Ernest Giles Road
Kings Creek
64 36
66 37
Henbury Meteorite Craters

Finke River

Luritja Road
68
70

Connellan Airport
Docker River 189 km
Lasseter Highway 85 12 41 51
Mount Ebenezer 58
Erldunda

Kata Tjuta
Yulara
Uluru
Curtin Springs
Mt Conner
ULURU-KATA TJUTA NATIONAL PARK

Stuart Highway

67
70

Mulga Park
20 Kulgera
Mt. Cavenagh

NORTHERN TERRITORY
167
2
SOUTH AUSTRALIA

To Adelaide

WATARRKA NATIONAL PARK
see also p.176

EMERGENCIES
Contact rangers at
Ranger Housing
or the Park Headquarters
for assistance

Mereenie Loop Road
(Permit required)
Hope Valley
Johnny Creek

Carmichael Crag

Dry Creek

Kings Canyon Resort
i ⚕ T
Kings Canyon
4
P T
i ⍭
6
1.5
Ranger Housing
Kings Creek
Reedy Creek
George Gill Range
Stokes Creek

14
Kathleen Springs
T ⬤ ⍭
2.5

Park Headquarters
i ⬤
T

13
T ⬤
Kings Creek Station

To Stuart Highway
165 km

0 — kilometres — 5

KEY
- ⬤ Camping sites
- ⊕ First Aid
- ⬛ Fuel
- *i* Information
- P Parking
- ⍭ Picnic tables
- T Toilet
- ⬤ Water
- ☆ Viewing point

- ∼ Creek or river
- - - - Park boundary
- ═══ Sealed road
- ——— Unsealed road
- — — 4WD Track
- ▾4▾ Road distance, kilometres

ACKNOWLEDGEMENTS

Many people have given me assistance and encouragement in the writing of this field guide.

I am indebted to my colleagues in Alice Springs for freely giving me their time in providing information and checking the accuracy of the manuscript. In particular I wish to thank Mike Fleming, Jon Willis, Gresley Wakelin-King, Peter Latz, Steve Morton, Dick Kimber, Jim Cotterill, Mike Gillam, Gerry Gerard and Greg Fyfe. Suzanne Hamilton provided a remarkably rapid and accurate word-processing service and Mike Fleming supplied many necessary computer skills. Wendy Dabourne valiantly read the entire manuscript as an 'interested visitor'.

The high quality of photographs provided by Mike Gillam and Ken Johnson, and of drawings by Christine Bruderlin, are vital to the success of this book. Mike Gillam gave hours of help and support in the careful selection of the photographs.

The Mutitjulu Community and Parks Australia at Uluru–Kata Tjuta National Park and the Parks and Wildlife Commission of the Northern Territory (PWCNT) have assisted in the preparation of this book. Jon Willis, members of the Mutitjulu Community, Bob Seaborne (ANCA) and Ian Cawood (CCNT) commented on some of the text. Carmel Leonard cheerfully provided access to the considerable resources of the CCNT (Alice Springs) library and Mike Fleming, Hilary Coulson and Michael Barritt supplied plant and animal checklists from the CCNT Biological Records Scheme and Herbarium Data Base.

I am grateful to the Mutitjulu Association Inc. and ANCA for permission to reproduce the stories from the Tjukurpa presented in Chapter 2, and the information in Figure 2.2; and to Billy Marshall Stoneking (http://stoneking.org) for permission to include his poem 'Sky' from *Singing the Snake* (http://singingthesnake.cjb.net).

Most of all to Mike, Catharine and Alison, thank you for your pride in me, your encouragement and your forbearance during the extended period of writing this book.

1
A LAND
OF EXTREMES

I can't properly talk about the country, teach about the country unless I am in it, walking on it, touching it, looking at it.[1]

For the traditional inhabitants of Central Australia, their land is everything — a feeling so clearly expressed here by a senior Aboriginal man while working on the Uluru fauna survey. The land provides food for both body and soul. It is not a barren desert; it is filled with wonderful plants and animals. The early white visitors to Central Australia, who came from green forested lands, saw it through different eyes: 'Whatever their past history may be, the two rocks in their present aspect may well stand as symbols of the land itself: huge; red; bizarre'.[2] For these visitors the land was an enigma, hard to comprehend and more than a little frightening. Now this has changed. The magic of the country can be understood and enjoyed by everyone.

Uluru (Ayers Rock) is undoubtedly one of Australia's most famous natural attractions. Kata Tjuta (The Olgas) and Watarrka (Kings Canyon) are amongst our best kept national secrets. Each of these has its own special appeal. Uluru (oo-loo-roo) is massive and majestic, rising out of the plain; Kata Tjuta (kaht-a-djurt-ah) has beauty and symmetry amongst a tumble of domes which seem to have been thrown together; and Watarrka (watt-ark-a) has the grandeur of its cliffs and 'lost city' formations — it is a haven in the desert.

Woven in with the natural fascination of these three features is an overriding 'sense of place' in the Australian desert and a remarkable history — geological, Aboriginal and recent. Central Australia is a land of extremes, of contrasts and surprises. It is an arid land, but the lush valleys of the Garden of Eden in Watarrka

FIGURE 1.1 Rivers, sand dunes, rocky outcrops — vital features in a vast wilderness. *M. W. Gillam*

FIGURE 1.2 Kata Tjuta, whose smallest dome would tower over the world's greatest cathedrals. *M. W. Gillam*

FIGURE 1.3 Uluru, a rock with many moods — sometimes looming, red, bizarre and at other times brooding and silver. *J. A. Kerle*

FIGURE 1.4 Kings Canyon, a haven in the desert with grand cliffs and barren domes. *J. A. Kerle*

are a sign of a much wetter climate in the past. The sun can be brightly shining, but vehicles are bogged after a recent storm. A dry landscape is transformed into a spectacular wildflower show within a few short weeks.

Why do these landscapes and land forms exist? The geological history of this country — spanning at least 1000 million years — can help to answer this question. Indeed, thanks to the sparsity of plants and soil over much of the ground, the underlying rocks can kindle a genuine interest in geology. The rock types, colours, varying strata and the changing land forms are all very visible. Because of this the geological explanation for the landscape can be readily appreciated in the Centre (as Australians often call Central Australia). The greatest difficulty lies in comprehending how long 1000 million years really is and in visualising how the enormous changes that occurred could happen. Our lives represent such a speck in time!

Aboriginal people have a different answer as to how these land forms came to be. For them the answers are in the Tjukurpa (djook-oor-pah) — the religious philosophy which underpins their existence. Like all religious philosophies the Tjukurpa provides explanations for the most fundamental of questions. It defines what is true, what is real and what is right. All the land forms, all the features and all life were created during the Tjukurpa when ancestral beings travelled widely and left their marks on the surface of the earth. Nothing existed before this. This rich Aboriginal culture is evident in the Centre, both in the landscape and through the more recent celebration of Aboriginal spiritual history in stories and rock paintings.

Because of their close association with the Tjukurpa the Aboriginal inhabitants respected their country and understood its behaviour and its moods. They learnt how best to enhance its productivity and to maintain reservoirs of food for the tough droughts they had to contend with. They used fire to make the land more productive in some parts of the country and they carefully protected other sites for the same reason.

FIGURE 1.5 Rain can rapidly transform the desert into a brilliant wildflower show. *M. W. Gillam*

FIGURE 1.6 Sunset strip, Uluru. *J. A. Kerle*

The relatively recent movement of non-Aboriginal people into Central Australia brought about a rapid sequence of changes to the region. A new suite of animals was introduced, new land management strategies implemented and the Aboriginal way of life completely disrupted. It is not a 'European history', as it is often described, but one in which Aboriginal and non-Aboriginal people crossed paths, clashed or intermingled. A lot of the country was transformed into pastoral leases. Permanent settlements were established to service this new industry. Minerals were discovered and mining activities commenced. And the desire of people from all over the world to see Uluru eventually led to the establishment of tourist facilities.

Despite these changes, the natural wonders of Central Australia still create a sense of awe and wonder. Some of the early non-Aboriginal visitors were especially eloquent in their description of the region — sometimes to such an extent that they painted an exaggerated picture of it. Of course these early travellers had traversed vast distances through dry, dusty and absolutely forbidding sand and gibber desert — on camels or horses — and the dramatic contrast of the central ranges provided a welcome relief. This reaction is well portrayed by Baldwin Spencer, who travelled mostly by camel, an animal he completely despised:

> The fact is that travellers, struck with the beauty of certain spots, after passing for long weary weeks or even months over desert country have unconsciously exaggerated their beauty and fertility. In reality the ranges form bare and often narrow ridges separated from one another by dry and sandy scrub covered flats varying in breadth from a few hundred yards to many miles, and there is nothing like a great mountain mass with sheltered, well watered and fertile valleys such as we had pictured in imagination.[3]

In this modern age of fast cars, buses and aeroplane travel, as well as comfortable accommodation, it is easy to be insulated from the harsh reality of desert country. Reflecting on the impressions of early travellers induces a greater feeling for the natural conditions of Central Australia The region is in an arid zone. It is very dry; rainfall is unpredictable. It can be extremely hot in summer and cold and frosty in winter. The Aboriginal occupation of such a harsh environment with none of our modern conveniences is remarkable. The early non-Aboriginal explorers and settlers, women and men, had to be tough to survive — and some didn't. Despite this, the country can awaken a fierce love and loyalty and most of its residents would never live anywhere else.

Like the first human inhabitants the plants and animals of the Centre are astonishing in their ability to survive in the desert. Diversity abounds together with examples of remarkable adaptation. Small changes in the slope of the land or soil type, barely perceptible to our eyes, can introduce a new environment, enabling another plant species to grow or an insect species to flourish.

The most important factors controlling the occurrence of plants and animals across the landscape are topographic variation, moisture, soil fertility and fire. The combination of these factors results in a mosaic of plant and animal habitats and greatly increases their variety.

The topography is a product of the geological history of the area. This, in turn, strongly influences the rainfall distribution and retention of soil moisture. Fires have long been a formative force on the landscape, both as wildfires and as a tool used by Aboriginal people. The soils of the Centre are ancient, weathered and highly sorted and are unusually infertile. The levels of nitrogen and phosphorus are exceptionally low (especially in my garden in Alice Springs!). But these nutrient levels are not universal in the arid zone. Places with greater topographic diversity, for example, contain run-on areas where the water flow produces richer patches. These become fertile islands in a sea of infertility.

ULURU

> Standing out there in the stark desert, its weather scarred walls rising sheer and bare to a height of 1100 feet, it seemed to dwarf the mind by its presence... Yet drop your eyes from it you cannot... You feel as a little thing and of no account... It looks like some deliberate trick of nature ... dropped there to guard and sentinel for ever the great western deserts that lie beyond.[4]

Alan Breaden, who wrote these lines, was one of the very early pastoral pioneers in Central Australia. In 1897 he led an expedition to Uluru (or Ayers Rock as it was then called) and the country beyond. He well understood how hazardous and desolate this desert could be and yet he found the imposing presence of Uluru quite overwhelming.

The Yankunytjatjara and Pitjantjatjara people, whose association with Uluru goes back at least 10,000 years, do not focus on it in the way that non-Aboriginal visitors often do. For them it is but a part of the many interconnected stories from the Tjukurpa and each of its features is accounted for by these stories (pp.14–22). The name Uluru is just that, a name, and it is not translatable as a descriptive term as many other Aboriginal names are.

Uluru is an enormous monolith — a single rock. It rises to 348 metres above the vast surrounding sand plain and dune fields and is 867 metres above sea level at its highest point. It is composed of a coarse-grained sedimentary rock. Faulting and tilting of the sedimentary strata resulted in their near vertical alignment; a very long period of weathering has moulded Uluru into the present shape.

From the air, it is roughly kidney-shaped. The parallel alignment of the vertical rock strata and the valleys, gnawing their way in from the edges, are clearly visible. The Rock's circumference is 9.4 kilometres. The sheer walls are steep, mostly at an angle of 80 degrees to the ground. The 'climb' at the north western corner of Uluru is not quite as steep as this, but for both spiritual and safety reasons the Aboriginal custodians would prefer that people did not climb the Rock at all (see box, p.13).

The first white person to visit Uluru was the explorer William Christie Gosse. Gosse reached the monolith on 19 July 1873 and named it Ayers Rock in honour of Sir Henry Ayers, Governor of South Australia. Although Gosse was generally not an effusive writer he could not contain his excitement on this occasion: 'This rock is certainly the most wonderful natural feature I have ever seen. What a grand sight this must present in the wet season, waterfalls in every direction'.[5]

The wet season may not have been what Gosse expected in this desert country, but a thunderstorm did occur while he was camped at the Rock and must have given him an

appreciation of the extraordinary contrasts of Uluru. When thunderstorms occur Uluru becomes more than just a visual wonder. The noise can be suddenly deafening with lightning cracking and the roar of water cascading down the sides. Then it can stop as quickly as it started, returning the country to stillness.

Uluru is most famous for its marvellous colours at sunset. When Arthur Groom visited Uluru in 1948, he was overwhelmed:

> I stood apart from the camp, and watched the setting sun colour Ayers Rock in a fiery red. The crevices and hollows, caverns and overhangs and blackened line of watercourses stood out in dark shadow and mystery against the the blaze of light over everything else; then I raced across the near sandhill and saw the sun go down in a fan of crimson behind the dark silhouette of Mount Olga.[6]

Of course it isn't always as dramatic as this. The colours vary with the weather but it is always an impressive sight.

If you do decide to climb Uluru the view reinforces both the feeling of solitude and the vastness of the landscape. It sets Uluru in the context of the country. Beyond the rolling sand sheet there are several peaks and ranges which interrupt the horizon. These features stand out as beacons in the sea of sand and were used for navigation by the Aboriginal people and the explorers. But all of the landscape was a map to the Aboriginal people — dune shapes, plant life, small changes in ground surface. Their navigation during daylight hours was incomparable.

FIGURE 1.7 A silver cascade at Mutitjulu. *J. A. Kerle*

FIGURE 1.8 Mount Olga, the highest point in Uluru–Kata Tjuta National Park at 546 metres above ground level. *M. W. Gillam*

KATA TJUTA

> We stood awhile before what was surely the organic heart of Australia, with tremendous life and power. Surely all the winds and moods and storms of the continent find birth in the Olga chasms, to move out north, east, south and west. *Arthur Groom*[7]

For many of the early white travellers the dramatic domes of Kata Tjuta were the most remarkable of the desert tors. More so than Uluru, amazing though it was. The colour and the rise and fall of the domes were described in terms with spiritual overtones. Needless to say, the Aboriginal people place great spiritual significance upon this feature. As with Uluru there are many interconnected stories from the Tjukurpa associated with Kata Tjuta, but they are of such significance that they are not available for general knowledge. The name Kata Tjuta can be translated as 'many heads'.

After he had found and named Ayers Rock William Gosse travelled to Mount Olga to look for water. This outcrop had already been named by Ernest Giles in October 1872, but from a distance. Giles had been blocked in his efforts to reach Mount Olga by the extensive, boggy Lake Amadeus (map, p.138) and did not return until September 1873, after Gosse had been there. Giles named both Lake Amadeus and Mount Olga, in honour of 'two enlightened patrons of science', the King and Queen of Spain at that time.[8]

Ernest Giles described the composition of Kata Tjuta as 'being composed of untold masses of rounded stones of all kinds and sizes, mixed like plums in a pudding and set in vast rounded shapes upon the ground'.[9] This 'pudding stone' is a conglomerate, made up of large pebbles, boulders and cobbles. The formation appears to extend some five or six kilometres below the surface and, like Uluru, is a residual mass of rock left standing above the surrounding sand plain. Over eons of time the

FIGURE 1.9 Sunset silhouette of the many heads of Kata Tjuta. *J. A. Kerle*

conglomerate has been eroded along many joints and fissures, giving rise to the 'many headed' formation. Arthur Groom wrote: 'The smallest dome could have crowned the world's greatest cathedral and the greatest was a red immensity of rock that would have completely dwarfed the same edifice'.[10]

There are 36 domes, varying greatly in size. The highest, Mount Olga, at 546 metres above ground level, is the highest point in the national park. The whole group covers 35 square kilometres and is about 24 kilometres in circumference.

The dramatic changing of colours on Uluru produced by the setting sun is strongly promoted, and justifiably so. The scene at Kata Tjuta is just as dramatic and is fantastically enhanced by the silhouette of the 'many domes splitting the horizon like the temples of an ancient city'.[11] The beauty of the colours of Kata Tjuta is nowhere more eloquently described than by H. H. Finlayson, honorary curator of mammals at the South Australian Museum, who travelled through this country in 1936:

In the finished symmetry of its domes it is beautiful at all times; but now the sunset works upon it a miracle of colour, and it glows a luminous blue against an orange field, like some great mosque lit up from within. Five times I saw the sun set beyond Mt Olga but in five hundred times it would not pall. It is the most delicate sight in all the land.[12]

It is not just its shape, size and isolation that create the appeal of Kata Tjuta. It also has a surprising plant life. Soil has accumulated in the valleys, cracks and crevices of the conglomerate. The exposed rockfaces support a characteristic arid zone flora of shrubs and spinifex. Tucked away in the sheltered valleys and on patches of swampy ground are some unusual plants which defy the desert conditions. There can be masses of the delicate pink lily early nancy carpeting the ground and very dense stands of tall willowy wattles filling some of the narrow valleys. Even the stony ridges can be covered with pink daisies.

Birds also abound amongst the domes. It is a treat to hear the beautiful call of the grey shrike-thrush, echoing between the walls. Painted firetails and zebra finches drop in to drink at the waterholes, singing and grey-headed honeyeaters forage for insects amongst the foliage of gums and shrubs, and kestrels nest in rocky hollows high up on the domes.

Water can remain in the channels and creeks for quite a long time after rain. The presence of water and the shelter of the valleys make this an attractive place — especially in the heat of summer.

ATILA — MOUNT CONNER

The seemingly flat-topped mesa Atila is another part of the Tjukurpa, woven as it is into the storylines which travel through Uluru, Kata Tjuta and other parts of Central Australia. The importance of all these landmarks to the survival of Aboriginal people in this hostile environment cannot be underestimated. For the visitor travelling to Uluru–Kata Tjuta National Park today, Mount Conner is the first vision of a spectacular, rocky desert outcrop.

Mount Conner, which rises more than 300 metres above the sand plain, was named by William Gosse. The objective of his government-sponsored expedition of 1873 was to find a route from the Centre to the far distant west coast. The desert defeated him in this quest, but his place in history is assured by his being the first white man to see and to name Ayers Rock and Mount Conner. Mount Conner is now within the Curtin Springs Pastoral Lease and is close to the western boundary of the cattle country.

FIGURE 1.10 Round-leafed wattle in the Valley of the Winds, taking advantage of extra moisture in the sheltered valley.
J. A. Kerle

ULURU–KATA TJUTA NATIONAL PARK AND AYERS ROCK RESORT

Uluru and Kata Tjuta are protected within the Uluru–Kata Tjuta National Park (see map on p.vi). Although the two massive rock formations are the primary attractions, the park is also vitally important for the conservation of a range of arid Australian ecosystems. Its importance is formally recognised nationally and internationally. It is one of twelve Australian parks identified by UNESCO as Biosphere Reserves. This places it within an international reserve network designed to conserve significant ecosystems. It was an uncontroversial nomination on the World Heritage list and is listed on the Australian Register of the National Estate.

Located close to the very centre of Australia, the park covers 1325 square kilometres and is surrounded by Aboriginal freehold land. The south-western corner of the Northern Territory was originally declared as the 'South-west Reserve' in 1920. Pastoralists had no interest in this vast area of arid, inhospitable and unpredictable

FIGURE 1.11 (above) Mount Conner, or Atila, the first sight of a dramatic desert mountain for a visitor approaching Uluru from the east. *J. A. Kerle*

FIGURE 1.12 26 October 1985, a day of celebration when the Aboriginal custodians were granted freehold title to Uluru–Kata Tjuta National Park. *Courtesy of Mutitjulu Community*

'corner country', enabling it to be given away as a 'sanctuary' for the 'desert nomads'. The so-called 'desert nomads', of course, viewed their country very differently!

The park itself was excised from the reserve and declared in March 1958 by the Commonwealth of Australia. Prior to that time visits to Uluru were limited because of the need to obtain permits from the government's Native Welfare Branch for entry into the Aboriginal Reserve. From 1958 onwards, the popularity of Ayers Rock as a tourist destination rapidly increased. In that year there were 2296 visitors. There were 18,963 in 1967 and 80,000 in 1980. The park now caters for 300,000 visitors per year, and this number is continuing to grow.

Until 1985 the park was managed by the Australian National Conservation Agency (ANCA) — or Australian National Parks and Wildlife Service as it was known at the time. The day-to-day administration was the responsibility of the Parks and Wildlife Commission of the Northern Territory. On 26 October 1985 inalienable freehold title to Uluru–Kata Tjuta National Park was granted to its traditional owners. The park was then leased back by the owners to the Commonwealth, for 99 years. A Board of Management, with a majority of Aboriginal members, was established; this arrangement ensures that Aboriginal concerns are properly incorporated into management decisions.

The Ayers Rock Resort, within the Yulara Village, is discreetly set amongst sand dunes to the north of the park boundary. Early tourist developments had grown haphazardly and close to the Rock. As the number of visitors rose dramatically it became obvious that expanded tourist facilities would cause irreparable ecological damage and impinge upon the majesty of Uluru. As a result the resort is located 19 kilometres from Uluru and 55 kilometres from Kata Tjuta. Although it is located outside the national park, you can clearly see both Uluru and Kata Tjuta, and feel the dominance of these two features over the surrounding landscape.

For many years Ayers Rock and Alice Springs were virtually synonymous. On one occasion in Alice Springs an international visitor asked me which street he would find Ayers Rock in! In fact, Uluru is south west of Alice Springs — 447 kilometres via high standard sealed roads. Access was first opened in 1948 and in those days it took two long rough days of travel to get there. Now it can take only four or five hours by road or one hour by air.

WATARRKA NATIONAL PARK — KINGS CANYON

> So far the George Gill Range had been somewhat monotonous and less spectacular repetition of the curving red bluffs and intervening gullies so common to many of the ranges within a hundred miles; but west of Stokes' the escarpments changed rapidly. Oddly grotesque shapes and huge domed outcrops of sandstone stood up above the plateau. Some were like mammoth red animals of a prehistoric age; some were isolated monoliths, hollowed with caves and terraces. It was like looking up to a gallery of leviathan figures modelled from the past. *Arthur Groom*[13]

Kings Canyon does not stand out on a sand plain and beckon to the traveller. It is tucked away in the George Gill Range waiting to be discovered and rediscovered. It is within the part of Central Australia known as the central mountain ranges, covering some 168,000 square kilometres. Hidden amongst these rocky ranges are gorges and waterholes: Kings Canyon is one of the most dramatic of these. To properly appreciate the beauty and spectacle of Watarrka National Park it is essential to take time to walk into the range (map, p.vii). The attractions of the George Gill Range are many.

FIGURE 1.13
Carmichael Crag and
the George Gill Range,
glowing in the sunset.
J. A. Kerle

FIGURE 1.14 Skeleton
fork fern, a 'living
fossil' fern species
which was abundant
over 300 million years
ago; it is now found in
only a few localities,
including the George
Gill Range. *M. W. Gillam*

There is the sculptured scenery on top of the range so aptly described by Arthur Groom, the water-worn spectacle of Kings Canyon itself, and the unexpected oases of the waterholes and valleys both on top of the range and down below.

Watarrka National Park incorporates the western end of the Range. It covers 724 square kilometres and mostly consists of range country with some sand dunes. The highest point, near Carmichael Crag, is 908 metres above sea level. Kings Creek is 650 metres above sea level and the walls rise 100–150 metres above the creek.

Through the ages people have depended upon the reliable waters of the George Gill Range. It has long been an exceedingly important area for the Luritja Aboriginal people and there are many places of special significance, including caves with paintings. 'Watarrka' is the Luritja name for the umbrella bush, *Acacia ligulata*, a plant species of considerable value to these people.

The early explorers also relied upon these waters, establishing base depots or retreating there from the waterless reaches of the sandy deserts. Although Ernest Giles did not earn the prestige of naming Ayers Rock or being the first white visitor to Mount Olga, he was the first to explore and name the George Gill Range, Carmichael Crag and many of the creeks. The range was incorporated into Tempe Downs Pastoral Lease in the late 1890s and was used for cattle production until 1983 when the National Park was declared.

It is not just the scenery that makes Watarrka National Park special. There is also a wonderfully rich plant life. Some 600 plant species have been found there and several are either rare or relict species. Most of these occur in the moister, well-protected valleys and around waterholes. The relict species are survivors from the much wetter environment that once existed in Central Australia. Part of the plant species diversity results from the location of the George Gill Range at the edge of three distinctive regions — the Simpson Desert to the east, the Western Desert and the central ranges.

The mountain ranges of Central Australia are not like those of eastern Australia's Great Dividing Range; nor are they like the beautiful snow-covered mountains of Europe or New Zealand. They are sparsely vegetated rocky ridges. But their importance within the Central Australian environment is immeasurable. They have endemic flora and fauna, including both rare and relict species. Along with the great variety of plants in Watarrka National Park there are many invertebrates living in the moist areas and waterholes. The ranges also act as a drought refuge for some species. The brushtail possum and Alexandra's parrot, for example, maintain populations in these ranges or retreat there during droughts, though under better conditions they may live in the less reliable habitats away from the ranges. Aboriginal people utilised the resources of the ranges in much the same way, moving away in good times and protecting the food supply from overuse.

The central ranges provide a greater variety of habitat types than the surrounding regions do and consequently can support a much greater diversity of plants and animals. The presence of sand dunes with desert oaks sitting on top of the George Gill Range is a good example of this. The ranges are a critical source of nutrients for the impoverished soils. The infertility of Central Australian soils is well recognised: it is a very old landscape and the soils have been leached of nourishment. In general the nutrient-rich habitats are in and around the rocky ranges where the nutrients are released from the eroding rocks.

Finally, the ranges provide a moister and more stable microenvironment. The rainfall on the ranges appears to be higher than on the surrounding lowlands and the water that falls there is concentrated and retained within the rock formations. Runoff is quickly channelled into creeks, filling waterholes. Because it is a more protected environment evaporation is reduced and the water has time to infiltrate the rock strata.

Watarrka National Park is about 300 kilometres from Alice Springs and 280 kilometres from the Ayers Rock Resort. Declared in 1983, the park is managed by the Conservation Commission of the Northern Territory under direction from a Board of Management which includes members of the local Aboriginal community. The Kings Canyon Resort is ten kilometres west of the canyon.

FIGURE 1.15 The mountain ranges of Central Australia are drought refuges for plants and animals, including some rare species. *M. W. Gillam*

EXPLORING ULURU AND WATARRKA WITH THIS FIELD GUIDE

A visit to Uluru and Watarrka is an essential part of any trip to the centre of Australia. If you take enough time you will find much more of interest than just a view of the spectacular scenery. And this book will help you.

There are many fascinating aspects of the region which are detailed in each of the chapters. Chapter 2: formation of the landscape — why is it there? Chapter 3: the marvellous array of stars blanketing the sky on a cloudless night; the weather patterns. Chapter 4: the variety of plant life, clinging to life in a harsh climate. Chapter 5: the cryptic and diverse animal life — birds, mammals, reptiles and insects. Chapter 6: human history — Aboriginal and non-Aboriginal.

Each of these facets is discussed in detail. As far as possible the Aboriginal people's interpretation of their country is woven throughout, to enrich and complement the perceptions provided by white explorers and scientists. The Aboriginal people have learnt to live with the land and they can teach us much. The Aboriginal words used in the text are from Pitjantjatjara. (In order to pronounce these words it is important to remember that they all have a stress on the first syllable.) The Yankunytjatjara and Luritja people who come from around Uluru and Watarrka use many of the same words or similar ones. (There are also some substantial differences, but all three are a part of the wider Western Desert language and culture.)

The final chapter (Chapter 7) details walks and tours and the safety requirements of a visit to Uluru and Watarrka national parks. It is necessary to adhere to park regulations, both for your own safety and for the protection of the natural and cultural environment. But there is so much to do and see that you are assured of a thoroughly enjoyable visit.

The Appendix provides a summary of basic information about the parks set out under easy-to-find headings. It is followed by a checklist and index of plant and animal species found in the park.

To climb or not to climb?

Since obtaining title to their land in 1985 the Aboriginal custodians of Uluru have clearly stated that they would prefer visitors not to climb to the top of the Rock, but they have not sought to prevent people from doing so. Their attitude reflects both their spiritual relationship with Uluru and a genuine concern for the well-being of the visitor:

- For the custodians, Uluru was never a place to be climbed but one to be respected and cared for. The act of climbing the Rock is not permitted within Aboriginal Law and is degrading of its spiritual importance;

- Safety for the visitor — heat stress, heart attacks and accidents regularly occur to people attempting the climb. It is a strenuous activity and the desert climate is unforgiving. (The climb is now closed between 10 a.m. and 4 p.m. if the forecast maximum temperature is above 37°C.) The strain of the climb can cause heart attacks up to a week or more after the event. Unsuitable footwear and careless behaviour cause people to slip and severe injuries or death can result.

2
A SPECTACULAR LANDSCAPE

Where did Uluru come from? Why are Uluru and Kata Tjuta different? How has this spectacular landscape been shaped? There are two stories. There is the spiritual story based on the Tjukurpa of the Aboriginal people. There is also the pragmatic geological story. Both provide an insight into the country and its history.

In western cultures the Tjukurpa is frequently described as 'dreaming' or 'the dreamtime'. This translation is inaccurate because the Tjukurpa does not refer to ideas obtained as a dream. It is a living philosophy of life which directs Anangu (arn-ahng-oo), as the local people call themselves, in their daily life. It is not simply a collection of fascinating stories of long ago, but rather the basis of the Law governing all aspects of traditional behaviour.

In many ways the geological history is equally steeped in mystery. The concept of a period of time spanning hundreds of millions of years is beyond easy comprehension.

FIGURE 2.1 Where did Uluru come from? *M. W. Gillam*

The concept that erosion during this vast period lowered the land surface by a few kilometres is difficult to visualise. And the fact that this was determined by examining the present land surface and various geological processes is also a matter of mystery for many of us. Nonetheless, the geological history of Uluru and Kata Tjuta has been described by means of well-established rock dating techniques and geological principles. It too is a fascinating story.

Uluru has been described in many different ways and stories of its formation were told by a variety of people. Consequently, names such as 'the brain', 'the kangaroo tail' or 'the digging stick' have become common usage. While features on Uluru may bear a superficial resemblance to such things they have absolutely no meaning. Many of the early records of the Aboriginal stories, especially those collected by Bill Harney and Charles Mountford, are unacceptable to Anangu as they are both incorrect and inappropriate for visitors to the culture. The Aboriginal and geological explanations are far more meaningful.

STORIES FROM THE TJUKURPA

There is no single story describing how Uluru, Kata Tjuta or any other landscape feature came into being. Anangu do not look upon Uluru as a single spiritual object. Its formation and the creation of its specific characteristics are the outcome of several stories which are not necessarily connected (see map below). Prominent formations such as Uluru and Atila (Mount Conner) are regarded as an integral part of the landscape which was criss-crossed by the characters of the Tjukurpa stories.

FIGURE 2.2 Some of the sacred sites at Uluru and the routes travelled by characters in the Tjukurpa; a number of independent Tjukurpa journeys meet at Uluru and their tracks link Anangu to others living hundreds of kilometres away. *Reproduced with permission of the Mutitjulu Community*

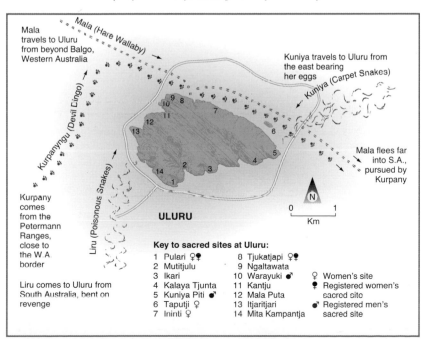

Mala travels to Uluru from beyond Balgo, Western Australia

Mala (Hare Wallaby)

Kuniya travels to Uluru from the east bearing her eggs

Kuniya (Carpet Snakes)

Kurpanyngu (Devil Dingo)

Mala flees far into S.A., pursued by Kurpany

Kurpany comes from the Petermann Ranges, close to the W.A. border

Liru (Poisonous Snakes)

ULURU

0   1
Km

Liru comes to Uluru from South Australia, bent on revenge

Key to sacred sites at Uluru:

1 Pulari ♀♂
2 Mutitjulu
3 Ikari
4 Kalaya Tjunta
5 Kuniya Piti ♂
6 Taputji ♀
7 Ininti ♀

8 Tjukatjapi ♀♂
9 Ngaltawata
10 Warayuki ♂
11 Kantju
12 Mala Puta
13 Itjaritjari
14 Mita Kampantja

♀ Women's site
♀ Registered women's sacred site
♂ Registered men's sacred site

The characters of the Tjukurpa are many and varied. Some were human, others were equivalent to plants or animals and still others were unlike any known creature. These characters arose from the earth while it was still featureless. They then travelled widely, leaving behind an altered landscape as a result of their activities. The features of the landscape are the places of great ancient battles, shelters, grinding stones, digging sticks or the ancestors themselves. The journeys undertaken by the people of the Tjukurpa are perpetually relived through stories and songs. Sites of special importance along the paths they travelled are often named and retain special significance .

The details of all these stories, however, cannot be told to everyone. For Anangu, this is one of the most crucial aspects of understanding the Tjukurpa. To provide details of stories to the wrong people is to break the Law. A visit to a place as rich in Aboriginal culture as Uluru can only provide a glimpse into the depths of their philosophy of life. It is neither possible nor permissible to fully understand the complexities of the Tjukurpa. The knowledge is gradually given to the right people as they grow and become ready to accept the responsibility that such knowledge bestows upon a person.

The closed, fenced-off sites of special importance around the base of Uluru are a clear demonstration of the difference between publicly available information and restricted knowledge. For Anangu, access to any of these sites by the wrong people is a desecration of that site. The restrictions do not apply only to non-Aboriginal people. Two of the sites are a part of the Tjukurpa celebrated by women and must not be entered by men or unprepared girls. Likewise women must not enter sites restricted to men's ceremonies.

Kata Tjuta is a particularly important area, managed only by initiated men. For this reason there are no Tjukurpa stories which can be told to the casual visitor. Some stories supposedly relating to Kata Tjuta have been published, but they are not considered to be either accurate or appropriate by Anangu. The stories included here relate to Uluru and Watarrka and are available to the general public — anyone who is newly learning this information, as I am.

In the Tjukurpa, Uluru was formed by Two Boys piling up mud when playing at Kantju waterhole. It has been remodelled and reshaped as the various characters of the Tjukurpa passed that way. Several stories and many characters were involved in this. There were Mala (hare-wallabies) and Panpanpalala (bellbird men), Kuniya (the python woman) and Liru (poisonous snake men), Lungkata (blue-tongue lizard), Itjaritjari (marsupial mole), the terrifying Kurpany (devil dingo), Linga (the central netted dragon) and several others that have all left their marks. The places in the stories are named on the map on p.15. Not all these stories can be told.

The stories of the Two Boys, Mala and Kuniya all take place around the two most permanent waterholes at Uluru — Kantju (kahrn-djoo) and Mutitjulu (moor-ti-djoo-loo).

FIGURE 2.3 Mala wallaby — in the Tjukurpa, all the features across the northern face of Uluru are part of the Mala story. *K. A. Johnson*

THE MALA STORY

The best way to fully appreciate the Mala story is to walk around the base of the Rock to Kantju Gorge. Starting from the bottom of the climb, the walk will take you past caves and other features involved in the story. Indeed, all the features across the northern face of Uluru are part of the Mala story — as told here by the custodians:

In the beginning, Mala men, women and children must travel a long way from the west and the north to reach Uluru. When they arrive they camp at separate sites from one another in groups of young men; old men; young and single women; and old and married women. They do this because they are here for an Inma [religious ceremony].

Some Mala men, who come from the west, carry the ceremonial pole, Ngaltawata [nahrl-ta-wahr-tah]. They scramble quickly to the top of Uluru and plant the pole in the ground at the most northern corner to begin the Inma. From this moment on, everything becomes a part of the ceremony. Even everyday jobs like: hunting; gathering and preparing food; collecting water; talking to people; or just waiting, are now done in a proper way for ceremony. This has become Law for men, women and children ever since.

The Mala are happy and busy. Suddenly people from the west come with an invitation to join another Inma. The Mala must refuse, as they have already started their own ceremony. The people from the west return home in great anger at the insult. They plan to wreak vengeance upon the Mala in a terrible way.

Across the land comes an evil, black dog-like creature: Kurpany. He has been created by these people in the west to destroy the Mala ceremony. Lunpa, the kingfisher bird, cries a warning to the Mala. It is ignored, and Kurpany attacks and kills many Mala men, women

FIGURE 2.4 Women collecting and preparing witchetty grubs while a child enjoys the feast. *Christine Bruderlin*

and children. In terror, the remaining Mala flee to the south with Kurpany chasing them all the way.

On the Mala Walk, you will see some of the very places where the Mala prepare for ceremony. As you walk through this area you will be surrounded by the Mala Tjukurpa.

The Mala Walk has been described in detail by the custodians in an excellent booklet which can be purchased from the Park Visitor Centre. The booklet tells about the Itjaritjariku Yuu, the shelter built by Itjaritjari (the marsupial mole); Malaku Wilytja, a shelter built by Itjaritjari for the Mala women; and the very significant Mala Puta which you must not enter or photograph.

Around Kantju you are close to some sites of great significance to Anangu men. They ask that you move silently through this area as they themselves would. It is a privilege for visitors to walk through or past these sites and learn about the story. Please show respect for these places and the living culture of Anangu.

FIGURE 2.5 Lunpa the kingfisher woman. *Dennis Chinner*

THE FORMING OF ULURU BY TWO BOYS

This story of the formation of Uluru was told by Tommy Manta to Jon Willis at the Mutitjulu Community in October 1994.

The Two Boys came up from South Australia, and travelled towards Uluru across the southwest corner of the Northern Territory. They stopped for a while at Itarinya, a site on the Uluru side of Pirurpakalarintja, the cone-shaped peak to the west of the park. They were hunting and travelling together, and as they continued on towards Uluru, they heard the sound of the Mala at ceremonies around the rockhole that is now part of Kantju Gorge. The Mala had initially erected the Ngaltawata, their ceremonial pole at this site, but the ground was too boggy and the pole lurched sideways. They pulled it out, and replanted it in the more secure location where it still stands, turned to stone. The Two Boys travelled towards the ceremony, to see what was happening. They were uninitiated boys, and had no knowledge of men's ceremonies. They were very curious.

The Mala, meanwhile, were separating into their men's and women's camps to get ready for inma the next morning. They didn't know it, but already Kurpany was heading towards them from the west intending to destroy them. The men were resting at Mala Wati and preparing their decorations for the Inma, and the women were asleep at Tjukatjapi.

The Two Boys began playing in Kantju waterhole, mixing the water with the surrounding earth. They piled the mud up, getting bigger and bigger, until it was the size that Uluru is now. Then they started playing on it. They sat on the top, and slid down the south side of their mud pile on their bellies, dragging their fingers through the mud in long channels. The channels have hardened into stone, and now form the many gullies on the southern side of Uluru.

Their play was interrupted, as Kurpany attacked the Mala, killing two men, and driving the rest of the Mala south in a panic towards Ulkiya (Mt Caroline) in South Australia. The Two Boys headed southeast, towards Mt Woodroffe. They resumed their hunting and searching for water, eventually encountering a Wanampi (water serpent). This encounter resulted in the formation of Atila (Mt Conner) and Pantu (Lake Amadeus).

Figure 2.6 The ribbing on Uluru was created by the Two Boys dragging their fingers while sliding down the surface of their mud pile. *J. A. Kerle*

THE STORY OF KUNIYA

The story of Kuniya the python woman travels west to Uluru from near Erldunda (see map on p.vii). If you drive to Uluru from there, the journey will take about three hours. The expectation and excitement of arriving at Uluru often means that visitors absorb very little of the country in between. This is unfortunate as that country is also part of the Tjukurpa. The Kuniya Tjukurpa — her journey, resting places and troubles — is known and sung by Anangu from communities through parts of the Northern Territory, South Australia and Western Australia. This is the story of Kuniya as told by the custodians:

Kuniya has been away for a long time during which she has become an adult and a mother. She sorely misses her home; but, above all, she wishes her children to be born in her own country. She has a long way to go; she is vulnerable to predators; she has no arms or legs; and she is burdened with many eggs which she carries in a bundle around her head. Her journey is very long and very hard.

Every night she must stop and curl up around her eggs to keep them warm. Each day she resumes her journey west. She is burdened and dispirited; for, being very low to the ground, she cannot see very far ahead. Each time she reaches the top of the sandhill she peers carefully over the top, looking anxiously for a sign of home until finally Uluru appears on the horizon. But still there is a very long way to go, and she must go, snake-like, up every sandhill and down the other side. And up and down and up and down, who knows for how long a time.

She travels and travels and travels and travels until she finally emerges on the eastern side of Uluru in the vicinity of Taputji ["Little Ayers Rock"]. She is exhausted and starved, but she has brought her children to be born in her country. She has arrived, and she is home where her body and spirit will be renewed. She dives into the ground, leaving the eggs behind on the surface in a ring.

You can see her on the northerly face of Uluru, heading for Kuniya Piti. She camps herself on the north side of Taputji and goes off each day into the sandhills in search of food. The huge grooves she makes as she comes and goes on her search are visible on the north side of Taputji.

While Kuniya is there, she becomes involved in a terrible family tragedy. Her young nephew, also a Kuniya, has enraged a group of Liru who are travelling out of the West to take revenge on him. They come south of Kata Tjuta, missing the often misnamed Liru wall which is not connected with the story of Liru at all.

The Liru spot their target resting just to the west of where tourists now climb Uluru, and rush on him hurling their spears. The indentations of the spears are obvious here in the side of the rock.

The poor Kuniya, outnumbered, dodges what he can but eventually falls dead.

His aunt, overwhelmed with grief and anger travels under the ground from Kuniya Piti to Mutitjulu. There she comes across one of the Liru warriors who mocks her grief and rage.

As Kuniya approaches Liru in her righteous anger, she performs a ritual dance to make it publicly known that a woman of power is seeking to punish the person who has offended her. Kuniya is furious, and in an attempt to control the dark forces that her ritual anger is unleashing, she picks up a handful of sand and lets it fall to the ground. This is to settle the forces she is disturbing, so that they will not harm others.

However, Kuniya's rage is too strong, and a great battle takes place. Kuniya strikes Liru and he receives a small wound as he deflects the blow with his shield. Then Kuniya delivers

FIGURE 2.7 Kuniya the woma python.
M. W. Gillam

FIGURE 2.8 Liru the poisonous snake.
M. W. Gillam

Liru a second strike and he receives a deep, long and fatal wound. Liru's shield falls with him to the ground.

Kuniya has avenged her honour, but in her furious rage every plant near the battle has become poisoned. The spearwood bush here is particularly poisoned.

Evidence of Kuniya's actions as she rushes towards her insulter and destroys him, is clear in the features along the Mutitjulu walk. You will not just be looking at rocks and walls; you will be walking in the midst of creation and the record of events which continue today to be celebrated in story, song and ritual dance.

Evidence of the Kuniya and Liru battle (below) can be seen clearly from the Liru Walk, the walk into Mutitjulu and from the car park. Details are given in a booklet produced by the Mutitjulu Community and sold in the Information Centre in the Park, titled *An Insight into Uluru — The Mala Walk and the Mutitjulu Walk*.

While walking into the Mutitjulu waterhole you will pass two caves. The art work in the first of these is not directly connected with the Kuniya story. This large cave was a well-used camp site, close to the reliable waterhole. This critical water supply was controlled by Wanampi, an ancestral water snake. Anangu are always respectful in this area in order to ensure the water supply.

Kuniya moving in to strike Liru

sand dropped to control the forces of anger

FIGURE 2.9 Evidence of the battle between Kuniya and Liru above Mutitjulu. *J. A. Kerle*

FIGURE 2.10 Cave art, Uluru. *J. A. Kerle*

LUNGKATA — THE BLUE-TONGUE LIZARD MAN

The Lungkata story is another part of the Tjukurpa around Uluru. The origin of the boulders on either side of the circuit track to the west of the Mutitjulu car park is described in this story. It also contains an important moral message which all people — both Piranpa (white people) and Anangu — should heed.

Lungkata travelled to Uluru from the north, from near where Mt Liebig Community is today. He came via Mt Currie and the Sedimentaries, burning the country as he walked and providing the impetus for traditional fire management of country.

At Uluru, Lungkata camps in a cave high on the western face, looking out over where the Ranger Station is today. He hunts around the southern base of the rock, where he comes upon a wounded Kalaya (emu), still dragging a spear from another hunt. Dishonourably, Lungkata finishes off the bird, and begins cutting it up and cooking it.

The two Panpanpalala (crested bellbird) hunters were not far behind their quarry, however. Losing the track of the wounded emu, and seeing the smoke from Lungkata's fire, they come up to him and ask if he had seen their wounded bird. Hiding the pieces of Kalaya behind him, and lying through his teeth, he told the two hunters that he'd seen nothing. Disappointed, they walk off but swiftly locate the tracks of the emu and guess what has happened.

Lungkata, meanwhile, gathers up what he could carry of the bird and races west along the bottom of the rock towards his permanent camp leaving a trail of meaty chunks behind him. At Kalaya Tjunta, just north of Ikari, the emu's thigh is clearly visible. Just west of Mutitjulu, the circuit walk snakes its way between huge blocks of emu meat.

The trail was easy to follow, and the two Panpanpalala catch up with Lungkata as he climbs up into his camp. They make a huge bonfire under the camp, and the smoke and ash of that fire still stain the side of the rock. Lungkata, the lazy, greedy and dishonest thief, was burned up.

STORIES FROM WATARRKA

Many Tjukurpa stories are woven through the land forms of the George Gill Range and surrounding country. The stories relating to Kings Canyon itself appear to be more closely connected with country to the south, especially the Kings Creek floodout, rather than with sites such as Lilla or Kathleen Springs. These places have their own stories.

There are stories about the willy wagtail, Papa the dingo, the two women Kunka Kutjarra, the carpet python Inturrkunya, the native cat and the possum Wiuta and many others. They have not been written down and are told by the Aboriginal Guides conducting Kurkara tours — in the oral tradition of their forefathers.

THE GEOLOGY: A STORY OF UPHEAVAL, WIND, RAIN, ICE, SEDIMENTS AND ROCKS

If you were to connect the three desert tors — Mount Olga, Uluru and Mount Conner — on a map, you would find that they lie along a straight line (see map on p.vii). Is this surprising fact simply a quirk of nature or is it related to the geological history of the region? We do not really know the answer to this question. But it does challenge us to view these spectacular features in the context of the complex geological formation of the whole region, not as isolated oddities. In doing this, we are following the Anangu way of looking at the land; the way of the interconnected stories of the Tjukurpa. Unlike these stories, the geological interpretations are still evolving and being refined. While there is general agreement on the broad principles of the processes involved in the formation of the landscape, there is still debate about the details.

FIGURE 2.11 Lungkata the greedy blue-tongue lizard. *J. A. Kerle*

FIGURE 2.12 Panpanpalala the crested bellbird. *G. Anderson / NPIAW*

FIGURE 2.13 Tjintir-Tjintirpa the willy wagtail. *G. O'Neill*

THE SHAPING OF THE LAND

In looking at the geological history of the region, we will begin with the relatively recent shaping of Uluru, Kata Tjuta, Mount Conner and Kings Canyon and consider how the caves, valleys and scars were formed. Then, in the following section we will turn the clock back a mere thousand million years and trace the overall evolution of the landscape of this part of Central Australia. It is a story of unimaginable continental upheavals, active and extensive erosion, formation of inland seas, deposition of sediments and remnants of some early forms of life.

Uluru — the monolith

> I felt like an ant at the door of a cathedral... *Arthur Groom*[1]

The most striking feature of Uluru is its monolithic character, appearing to rise sheer from the surrounding sand plain. From a distance it presents as an integral unit, without seam or cleavage. Move closer and you will notice the ribbing, valleys and caves. These features are the product of millions of years of erosion and weathering, but because there are no joints through the rock mass it has been able to persist as a monolith.

In the writings of the early European explorers Uluru was often described as a great pebble. While this is certainly the impression it gives, it does not just sit on the surface. It is the exposed tip of an almost vertical slab of rock. Just how far down it goes is as yet unknown. Perhaps six kilometres? There is some suggestion from information obtained from water bores and from other outcrops that the Uluru rock extends to the north-west beneath the sand, but this is conjecture. Its ability to remain standing above the sand plain occurs because the different rock types surrounding it are generally softer than the unjointed rock of Uluru.

The monolith itself is a sedimentary rock called arkose — Uluru Arkose. It is made up of a mixture of small particles and pebbles of sand, quartz and feldspar with traces of iron oxides, clay and fragments of other rocks. When William Gosse first visited Uluru in 1873, he described it as a granite, metamorphic rather than sedimentary. He could be excused for this error: the mountains which were eroded into the sediments that ultimately became Uluru Arkose were probably made of a granite or something similar.

Mostly Uluru is red but inside the caves it is grey. (No, it is not made of polystyrene, as I have heard suggested!) The unoxidised grey arkose becomes coated with reddish iron oxide after its exposure to oxygen and to the weathering process. Overall, this rock is relatively resistant to weathering which has been very even, resulting in its familiar broad rounded faces. Taputji (also known as Little Ayers Rock) and a flat rock pavement to its north-west are an enigma, however. They are made of equally hard Uluru Arkose yet they have been eroded right down. Perhaps there are joints along this edge, creating a weakness which allowed weathering to occur at a faster rate.

The parallel ribbing across the surface of Uluru, which is so clearly evident from the air is a product of the original layering of the sediments — or 'bedding' as the geologists call it. These layers were once horizontal but tilting of the whole rock stratum has brought them into an almost vertical alignment. The ribbing is a product of variation in the resistance of the beds to weathering. Some layers are just a little softer than others. The reasons for this difference are unknown but may be due to subtle variation in the grain size of the arkose.

The configuration of the bedding tells a story. The whole rock stratum has been upended almost 90 degrees from its original horizontal position, creating the question: which end of Uluru was originally on the bottom? Which end is the oldest? The answers to these questions can be found by careful examination of the fine layers in the rock. These layers, or beds, are the original sand and gravel deposits but they are not simple parallel layers. They are made up of many small curved segments called crossbeds. The curving of the crossbeds indicates that Taputji is older than Uluru and you approach the youngest strata as you drive from the Park Visitor Centre towards the ring road — the south-western end of Uluru. The traverse from there to Taputji covers a period of 50 million years —approximately!

Close up, the old, outer exposed surface of Uluru is flaky red with greyish patches. Slowly but surely, Uluru is being worn away by water and by oxygen from the air which together cause chemical decay of minerals in the rock. The presence of silica and iron at the surface creates a 'skin', making this a slower process than it is for many other rocks. Sand-blasting by wind borne sand grains is often thought of as a primary weathering agent. This is unlikely in the case of Uluru. Sand-blasting would produce a roughened or polished surface, not a flaky surface, and would affect only the first few metres above ground level.

But if Uluru has a toughened skin how do caves form? There are two different types of cave: the honeycomb caves high up on the walls and those at ground level which have a waveform shape (below). The precise mechanism for the

FIGURE 2.14 Slowly the surface of Uluru is flaking away as a result of chemical decay of minerals in the rock. *J. A. Kerle*

FIGURE 2.15 Possible mechanisms for the formation of 'honeycomb' and 'wave' caves around Uluru

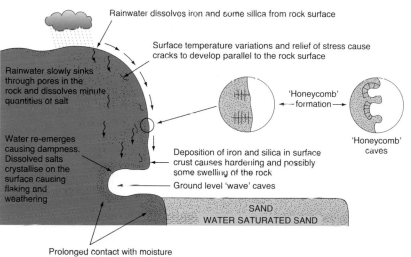

Rainwater dissolves iron and some silica from rock surface

Surface temperature variations and relief of stress cause cracks to develop parallel to the rock surface

Rainwater slowly sinks through pores in the rock and dissolves minute quantities of salt

'Honeycomb' ← formation →

'Honeycomb' caves

Water re-emerges causing dampness. Dissolved salts crystallise on the surface causing flaking and weathering

Deposition of iron and silica in surface crust causes hardening and possibly some swelling of the rock

Ground level 'wave' caves

SAND
WATER SATURATED SAND

Prolonged contact with moisture weathers and softens the rock which then erodes away

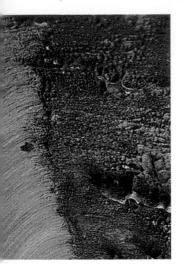

formation of these caves is a matter of debate between geologists. One idea is that, in places where the chemical weathering has broken through the toughened skin, the rate of weathering of the underlying arkose (which has not been toughened) is faster. Small pits become hollows and eventually caves. In essence the inside is eaten out! Once a cave formed, the surface became toughened and then smaller caves formed inside by the same process, producing a honeycomb effect.

The most spectacular of the ground level caves is undoubtedly Malaku Wilytja (above), the Wave Cave on the Mala Walk, which could have formed through a similar process. When the flaking is more active in the shadier higher parts of the hollow the cave grows backwards and upwards. The grey parts of the cave indicate the places where weathering is still active, but the red surfaces have been coated with iron oxide and are not being actively weathered.

An alternative hypothesis proposes that the ground level caves are the product of chemical weathering by water trapped in the surrounding sand when the soil surface was a few metres higher than at present (Fig. 2.15). After the level of the surrounding sand plain dropped the weathered rock was eroded away. This hypothesis also suggests that the active sub-surface weathering of the rock maintains the steepness of the slopes.

The ceiling and upper wall of Malaku Wilytja are sculptured into grotesque shapes. These were probably formed by the movement of water through the rock, depositing a harder cement onto the arkose. These bits become more resistant and are used by birds as perches! This cave is also a good place in which to examine both the composition of the Uluru Arkose and its bedding. The bedding is visible as green-grey streaks which slope slightly (85 degrees) to the right as you look into the cave. The older beds are to the left. The fine crossbeds are concave in the direction of the younger beds — to the right.

Other caves are formed by slabs of the surface of Uluru breaking away. These curved cracks are called topographic joints (Fig. 2.18); the best example is Ngaltawata, the ceremonial pole of the Mala men (Fig. 2.2). The cracks are thought to form as a result of elastic outward expansion of the rock when the surrounding rock is eroded away. The pressure on the compressed rock underneath was released and a crack parallel with the surface is formed. Eventually the connecting rock above the crack or topographic joint erodes away, freeing the layer which can then split off and fall in blocks to the ground. This is the source of the blocks around Taputji, and the so-called 'chicken rock' at the bottom of the climb.

The valleys eating their way into the sides of Uluru are a product of weathering and erosion of the softer bands of arkose. Often one valley can be paired with another if you follow the bedding from one side of the monolith to the other (Fig. 2.2). For example, Mutitjulu can be paired with the valley near Malaku Wilytja. Kantju Gorge appears to have formed in a slightly different way. There is a vertical fracture in the wall at the deepest point of the gorge. This probably assisted its erosion.

From the air the south-eastern side of Uluru appears to have a straight boundary (see map on p.165). Drilling for water in this area has indicated that there is no Uluru Arkose below the surface. This suggests that, while there are no joints or faults in Uluru itself, there may be one along this south-eastern edge, labelled 'fault line' on the map.

FIGURE 2.18 Curved cracks parallel with the surface of Uluru are called topographic joints. *J. A. Kerle*

The product of one of the most unusual of erosional forces is visible on Uluru, especially between the ends of the two hand chains running up the climb. This force is lightning. If lightning strikes the rock it produces a scar. The heat of the bolt of lightning boils water trapped in the rock surface and flakes of rock are exploded off. Beware of climbing Uluru during stormy weather!

The Many-headed Kata Tjuta

> ... Mt Olga is composed of pudding stone so heterogeneous that its constituent particles vary in size from a motor car to a walnut. *H. H. Finlayson*[3]

Kata Tjuta's rock type is different from Uluru's. It is a conglomerate, not an arkose. Its component particles vary greatly in size, yet its outline and surface are smooth, sometimes smoother than Uluru's. As you approach, Kata Tjuta appears as a tumbled clump of domes thrown together. From the west, the full height of the bluffs is more dramatic. It is almost as if a longer and higher Uluru has been slashed with giant vertical cuts from the top right to the bottom.

The Kata Tjuta conglomerate is called Mount Currie Conglomerate, having been found first at Mount Currie, 35 kilometres north-west of Kata Tjuta. It is made up of large smooth boulders held together by a matrix of grains and pebbles. The boulders are formed from a variety of rock types — igneous (dark blue-green basalt and pale speckly granite), metamorphic (streaky gneiss) and sedimentary (sandstone). All of these are cemented together by a fine greenish matrix. The green colour is produced by the mineral epidote. Amongst the boulders there are occasionally greenish epidote-rich sandstone lenses. Some are visible just before you begin the descent into the creek in Olga Gorge but one of the largest has become a sandstone pavement which is traversed by the Valley of the Winds track as it descends from the first lookout (p.81).

FIGURE 2.19 (right)
Kata Tjuta, a tumbled
clump of domes.
J. A. Kerle

FIGURE 2.20 (below)
The conglomerate or
pudding stone of Kata
Tjuta.*J. A. Kerle*

FIGURE 2.21 (below
right) Not all the
boulders in the
conglomerate are
rounded; some have
been cracked in half as a
result of extremes in
temperature. *J. A. Kerle*

The highest dome, Mount Olga on the western end, rises 546 metres above ground level. From there the height of the domes decreases to the east. Why have these majestic domes remained to dominate the landscape and what happens under the ground? The Mount Currie Conglomerate is quite extensive. It is found under the sand for 40 kilometres to the north-west and 15 kilometres to the north east of Kata Tjuta, but only the portion that is Kata Tjuta has resisted being weathered away. The reasons for this are another puzzle to geologists. The Mount Currie Conglomerate ends abruptly south east of Kata Tjuta along a fault line and abuts the younger, softer and more fractured Proterozoic rocks of the Amadeus Basin (p.32). This was probably eroded away more quickly, leaving the more resistant conglomerate. Geologists have estimated that under the ground the conglomerate continues to a depth of five to five and a half kilometres, making this layer up to six kilometres thick if measured from the top of Mount Olga.

Unlike Uluru, the conglomerate strata of Kata Tjuta have not been upended and they tilt only slightly. The tilt of the bedding is best viewed from the western end and the angle, or dip, is 12–15 degrees to the south-west.

A series of joints or fractures cracked through the rock probably as a result of a massive upheaval about 400 million years ago. They formed at right angles to the bedding. From that time on, weathering and erosion have slowly but surely worked on the joints, forming the valleys and gorges that split the conglomerate into domes. The number of joints is greater at the eastern end of Kata Tjuta. This would have enabled the weathering and erosion to be more rapid there and explains why those domes are smaller and lower. As well as the major joints there were some small vertical cracks in the more rigid and brittle beds which now appear as indentations on the domes.

The huge blocks of conglomerate scattered around Kata Tjuta have fallen from the walls of the domes, probably from around cracks in the rock. While most of these rock falls are old, the weathering is an ongoing process. Like Uluru, Kata Tjuta is coated with red iron oxide, except on surfaces or blocks that have been exposed in 'recent' history.

Topographic (curved) joints, as described for Uluru, can also be seen at Kata Tjuta. These strongly influence the erosion pattern and produce the attractive rounded shapes. But not all features are rounded. Many of the boulders are cleanly cut — as if they have been sliced by a knife — rather than protruding from the surface. They did protrude originally, but the exposed portion expanded and contracted in response to temperature changes much more than the protected portion did. This created tensions which split the boulders.

Mount Conner — tabletop mesa

Mount Conner is usually the first of the 'desert tors' to be seen by a visitor to Central Australia. Standing 300 metres above ground level, it doesn't have the familiar rounded features of Uluru, but is a classic flat-topped mesa. It is visible from the Lasseter Highway between the Luritja Road and Mulga Park Road intersections with the highway (see map on p.vii). The rest area 26 kilometres west of the Luritja Road (Kings Canyon) turnoff is a good vantage point for photography. If you cross the road and climb the sand dune you have the dual view of an extensive salt lake to the north and Mount Conner to the south. If you venture down the Mulga Park Road you will see that the cap of the mesa is dented by a creek line.

Geologically, Mount Conner bears no relationship to either Uluru or Kata Tjuta. It is the product of more resistant beds lying within almost flat Winnal beds of silica sandstone, which are thought to be 650–750 million years old. As the sandstone was eroded away the more resistant bed persisted, the steep sides being formed by undercutting of the capping (below).

FIGURE 2.22 The formation of Mount Conner. The more resistant bed has become a capping which has been undercut to form the Mesa.

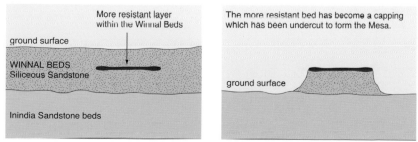

FIGURE 2.23 The beehive domes above Kings Canyon result from joints or cracks being eroded out over millions of years.
J. A. Kerle

The Winnal beds appear to have older sandstone beds, called the Inindia beds, lying under them. Tillite, which is a glacial deposit, has been found between the two sandstone beds. It was probably deposited during the glacial period 750 million years ago. Large-scale crossbedding is also visible on Mount Conner.

As Mount Conner is on the Curtin Springs Pastoral Lease visits can be organised only through the property owners or with a recognised tour operator. Enquiries may be made at the Curtin Springs Roadhouse.

Kings Canyon and the beehive domes

The formation of Kings Canyon and the beehive domes is another story of jointing and differential weathering between rock types. The top 30–50 metres of the canyon and domes are Mereenie Sandstone. Below this, where the slope of the canyon sides is more gentle, is the softer and older Carmichael Sandstone. In between the two, right at the change of slope, is a thin layer of purple shale or mudstone. This shale is more flexible than the sandstones and is unjointed. It is impervious to water (Fig. 2.24).

The present land form is a direct result of jointing or fractures in the upper layer of Mereenie Sandstone. Unlike Kata Tjuta, where the joints were all roughly in the same direction, the Mereenie Sandstone was cracked into strong joints which run WNW

FIGURE 2.24 A geological cross-section through the Garden of Eden, Kings Canyon

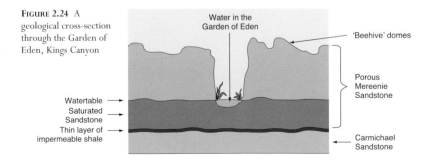

FIGURE 2.25 The sheer south wall of Kings Canyon. *J. A. Kerle*

and weaker joints which run at right angles — NNE. The most spectacular demonstration of this right-angle jointing is Kings Canyon (WNW) and the Garden of Eden (NNE), shown in Fig. 7.25. Mostly the cracks did not penetrate into the lower Carmichael Sandstone which is protected by the more plastic layer of shale in between.

The sheer south wall of Kings Canyon is an almost vertical jointface. On the other side, the yellowish north wall is gradually receding and widening the valley. The softer Carmichael Sandstone is being eroded out from under the Mereenie Sandstone, which then breaks away along smaller fracture lines. The huge sandstone boulders in the valley of Kings Creek, some of which are larger than a house, came from the top — the Mereenie Sandstone.

The beehive domes are also a product of jointing. The sandstone was broken into large rectangular blocks and then weathered and eroded into the characteristic beehive or 'lost city' shapes. A close look at the beehives provides an insight into the environment which existed when the sands which formed the Mereenie Sandstone were deposited. Geologists believe that the country was an inland dune field with rivers and small freshwater lakes. The dramatic examples of crossbedding (Fig. 2.26), the even grain size, the occasional ripple beds and an almost complete lack of fossils in the sandstone are some of the evidence used to reach this conclusion.

Crossbeds, many of which are large and exposed on the beehives, are probably relics of the sand dune slopes. Some of these are cut off by a horizontal layer which may reflect a time when the sand dunes were inundated with water and wave action levelled the surface of the sand. Size of the sand particles in a dune environment tends to be highly sorted. The lightest, very fine particles are lost as dust and the larger heavier grains don't move much. The dunes are formed from the remainder: sand grains which can be moved along the ground by the wind. This evenness in size creates a very porous sandstone. Indeed, the Mereenie Sandstone is the most important water-bearing rock in Central Australia and is the source of most of the Alice Springs town water supply.

FIGURE 2.26 Crossbeds are a feature of Mereenie Sandstone and can help to explain the type of environment that existed when the rock sediments were being deposited. *J. A. Kerle*

FIGURE 2.27 Tracks of the extinct squid-like cruziana can be seen in the Carmichael Sandstone on the descent from the range at the end of the Kings Canyon Walk. *J. A. Kerle*

The Carmichael Sandstone, on the other hand, is thought to have been deposited when the area was covered by shallow seawater. It is rich in fossils, including scolithus worm tubes, squid-like nautiloids and the fossilised tracks of cruziana, an animal like the Moreton Bay Bug. It was probably an estuary or delta where salts became highly concentrated by high evaporation rates. Evidence of the salt crystals remains as cubic casts in the sandstone. The grain size of this sandstone is not as well sorted as that of the Mereenie Sandstone, so it is not nearly as porous. In addition, the impervious mudstone layer prevents the water percolating down into this layer.

The surface colours of the sandstones in the George Gill Range are typical of the iron-stained reds of the region. Underneath, the Mereenie Sandstone is a bright white and free of any iron. The purity of the sand in the Mereenie Sandstone is indicated by the fact that it weathers to sand and very little soil has accumulated on the plateau. The Carmichael Sandstone is generally red to light brown on fresh surfaces. Sunset on Carmichael Crag is, like Uluru and Kata Tjuta, a spectacular sight.

The flat ground around the foot of the George Gill Range is a soft siltstone which does not leave many outcrops. The Kings Canyon Lodge, on the other hand is built amongst an outcrop of Carmichael Sandstone. Around the motel units the rocks are riddled with scolithus worm tubes.

THE LONG GEOLOGICAL HISTORY ... HOW DID IT ALL HAPPEN?

Let us now turn the clock back about 1000 million years (Fig. 2.28). Prior to that time the land surface over most of Central Australia was erupting with volcanoes, rocks were heated and changed in composition, severe folding and faulting occurred and huge mountain ranges formed. Gradually the land surface was eroded down to sea level and eventually sank below it.

The Amadeus Basin

Imagine, if you can, a vast shallow, inland sea covering most of Central Australia. Sometimes it was connected with the ocean surrounding Australia, at other times it was cut off. This was the Amadeus Basin, which was many times larger than Lake Amadeus, the ephemeral salt lake shown in Fig. 6.8. For the next 300 million years vast quantities of sediments were deposited by rivers into this basin — mud, sand and gravel. Intermittent changes in conditions led to changes in the type of sediments deposited — when the sea was blocked off from the ocean, evaporation increased and salts were deposited. Other climatic changes produced layers of lime muds.

Some 700 million to 650 million years ago the climate cooled, the land subsided again and there was a period of extensive glaciation. The unsorted sediments deposited by glaciers (glacial till) can be found in areas ranging from near Adelaide right through Central Australia, including Mount Conner, to the Kimberleys in the north of Western Australia. The Winnal beds, which form the top layer of Mount Conner, above the glacial till, were deposited around 650 million to 600 million years ago.

In this period of about 300 million years, some three or four kilometres' depth of sediment accumulated, but the land surface was not necessarily raised by this amount. It seems that the floor of the Amadeus Basin was sagging as quickly as the sediments were building up. Compression and cementing of these sediments ultimately turned them into sedimentary rocks — sandstone, mudstone, limestone and rock salt. The rock salt can no longer be found on the surface because it has been dissolved out by rain and surface waters but it is still present in the deep strata. A layer of rock salt 800 metres thick has been discovered at a depth of 2000 metres by exploratory drilling in this region.

Upheavals and another inland sea

The sedimentation sequence was abruptly halted by dramatic movements in the earth's crust heaving up a huge mountain range. This event occurred about 550 million years ago and is called the Petermann Ranges Orogeny. It affected a vast area to the south and west of Uluru. This was during the Cambrian Period of geological history when many of the earliest, most simple forms of life were evolving. At that time the earth was still bare and a period of very rapid erosion followed.

The sediment from the rapidly eroding mountains was disgorged by rivers onto the lowlands as alluvial fans (Fig. 2.29). The sediments were dumped rapidly and were completely unsorted — a feature clearly visible in the Uluru Arkose and Mount Currie Conglomerate as they are both made up of particles which vary greatly in size. Theories about the relative positions of the Uluru and Kata Tjuta sediments have differed. Earlier hypotheses postulated that these two sediments occurred at different points along the same alluvial flow — the conglomerate of Kata Tjuta being deposited closer to the ranges than the finer grained Uluru sediments. More recent ideas suggest that they were formed from two separate alluvial fans.

Not only were these sediments deposited rapidly but they became very thick. The layers at Uluru were at least 2.5 kilometres thick, indicating that the ranges they came from must have been uplifted by at least that much. As the mountains were not instantly uplifted to their full height — it was a gradual process over some 50 million years —they were never standing 2.5 kilometres above the surrounding lowlands. The fans of the Mount Currie Conglomerate were perhaps six kilometres or more thick by the end of the deposition phase.

Circumstances changed again about 500 million years ago. Another shallow inland sea formed and new sediments were deposited — vast quantities of sand to begin with and then mud. Prolific marine life must have existed throughout this period. The rock layers contain many fossils and are also the source of the rich oil and gas fields in Central Australia. The flat ground surrounding the George Gill Range, Stokes Siltstone, is derived from mud layers deposited around 475 million years ago. This was overlain by the Carmichael Sandstone of Kings Canyon 440 million years ago.

Only a few million years later the inland sea retreated and deposition of sediment

FIGURE 2.28 *Timescale of major geological events* These events led to the formation of Uluru, Kat...

TIME million years ago *my*	PERIOD	CENTRAL AUSTRALIA
1.6 my —	Quaternary	Dune formation 30,000 years ago; Henbury meteorites
65 my —	Tertiary	Diprotodon fossils; crocodiles, reed swamps Tertiary weathering
100 my —	Cretaceous	Deep valley eroded between Uluru and Kata Tjuta Gosse Bluff crater Last inundation
200 my —	Jurassic	Erosion of a stable landscape Marine molluscs
	Triassic	Plant remains
	Permian	Glaciation, plant remains preserved
300 my —	Carboniferous	Alice Springs Orogeny (mountain building, lifting, folding, cracking of beds)
400 my —	Devonian	Inundation of the land Mereenie Sandstone deposited (wind) Sea retreated
	Silurian	Erosion — no sediments or fossils preserved
500 my —	Ordovician	Carmichael Sandstone deposited Stokes Siltstone deposited, trilobites, scolithus worms Formation of a shallow inland sea
	Cambrian	Deposition of Uluru Arkose and Mount Currie Conglomerate Petermann Orogony (mountain building upheaval)
600 my — 700 my — 800 my — 900 my — 1000 my — Before 1000	Pre-Cambrian	Winnal Sandstone (Mount Conner) deposited Land subsided, cooled, extensive glaciation ◀ Stromatolite formation ⊢ Sedimentation into the shallow inland sea of the Amadeus Basin Amadeus basin formed Earth and planets formed 4500 million years ago

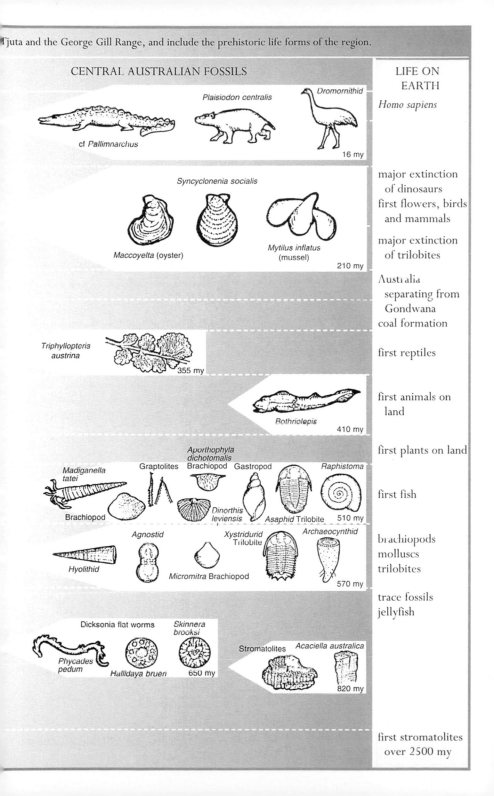

CENTRAL AUSTRALIAN FOSSILS

LIFE ON EARTH

Homo sapiens

Dromornithid

Plaisiodon centralis

cf *Pallimnarchus*

16 my

major extinction of dinosaurs
first flowers, birds and mammals

Syncyclonenia socialis

Maccoyella (oyster)

Mytilus inflatus (mussel)

210 my

major extinction of trilobites

Australia separating from Gondwana
coal formation

Triphyllopteris austrina

355 my

first reptiles

Bothriolepis

410 my

first animals on land

first plants on land

Aporthophyla dichotomalis

Madiganella tatei

Graptolites Brachiopod Gastropod

Raphistoma

Brachiopod

Dinorthis leviensis *Asaphid* Trilobite

510 my

first fish

Agnostid

Xystridurid Trilobite

Archaeocynthid

Hyolithid

Micromitra Brachiopod

570 my

brachiopods
molluscs
trilobites

trace fossils
jellyfish

Dicksonia flat worms *Skinnera brooksi*

Stromatolites *Acaciella australica*

Phycades pedum

Hallidaya brueri

650 my

820 my

first stromatolites over 2500 my

stopped. It became a desert and the surface of the Amadeus Basin was eroded and transformed to a low-lying plain with sand dunes, ephemeral lakes and some rivers. The clean white sands of Mereenie Sandstone were deposited during this period, around 360 million years ago.

All these deposited sediments were thrown into total disarray by the Alice Springs Orogeny. This major mountain-building event, impacted extensively on the region from 340 million to 310 million years ago, with the peak of activity being 315 million years ago. The land surface was lifted, pushed, folded and faulted. It was this event which upended the Uluru Arkose, tilted and faulted the Mount Currie Conglomerate to form Kata Tjuta and cracked joints into the Mereenie Sandstone in the George Gill Range.

A stable landscape — the last 300 million years

The Central Australian landscape was lifted back above sea level during the Alice Springs Orogeny — where it has since remained. The marine influence was removed. Extensive active erosion has shaped the landscape for almost 300 million years. The layers of rock above Uluru, Kata Tjuta and Mount Conner were worn down. These resistant land forms began to protrude and together formed a watershed between Lake Amadeus to the north and the country to the south.

Erosion continued to such an extent that by 70 million years ago a broad valley, deeper than presently exists, had formed between Uluru and Kata Tjuta, but we do not know if the two features looked the same then as they do now. Sediments carried by streams were deposited in this valley. Marshes and peat formed and ultimately became compressed into layers of brown coal. Many plants had evolved by this time and their distinctive pollens have been used in dating the more recent sediments of the valley. The sand in these sediments has a very practical importance: the sediments are the main water-bearing strata of the area and are the source of water for the Ayers Rock Resort.

FIGURE 2.29 Both Uluru and Kata Tjuta were formed from sediments deposited during the erosion of the Petermann Ranges; originally they probably formed as two different alluvial fans as illustrated in this reconstruction which is a view to the south.

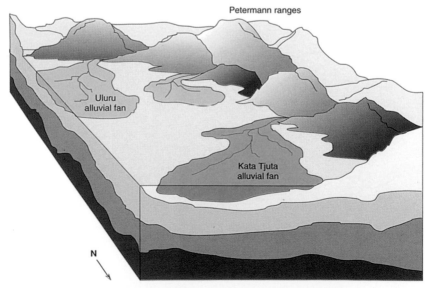

Throughout the last 250 million to 300 million years, Central Australia has been very stable geologically. So stable in fact that Tennant Creek, 500 kilometres north of Alice Springs, was once designated as a suitable site for the disposal of toxic wastes, especially radioactive wastes. The proposal was nullified by an earthquake in 1988 measuring 6.8 on the Richter Scale which moved the two towns half a metre closer together! A similar size earthquake in the populous Middle East killed around 100,000 people. Nevertheless, Central Australia is still a relatively stable portion of the earth's crust.

In the last half million years the climate has become drier but there has been some variation. For example, during the glacial periods conditions were much drier than they were during the periods between glacials. But it was still an arid climate. Chemical weathering of the rocks has continued and the winds have sculptured the land surface, developing the vast dune fields of the Centre.

Dunes

Uluru and even Kata Tjuta may be familiar images of Central Australia but the dunes of the desert are a far more extensive and persistent image. They cover 82 per cent of Uluru National Park and 35 percent of Watarrka. The rocky remnants are mere pinpricks in the desert by comparison. Dune fields form when arid or semi arid conditions prevail in areas where there is plenty of fine-grained, quartz-rich sediment available. This describes Central Australia.

The vision of a bare, rippled sand dune known from other parts of the world is an uncommon sight in Central Australia. The present

FIGURE 2.30 Stark red sand dunes of Central Australia — some are bare, most are well covered with vegetation; sometimes other features such as these blocks of calcrete are visible. *J. A. Kerle*

climate is wet enough for plants to grow, mostly stabilising the dunes. The tops of dunes can become exposed and destabilised by fires, resulting in a blowout of the sand, but generally this is neither extensive nor permanent. This was not always the case. During the extremely arid glacial periods the dunes did not support plant life, and active dune building occurred. The last significant phase of dune building occurred about 30,000 years ago, when the dunes of Uluru — Kata Tjuta National Park began to form.

But granite and other quartz-rich metamorphic rocks are still eroding to produce dune-building sediments. Periodically the ephemeral rivers disgorge a load of sediment onto their floodouts. Then the wind comes into play. The very fine dust particles become airborne as dust storms; the heavier grains are redistributed and sculptured into dunes. The dunes vary in height in both national parks and may reach 13 metres. The most spectacular dunes in arid Australia, though, are found in the Simpson Desert, south-east of Uluru. There they regularly reach an impressive 35 metres in height and can run for hundreds of kilometres in parallel formation.

The dunes are really only a sandy veneer over the underlying rock surface. This is most obvious in the swale, the low part between two dunes. In some places the bedrock is exposed. In others the swale is filled with richer, finer alluvial soils rather than sand, and mulga shrubland grows there. Or there may be calcrete and gypsite outcroppings, indicating that a watercourse once flowed there.

Rivers and salt lakes

The stark image of shining white salt lakes against a backdrop of red dunes is another familiar vision of Central Australia. The extensive salt lake system in the south-west of the Northern Territory is a distinctive feature of the region. While the lakes are not part of either national park they do have visual, biological and cultural significance. They were important places for the Aboriginal people and they greatly frustrated the early white explorers who found them difficult to cross. The most accessible place for you to see a small part of the salt lake chain is across the road and over the dune from the Mount Conner roadside stop (p.158).

The chain of salt lakes in the Amadeus system extends for more than 500 kilometres from Lake Hopkins in Western Australia almost to the Finke River east of Lake Amadeus, part of which is shown in the map on p.138. It is the remnant of a vast fossil drainage system which discharged into Lake Eyre via the ancestral Finke River during the Tertiary Period from 65 million years ago. The streams and wetlands which formed in the valley between Uluru and Kata Tjuta during that period were also a part of this drainage system. But the system no longer drains into the Finke River. There is a low ridge or divide in the vicinity of Curtin Springs which separates the western (Lake Amadeus) portion from the eastern (Karinga Creek) portion, which lies between Curtin Springs and Erldunda on the Stuart Highway.

FIGURE 2.31 Shining white salt lake and dune. *M. W. Gillam*

FIGURE 2.32 Lalgra Waterhole on the Finke River. *J. A. Kerle*

The past extent of the drainage system is indicated by the occurrence of calcrete masses which can be found well away from the present system. These masses, which are composed of gravel, sand or other debris cemented together by porous calcium carbonate, show that the lakes rose to very high levels during periods of higher rainfall. The most recent of these events occurred within the last 30,000 to 50,000 years and lakes probably then covered the whole area between Uluru and the George Gill Range.

The saltiness of the water underlying the Lake Amadeus system varies enormously. Brines several times more concentrated than seawater (greater than 110 grams of total dissolved solids per litre) are present immediately under the lakes. But good supplies of fresh water (1–5 grams of total dissolved solids per litre) are also present in the calcrete or limestone deposits which are remnants of the original Tertiary watercourses. Both these groundwater supplies are recharged by infiltration of rainwater.

The rivers in Central Australia are all quite short. None reaches the sea and most start and finish within the region. They are dry most of the time running for only short periods after heavy rainfalls. Mostly they end in a 'floodout' where the water spreads on to the plain and drops its sediment load as it evaporates or disappears underground. In the last 15 million years many of the ancient rivers have become buried by sand and the alignment of their original paths is now visible only from space!

When travelling through Central Australia you will cross a number of these dry riverbeds. One of the best known is the Todd River in Alice Springs, the site of the annual dry river boatrace, Henley-on-Todd, where the boats are carried rather than rowed! Between Alice Springs and Uluru or Watarrka you will cross Roe Creek, Hugh River, Palmer River and Finke River. Their waterless beds belie the ferocious and dangerous torrents which periodically transform them. They can rise incredibly quickly and it is not unusual for people to find themselves stuck in a river or creek crossing. They can be very deceptive. These rivers mostly stopped constantly flowing 30–40 thousand years ago.

The mighty Finke River (see map on p.vi–vii) is the longest of the watercourses in Central Australia. It runs south-easterly, meandering from the western MacDonnell Ranges to its floodout in the Simpson Desert. It no longer reaches Lake Eyre. It began its journey about 15 million years ago and is still an awesome sight when in flood. Analysis and dating of sediment deposits along the river indicate that prior to modern times, the largest floods in the Finke were in the 1200's, 700 years ago. Large floods in the Finke River also occurred in 1967, 1972 and 1974 and it is evident from the journals of John McDouall Stuart, as he followed the course of the Finke River in the 1860s, that he believed it to be a permanently trickling river.

Prehistoric Life

Among the first life forms to develop anywhere on earth were stromatolites. Some of the oldest in the world, at 3500 million years, have been found in Western Australia. Living specimens can also be found in Western Australia, growing in the shallow, highly saline seas of Shark Bay. Stromatolites are microscopic organisms which begin as large mat-shaped colonies. They produce a sticky surface which traps sediments. As it slowly grows, each colony divides into separate multi-layered columns, forming a composite dome. In Central Australia the fossil stromatolites are not quite as old as those in Western Australia, being found in the 800 million year old Bitter Springs formation on Ellery Creek in the West MacDonnell Ranges (map, p.vii).

Stromatolites are not the only fossils to be found in Central Australia. The age of the rocks and the lack of soil and dense vegetation help to ensure that a variety of interesting forms can be found. They range in age from the stromatolites to a deposit of fossil vertebrate bones which are about 15 million years old (mid-Miocene). These and other forms of life found in Central Australia are illustrated in Fig 2.28, pp.34–35.

Around 570 million years ago, at the beginning of the Cambrian Period, the abundance and diversity of animal life exploded. Trace fossils (tracks and burrows) of worms from this time can be found in rocks along the Ross River south of the Ross River homestead east of Alice Springs. Shelled animals also became common including trilobites (an extinct crustacean), brackiopods (lamp shells) and gastropods (snails).

In Central Australia, the most abundant fossil remains are from the Ordovician period (510–438 million years ago) when most of the country was covered by a shallow sea. The Pacoota Sandstone, Stairway Sandstone and Carmichael Sandstone contain a lot of fossils and trace fossils. Some of these can be seen around Kings Canyon. Scolithus worm tubes, trilobite tracks and casts of brachiopods, gastropods, nautiloids and bivalves (molluscs with two shells) have been found.

Vertebrates first appear in the Ordovician rock strata near Alice Springs as an imprint of *Arandaspis*, the oldest known fish. Remains of another fish, *Bothriolepis*, have been found in 340 million year old rock strata of the West MacDonnell Ranges. Perhaps the fishing in Central Australia was better then than it is now!

Probably the richest fossil beds in Central Australia occur in the Horn Valley

Siltstone and Stokes Siltstone where large nautiloids, trilobites, brachiopods, gastropods and bivalves are found. Some fossils can be found a few hundred metres from the Stuart Highway, on both sides of the bridge, at Maloney Creek 120 kilometres south of Alice Springs.

Very few fossils formed in the rock strata were deposited after the inland seas retreated about 430 million years ago. During the Tertiary Period (65 million years ago), the Central Australian landscape was much as it is now but the climate was wetter and cooler. It was at this time that the great ancient continent of Gondwana began to break up and the Australian Plate started to move north. Many of the low-lying areas, such as the valley between Uluru and Kata Tjuta, became marshy. The sediments deposited in those marshes contain fossil plant parts and pollens which can be identified and used to reconstruct the botanical environment of the time.

Early white visitors to Central Australia had written so glowingly of the central ranges that others following after gained a misleading impression. The botanist of the Horn Scientific Expedition in 1894, Ralph Tate, had '... pictured a vast mountain system capable of preserving some remnants of that pristine flora which had existed on this continent in Palaeocene times — probably a beech, possibly an oak, elm or sycamore'.[3] Unfortunately he was 40 million years too late!

Pollens taken from cores drilled near Uluru come from land plants which now grow in wetter climates such as that along the Victorian coast or in Tasmania. The oldest brown coals, dated at 65–70 million years, contain pollens from *Podocarpus* (southern conifer) species and from fern spores. *Nothofagus* (beech myrtle) pollens were abundant 40 million years ago, as were pollens from extinct members of the Proteaceae (banksias, grevilleas) and rainforest representatives of the Myrtaceae (eucalypts and others).

As the continent dried out, the rainforest vegetation retreated to the north and was replaced by savanna or woodland environments. The larger vertebrates had evolved and were well established on the continent. A rich fossil deposit on Alcoota Station north-east of Alice Springs provides one glimpse of the wildlife living in Central Australia at that time. Representatives of the so-called Australian megafauna are found there and include large grazing mammals such as *Diprotodon optatum* which was three metres long and two metres in height. These diprotodontids, which were part of the same group of marsupials as the kangaroos and possums, lived in open woodland. And lakes supported a variety of crocodiles, turtles and flamingoes.

The most common fossils found at Alcoota are those of dromornithid birds. These birds, known only from Australia, lived until about 26,000 years ago and were familiar to Aboriginal people. They were very large flightless birds but, despite some similarities to emus and cassowaries, may in fact be more closely related to the domestic hen! The biggest of them, *Dromornis stirtoni*, was three metres tall and weighed a massive 350–400 kilograms — the largest bird ever recorded.

The faunal record provided by the Alcoota fossils indicates a time of great change amongst the land mammals. The record contains a few members of animal groups which were to become dominant in Australia and one which persisted from earlier times. There were giant kangaroos (macropodids) and a variety of diprotodontids grazing in the region. They were preyed upon by the marsupial lion *Wakaleo* and early ancestors of the thylacine (Tasmanian 'Tiger'). Unfortunately, no plant remains have been found at this site to help us reconstruct the plant communities that were present.

3

THE SKIES ABOVE
THE CLIMATE AND NIGHT SKY OF
CENTRAL AUSTRALIA

'See Alice while she's hot!' was the cry from tourist brochures promoting Alice Springs. Central Australia is famous for the blistering dry heat of summer — and it is the quiet season for the tourist industry. It is hard to comprehend temperatures greater than 50°C, such as can occur in the heat of a midsummer day amongst the domes of Kata Tjuta. But of course that is not the time to go walking there. Indeed, the climb to the summit of Uluru is closed if the forecast maximum temperature is above 37°C. That forecast is for a temperature measured inside a shaded screen; the heat radiating from the Rock itself would be significantly higher on such a day.

While the hot summers may be well known, the frosty winter nights can be a great surprise to the visitor. And then there is the cold lazy wind which often blows, especially across the top of Uluru. But, if you are prepared for cool or cold nights, the weather for the six months from Easter onwards is delightful. Cloudless skies, balmy days and cold, clear nights. But, regardless of the time of year, always remember to carry water and to drink lots of it.

FIGURE 3.1 A turbulent Central Australian sky. *M. W. Gillam*

FIGURE 3.2 Henbury meteorite craters — the meteorites are thought to have landed within the last 10,000 years. *J. A. Kerle*

FIGURE 3.3 Gosse Bluff, west of Alice Springs, perhaps the remnant of a huge crater left by a comet about 130 million years ago. *J. A. Kerle*

When lying snugly in a swag (bedroll) on those cold clear nights, staring into the sky is a humbling experience. You are merely a speck in the sand under the wonderful brilliance of a sky full of twinkling stars. There are no city lights to spoil it and rarely are there many clouds. The Milky Way is like a well-lit highway across the expanse — indeed the sky is so black and the stars so bright that the Milky Way can cast a shadow. The constellations are very clear and there are lots of 'shooting stars'. A joy to children and adults, locals and visitors alike.

At the time of the passing of Halley's Comet in 1987 the clarity of the Central Australian skies attracted many people. While the comet was not the spectacular sight anticipated — it had diminished greatly from the brilliance of its passing in 1910 — the stars were still there in all their glory.

The comet's 1987 traverse merely boosted the tourist industry. Many other celestial objects have left a more lasting impact in the region. The Henbury meteorite craters north-east of the George Gill Range can be visited on the drive between Watarrka National Park and Alice Springs. Gosse Bluff, west of Alice Springs, is thought to be the central core of a comet or asteroid impact crater. It can be visited from the western loop road between Watarrka and the West MacDonnell Ranges National Park (see map on p.vii). There is also a scattering of tektites — small glassy rocks of meteoric origin — throughout the desert.

FIGURE 3.4 Uluru at sunrise. *M. W. Gillam*
FIGURE 3.5 (opposite page) Cascading water and the steely grey of Uluru in the rain. *M. W. Gillam*

THE CENTRAL AUSTRALIAN CLIMATE

The colours of Uluru are one of its most famous features. They vary from dramatic hues of orange-red to a brooding grey. Many brochures have been produced to demonstrate this incredible range of colours and visitors are sometimes disappointed because they have not been able to see a stunningly vivid sunset.

It is the influence of the earth's atmosphere, the clouds and humidity, that controls the colours of the sunset on Uluru and Kata Tjuta. The atmosphere splits the rays of the sun into the colour spectrum as a giant prism would. When the sun is low in the sky, at sunrise and sunset, the red end of the spectrum is predominant. Too much cloud or smoke haze will block the sun's rays and the sunset will not be as bright. The most vivid colours can be seen when there is enough cloud to re-reflect and intensify the sun's rays, but not block them too much. The iron oxide staining of the rocks and sand enhance the colour.

Because these factors vary, it is impossible to know how spectacular the sunset will be at any given time. Uluru has many moods. In the rain it can have a silvery sheen as sheets of water cascade down the sheer sides. After rain, the Rock becomes steely grey under a threatening sky. These colours can be just as impressive as the rich reds. At other times, the full moon appears to roll up the side and across the rock as it rises. And sunset on Kata Tjuta is just as magnificent.

The climate in Central Australia is arid — just as it is in 70 per cent of the Australian continent. An arid climate is broadly defined as one with insufficient rainfall for the regular production of crops. Such a description is undoubtedly appropriate for Central Australia! It is dry: it doesn't rain very often and the humidity is low. In order to highlight this some comparative figures for Sydney, Melbourne, London, New York and Tokyo are provided in Table 3.1.

The weather pattern is strongly influenced by the location of this region in the centre of the continent and by seasonal changes in the continental air pressure systems. Central Australia lies in a transition zone between temperate and tropical climatic forces. During winter the south-easterly high pressure belt is the major influence on the weather of the region. In summer the tropical depressions and convectional thunderstorms can cause heavy rainfalls.

From April to October the skies are mostly bright and clear, with excellent visibility. Periodically this is broken by a low pressure trough which can produce strong winds, frosty nights or some cloud. If it rains, the rain can be heavy and widespread. In the hotter parts of the year, from November to March, the sky is usually cloudier

Table 3.1 Comparative climate statistics for Alice Springs, Sydney, Melbourne, Perth, New York, Tokyo and London.

Seasons: S=summer, W=winter.

Location	Season	Average Daily temperature °C		Average Daily temperature °F		Relative humidity %		Annual average rainfall		Average daily sunshine	Average number of rain
		max	min	max	min	9am	3pm	mm	inches	hours	days
Alice Springs	S (Jan)	36	21	97	70	31	23	253	9.9	9.8	44
	W (Jul)	19	4	67	39	49	31				
Sydney	S (Jan)	26	18	78	65	68	64	1082	46.5	6.6	139
	W (Jul)	16	8	60	46	76	60				
Melbourne	S (Jan)	26	14	78	57	58	48	650	25.7	5.7	147
	W (Jul)	13	6	56	42	82	65				
Perth	S (Jan)	29	17	85	63	51	44	881	34.7	8.0	116
	W (Jul)	17	9	63	48	76	63				
New York	S (Jul)	28	19	82	66	77	58	1076	42.8	7.3	121
	W (Jan)	3	-4	37	24	72	60				
Tokyo	S (Jul)	28	21	83	70	91	69	1565	61.6	5.5	107
	W (Jan)	8	-2	47	29	73	48				
London	S (Jul)	22	14	71	56	71	59	593	23.3	4.1	153
	W (Jan)	6	2	43	36	86	77				

and there is more of a dust haze. When moist air masses drift south from the tropics the humidity can increase markedly. Tropical depressions, the product of tropical cyclones, can also pass through. They are no longer accompanied by the cyclonic winds that hit the northern coast, but they do cause higher humidity and lower temperatures and may bring lots of rain.

RAINFALL, DROUGHT AND HUMIDITY

The most important and obvious feature of rainfall in Central Australia is that it is highly unpredictable in space, time and intensity. Occasionally, heavy rains fall over large areas, but often storms are so isolated that they cause only one of two adjacent creeks to flow. Droughts can last for years. Describing the rainfall in the region with an annual average figure is highly misleading. The rainfall patterns of many other deserts of the world, have a regular annual cycle, but in Central Australia patterns or cycles can be detected only after records have been collected for many years.

Long-term weather records are rare in the Centre. Tempe Downs, the pastoral station adjacent to Watarrka National Park, has one of the best rainfall records which

FIGURE 3.6 Monthly mean maximum and minimum rainfall and temperature for Uluru; records were collected for 19 years from 1964 to 1983.

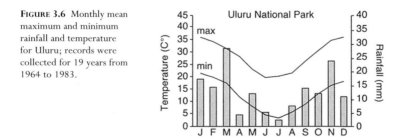

Table 3.2 Rainfall records for Uluru and Tempe Downs

For Uluru, the records cover the period 1964 to 1983 and for Tempe Downs 1883 to 1977; the Tempe Downs figures for the 15 year period 1964 to 1977 have also been presented to provide a closer comparision with the Uluru observations.

	Uluru	Tempe Downs	
Number of Years	19	15	94
Mean annual rainfall, mm	330	331	248
Coefficient of Variation	58%	70%	59%
Minimum annual rainfall, mm	82	41	41
Maximum annual rainfall, mm	935	980	980

covers the 94 years from 1883 to 1977. In that time the lowest annual rainfall was 41mm and the highest 980mm. The mean (average) rainfall was 248mm. At the Uluru Ranger Station, rainfall records were only reliably kept from 1964 to 1983 (Fig. 3.1). The rain gauge was then moved to Yulara and not re-established at Uluru until 1992 creating a ten-year break in the sequence of records. The period from 1964 to 1983, 19 years, included the end of a severe drought and several years of exceptional rainfall, with annual rainfall ranging from 82mm to 935mm. The 19 year average was 330mm. These data are summarised on Table 3.2.

Since records were only collected for a short period at Uluru, do these figures represent a true picture of rainfall patterns at the Rock? Comparison with the Tempe Downs records, particularly the records for the same period, demonstrates that 1964-1983 was probably a relatively wet period overall and that the likely mean rainfall for Uluru is perhaps 230mm or 250mm. But if you are in the middle of a drought or a flood, the average figure doesn't have much relevance! Even during the drought of the late 1950s and early 1960s Bill Harney, the first curator at Uluru recorded frequent storms: 'For two years my tent kept me dry and many a tourist who arrived late at night during a storm slept on its floor'.[1]

Storms occurring during droughts are much more likely to fall around the mountain ranges and outcrops. It is not unusual to travel through drought-stricken sand dunes, dry and brown, only to discover wildflowers blooming within 500 metres of a rocky outcrop. These storms are especially important because they replenish the waterholes. In the few months after his arrival at Uluru in 1957 Bill Harney noted that the water from Maggie Springs — Mutitjulu — had dried up but 'a few days later some rain came in from the west to fill Maggie Springs'.[2] The effect of the ranges and rocky outcrops on the rainfall of Central Australia is one reason why this area is not as dry as the Simpson Desert or the Lake Eyre region where the annual average rainfall is estimated at 75mm to 120mm.

While the irregular storms are important for sustaining plant and animal life it is the heavy rains which fall over large areas that can end a drought, fully replenishing the underground waters and saving long-lived plants. Rainfalls like this are very rare but when they occur the country changes dramatically. In March 1989 some 500mm drenched the Uluru area in about three days. It became impossible to travel off the formed roads for about two months! This rain certainly made it impossible to pursue field studies for a while. Rain can fall in any month of the year in the Centre but

FIGURE 3.7 The barren landscape during a drought. *NT Department of Primary Industries and Fisheries.*

the influence of tropical weather patterns induces higher rainfall in summer. Thunderstorms are most common in November.

A drought can be defined as a period of months or years when little rain falls, the country gets 'burnt up', grass and water disappear, crops become worthless and sheep and cattle die. It is a constant spectre of life in Central Australia. Even if some rain falls the average evaporation rate of around 2800mm per year ensures that most of it is lost to the atmosphere. Thus, the length of a drought is not easy to determine. Bill Harney believed that a fall of 175mm in 1959 provided a temporary break in the drought conditions at the time, but it is really only the fall of heavy rains over a large area, recurring for a few years, that provide a drought-breaking recharge to the country. Analysis of historical information indicates that until 1970, there were no true drought-breaking rains since 1922 — and perhaps even as far back as the 1870s.

The humidity in Central Australia is low. I have heard visitors to the Centre say they felt as if they had 'dried up like a potato chip'! Local sales of heavy duty skin moisturisers are high. Actual relative humidity readings range between 5 per cent and 45 per cent, except during and shortly after rainy weather. The general trend of humidity is almost opposite to that of temperature — it is highest in midwinter and lowest in summer.

The overall low humidity also explains why dew is less common here than it is in other deserts of the world. For example, humid onshore winds allow the regular formation of dew on the coastal Namib desert in the south-west of the African continent, and this is readily utilised by wildlife. In Central Australia, the atmospheric humidity is mostly too low for the dew point temperature to be reached; but the higher humidities in winter are instrumental in increasing the incidence of frosts from June to August.

TEMPERATURE

Unlike rainfalls, the temperatures of Central Australia are quite predictable. Typically, the temperature range, both throughout the year (Fig. 3.6) and within a 24-hour period is large. The maximum monthly temperature ranges from 40°C or more in January to 20°C in July, while the minimum ranges from 22°C in January to 4°C in July. Similarly, the air temperatures can change by 20–25°C within one day. It must also be remembered that these are average *air* temperatures. The temperature of the ground, the rocks and the radiant temperature of the rocks could be 10°C higher — raising the temperature amongst the domes of Kata Tjuta and Kings Canyon above 50°C.

The large daily fluctuations in temperature are a direct result of the extremely high levels of radiation. There is very little cloud or moisture in the air (humidity) to interfere with either the incoming or the outgoing radiation. The greatest fluctuations occur during winter and through to late spring. While people may enjoy the balmy days with cold to freezing nights, the plants do not thrive so well. The cold nights kill parts of the plants and then the daytime temperatures rise high enough to dry out the dead plant tissues. In association with the low rainfall, this restricts plant growth, enhances soil erosion and determines fire behaviour in this country.

WINDS

Most of the winds blowing through Uluru and Watarrka come from the south-east. The windiest time of the year is from August to November with ground velocities averaging about 1–2 kilometres per hour. But wind speeds of up to 90kph have also been recorded. On top of Uluru wind speeds are generally much higher than they are on the ground, so be prepared for that. It can also be much colder on top of the Rock because of the wind-chill factor. Make sure you carry warm clothing in such conditions to avoid risking hypothermia (severe exposure). It can be quite windy on top of the George Gill Range too, but detailed information on wind speeds does not exist for Watarrka National Park.

CLIMATE AND THE VEGETATION; THE EFFECTS OF FIRE

The intensity and timing of rainfall throughout the year is the most important climatic factor affecting the distribution and growth of plants. (The Wildflower Calendar on p.62 shows typical weather and plants in flower, by month.) It is summer rainfall that is most valued by the pastoralists of Central Australia because it stimulates the germination and growth of perennial plants, especially the grasses. Most of the perennial plants are sensitive to low temperatures and remain dormant throughout the winter, even after significant rains have fallen. This growth pattern is used by common arid zone plant species such as mulga *Acacia aneura* and spinifex (*Triodia* and *Plectrachne* species).

If winter rains have fallen the perennial plants grow rapidly as soon as the temperatures are warm enough, and they grow until all the available soil moisture is exhausted. They then continue to respond with intermittent bursts of growth after sporadic summer rains. Many of the ephemeral wildflower species, especially the daisies (Compositae), grow actively even in low temperatures. They grow rapidly after winter rains but, as their roots penetrate only to a depth of 150mm, they generally don't deplete the soil water reservoir which is available for the larger perennial species. Regeneration of the perennial species only occurs after extensive periods of rainfall.

Fires are also strongly affected by the weather. November is the worst time for wildfires, particularly if there have been winter and spring rains. Good plant growth produces a buildup in fuel (leaves and ground litter) and the high temperatures dry this out, ready to be ignited by lightning or accidentally by people. The fuel buildup is also assisted by frost damage and its flammability is increased by the low atmospheric humidity. Summer wildfires can decimate vast areas of Central Australia. One wildfire in 1950 burnt one-third of Uluru National Park (some 440 square kilometres), and in 1976 two fires burnt three-quarters of the park.

FIGURE 3.8 Small fires lit by Anangu created a mosaic of plant associations across the country which enhanced the diversity of plants and animals; here there is a clear distinction between recently burnt and mature spinifex grassland. *J. A. Kerle*

The incidence of extensive wildfires was undoubtedly much lower before the introduction of livestock to Central Australia. This is because the Aboriginal people regularly burnt the land, manipulating the environment to their advantage. Their burning was generally carried out in the cooler months. The fires were small and close together, breaking the country up into patches and creating a mosaic of vegetation. This had several advantages for the people. The patchiness of the country, generally reduced the extent of any wildfire and also enhanced the growth and abundance of plants and animals important for their survival. The severe reduction in Aboriginal patch-burning this century has resulted in vegetation communities being much more homogeneous, reducing the habitat diversity necessary for the survival of some of our wildlife species.

THE NIGHT SKIES

On those clear sparkling winter nights the enthusiastic stargazer at Uluru or Watarrka is treated to an extraordinary array of stars and constellations throughout the night. At that time of year the Southern Cross is visible for the first few hours after dark and then, if you wake during the pre-dawn glow, Orion is bright above the northern horizon. Stargazing in Central Australia is rewarding at any time of the year but it is exceptional during winter — so long as there are no clouds!

Stars have been a source of fascination for people of all cultures. Many traditions and stories have been ascribed to them. Australians of European origin and astronomers use the Greek names and myths to describe the constellations (groups of stars) and individual stars. Because the constellations were named by people in the northern hemisphere, they are mostly upside down when viewed from Australia, making them more difficult to recognise!

Of course, the Aboriginal people also have a rich cultural tradition deriving from the stars, a part of the Tjukurpa (p.14). The Aboriginal celestial world is where the people of the sky live and have eternal life, unlike the people down below. Many of these once lived on earth. Their sky world contains an abundance of food, shelter and water. Often the most important stars in Aboriginal stories are not the brightest and, predictably, they do not recognise most of the major groups of stars or constellations defined by the European tradition. In contrast to the superb ability of Aboriginal people to navigate during the day, they do not have a well developed system of star navigation. As a rule they did not like to move around at night.

How many stars are there in that blanket of lights? We can only see about 3000 separate stars with the naked eye but with a telescope or even binoculars, this number is greatly increased. There are many features to look for: bright stars, constellations of stars, other galaxies, nebulae, planets, meteors, comets and

FIGURE 3.9 Stargazing in Central Australia is especially rewarding on a clear winter night. *M. W. Gillam*

man-made satellites. And there can be special occurrences like an eclipse of the moon or sun.

The sun is the star of our solar system. All other stars — those blazing balls of fire, exploding like countless hydrogen bombs — are so far away from us that they appear as mere pinpoints of light. Even the closest of stars beyond the sun, Alpha Centauri, is 41 million million kilometres away from earth. To avoid the use of extraordinarily large numbers like this, astronomers talk in terms of a 'light-year' — the distance travelled by light in one year, or 9.5 million million kilometres. Alpha Centauri is therefore 4.3 light-years away.

Stars at the edge of the known universe are ten thousand million light-years away; in other words it has taken ten thousand million years for the light we can see to travel from them to us. Given the length of time involved, it is entirely possible that those stars are now completely different — if they still exist at all. Not all stars are the same age, either. The ageing, cooler stars are detected by their reddish colour while younger, hotter stars are blue. Our sun is middle-aged and a yellow colour.

OUR GALAXY — THE MILKY WAY

The brilliant band of starry light stretching right across the sky is the Milky Way. It contains some two hundred thousand million stars, is 100,000 light-years long and 10,000 light-years across at its widest point. Our solar system lies about 30,000 light-years from the centre of the Milky Way.

The Southern Cross and the pointers are also a part of the Milky Way. At times the Southern Cross seems to be embedded in the Milky Way, even though it is much nearer to us than the background stars. This illusion is caused by our changing line of sight as we rotate around the sun. Beside the two brightest stars of the Southern Cross —Alpha Crucis and Beta Crucis — is the Coal Sack. This is a black nebula — a cloud-like formation of gas and dust. It is so opaque that it hides the stars behind it and gives the impression of a black hole in the sky.

A Galaxy is an enormous group of stars clustered together, and others can be seen in our night sky. The nearest are the Magellanic Clouds which are adjacent to the Milky Way. These two cloud-like patches are smaller than the Milky Way and the mariners of the southern seas in the 16th century, who thought they were clouds of glowing gas, used them for navigating. The Large Magellanic Cloud contains some ten thousand million stars but because it is 170,000 light-years away it appears merely as a fuzzy patch. It also contains our nearest supernova, or exploding star.

For Aboriginal people the Milky Way can be a river or dry creekbed — sometimes seen to be dividing the camps of different clans, as indicated by the stars on either side. In another story it is the hair of an ancestor streaming across the sky, the ancestor being represented by the the Coal Sack near the Southern Cross. And some people refer to the Milky Way as smoke produced by the fires that are the stars. The two Magellanic Clouds are sometimes referred to as spirit brothers, the larger cloud being the older and kinder of the two.

THE SOUTHERN CROSS

In the southern hemisphere the Southern Cross is one of the brightest and most easily recognised groups of stars. It has been used by many travellers for assurance that they are travelling in the right direction. Its significance in Australia is highlighted by its inclusion on the national flag, albeit inaccurately! To find the Southern Cross, stand

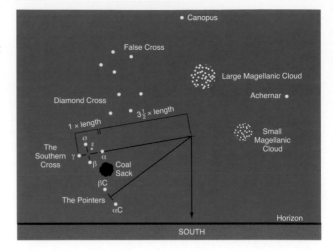

FIGURE 3.10 The Southern Cross and how to use it to find south; the pointers (αC and βC) are part of the constellation of Centaurus.

facing south (the sunset being on your right) and look up. It is a cross-shaped cluster with five stars and near it are the two bright stars called Pointers — Alpha and Beta Centauri (Fig. 3.10). Of course its position in the southern sky varies with the time of night and the time of year.

The brightest star of the Southern Cross is Alpha Crucis (α). The others, in descending order of brightness, are Beta Crucis (β), Gamma Crucis (γ), Delta Crucis (δ) and Epsilon Crucis (ϵ). They all vary a little in colour, with Alpha, Beta and Delta being bluish-white, the hottest. Close to Beta Crucis is the Jewel Box. This especially beautiful cluster is visible to the naked eye but is greatly enhanced with a telescope. There are more than 100 multicoloured stars in this group, surrounding a red star Kappa Crucis — a jewel in the sky.

There are two other cross-shaped groups of stars in the southern skies, the False Cross and the Diamond Cross, so be careful not to confuse them. Both of these have only four stars; the presence of the Coal Sack and the Pointers beside the Southern Cross can be used to verify its identification. The False and Diamond crosses are larger but not as bright as the Southern Cross. If you hold four fingers together at arm's length they will fit into the long axis of the Southern Cross.

In the northern hemisphere the Pole Star lies directly above the North Pole. The Southern Cross is not quite so well placed but it can still be used to find south as shown in the diagram. The long axis of the cross points to the South Celestial Pole. With your fingers at arms length, measure the length of the cross. South is directly below a point three and a half times this length from Alpha Crucis. Another method is to draw an imaginary line along the long axis, extending beyond Alpha Crucis, and then draw another line which perpendicularly bisects the pointers. South is directly below the point of intersection of these two lines.

One Aboriginal story about the Southern Cross concerns the wedge-tailed eagle and the black kite. In this story, some people suggest that the group of stars as a whole represents the eagle. Alternatively, the stars are the eagle's footprints, the Pointers his throwing stick, the Coal Sack his nest, and the footmarks of the black kite are the False Cross. In another story, four of the stars are four girls who won't marry an old man who passionately loves them. The old man is Alpha Centauri.

ORION AND THE SAUCEPAN

When the constellation of Orion the 'hunter' is high in the sky in the southern hemisphere he is standing on his head! This makes the constellation much more difficult to recognise. The Saucepan in the centre is more easily located. It incorporates the belt and sword of Orion (Fig. 3.11). These stars can be used to find directions too. When the handle of the saucepan is vertical it is directly above north. To find the Saucepan look towards the north.

In the middle of the saucepan handle, or Orion's sword there is a 'fuzzy star'. With a telescope you can see that it isn't a star at all but rather a vast area of gas and dust which is in a state of turmoil. It is the Orion Nebula — part of a 'stellar nursery' containing a cluster of four newly born blue stars called the Trapezium. The bright stars and star clusters in this area make it a rewarding view through binoculars.

Betelgeuse (pronounced beetlejuice!), or Alpha Orionis, is a red supergiant star which forms part of Orion's arm. Its orange-red colour indicates that it is quite cool — only 3,000°C! — and its brightness varies irregularly. It is so big that if it replaced the sun in our solar system it would eat up Mercury, Venus, Earth and Mars.

Orion's two dogs, Canis Major and Canis Minor, are to the east of him. They are separated by the Milky Way. Sirius (the 'shining one'), the brightest star in the sky, belongs to Canis Major and lies only nine light-years from our sun. Procyon is the brightest star in the smaller Canis Minor. Both Sirius and Procyon are double stars and their dwarf companions can be seen through binoculars.

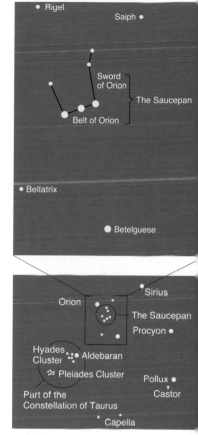

FIGURE 3.11 The stars of 'The Saucepan', the upside down 'Orion' and their near neighbours

SCORPIUS — THE SCORPION

Between March and October Scorpius can be seen in the southern evening sky. This magnificent formation is distinguished by a long line of stars which curve to form the scorpion's stinging tail (Fig. 3.12). In June, when Scorpius is overhead, it is upside down with the tail curving downwards. By August and September, when it is closer to the south-western horizon, the tail is standing upright. In the Greek myth it is the scorpion who killed Orion and so it rises as Orion sets.

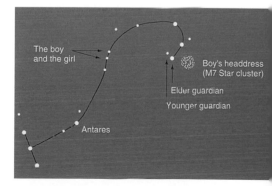

FIGURE 3.12 The stars of Scorpius (the Scorpion) and the characters from one Aboriginal story

Antares, or Alpha Scorpion, is the bright orange-red star in the body of the Scorpion. This is another red supergiant star which, with a diameter of 700 million kilometres, is even larger than Betelgeuse. The name Antares means 'rival of Mars', invoking a mythical rivalry with the red planet.

Instead of defining this group of stars as a scorpion, one Aboriginal story involves the guardians of the circumcision ceremony. The tale is about a young boy and girl at the time of his initiation. The girl broke one of the strictest of laws and stayed, hidden, to watch the ceremony. She then followed the boy to his camp and, after his guardian had fallen asleep, persuaded him to escape with her. Just as they left, the guardian awoke. Knowing that they had committed an unpardonable offence, the girl put her arms around the boy and 'flew' into the sky.

The guardian and his younger brother pursued them, climbing into the sky. Their feet slipped, creating many stars, but eventually they succeeded and strode along the Milky Way, leaving behind their footprints which became paired stars. A throwing stick thrown by the guardian knocked off the boy's headdress. Now they are all stars —the two guardians, the boy, the girl, the throwing stick and the headdress.

THE PLEIADES

The Pleiades, which is also called the Seven Sisters, is a very bright cluster of stars near Aldebaran and marks the shoulder of the (upside down) Taurus constellation. There are some 250 stars in the cluster, seven of which can be seen with the naked eye. About 30 can be distinguished with binoculars. In the Greek mythology Orion came upon the seven daughters of the giant Atlas while hunting in the forest. The girls were alarmed and cried for help, so the god Jupiter snatched them away and placed them in the safety of the heavens.

Like the Greek, the Aboriginal story is of seven sisters. The rising of this star cluster in May is an important event: the seven sisters are accompanied by many dogs — represented by stars — and this marks the beginning of the time when dingo pups are born. It is also the beginning of the cold season — a significant event in the Aboriginal calendar.

There are several stories recorded for this group of stars, but in broad terms they represent unmarried girls who are constantly sought after by a variety of suitors. One account suggests that the sisters are fleeing the attentions of men represented by the wandering planets. Another suggests that the suitor is the 'man of Orion', possibly Aldebaran or Betelgeuse. In yet another story, the sisters are ice maidens, tall and beautiful, who were being wooed by a family of brothers. Five of the sisters fled into the sky when an evil medicine man captured the other two. The two eventually escaped but not before the medicine man had melted some of their icicles away, which is why two of the stars in the group are not so bright. The heartbroken brothers were later transformed into part of Orion, probably the belt. Now the men hunt all day while the women gather food. When evening comes the women go over the horizon about an hour before the men, to prepare the evening meal.

THE SICKLE OR LEO THE LION

This readily identifiable group of stars in the northern sky is visible in the evenings from January to July. It can be identified either as an upside down lion or as a sickle. The sickle handle is at the top, above the curved blade. Regulus — Alpha Leonis — is the white star at the top of the handle. Seen as a lion, the hook of the handle forms the mane, Regulus (the 'little king') is the front paw or heart and a triangle of stars outlines the rump.

METEORS, COMETS AND SATELLITES

'Shooting stars' are a fascinating sight. They are not stars at all but meteors. Vast quantities of rocks, varying from huge boulders to grain-size particles, are travelling at great speeds through our solar system. If they strike the earth's atmosphere they become visible as white streaks. They may quickly be extinguished with their ashes floating to the ground, but if they are big enough to survive the pass through the atmosphere they drop to the ground as meteorites. The product of such a collision — a meteorite hitting the earth — can be seen at the Henbury Meteorite Craters northeast of Watarrka National Park.

Comets, on the other hand, have a head and a tail. The nucleus of the head is made of rocky material and frozen gases, and the tail consists of gases and dust. This configuration occurs only when the comets are close to the sun and their ice is melting. Away from the sun they are simply a dirty block of ice. To the naked eye the head appears as a fuzzy patch with a long faint tail. Indeed, the word comet has its origin in the Greek word for hair, because they were known as hairy stars. Some comets orbit the sun regularly although each orbit may take many years. Halley's Comet has been noted many times through recorded history but its last appearance in 1987 suggested that it may be fading. Other comets are seen only once and then disappear. Perhaps they collide with a planet such as Earth — this provides one explanation for the formation of Gosse Bluff in the Western MacDonnell Ranges. Alternatively, they may leave the solar system.

There are also 'stars' that move steadily right across the sky. These are either man-made satellites or the rubbish that remains from space programs. They can only be viewed during the first few hours after sunset. At that time they are high enough above the dark earth's surface to still be illuminated by the rays from the sun. Satellites are mostly used for communication but some are employed to photograph the earth's surface in astonishing detail. For example, they may distinguish something on the ground the size of a tennis court.

In Central Australia satellite photographs are used to detect fire scars and changes in land condition and they are one of the tools used in developing land management programs. The NOAA weather satellite has an additional use in Central Australia — it records the signals from radio-collared camels roaming the desert, providing detailed information about their movements.

THE PLANETS

The planet Venus is the Morning Star or Evening Star — the name depends on when it is visible. At its brightest it can outshine all the other planets. It is the 'star woman' and, with the Southern Cross, was one of the few objects used by the Aboriginal people for evening navigation. The sun and the moon feature in the traditional Tjukurpa stories too. The stories vary in detail between the groups of people, but the sun is generally a woman and the moon a man.

One useful distinction between stars and planets is that the planets do not 'twinkle'. They are solid bodies and shine only because they reflect sunlight, rather than making their own light as the stars do. The Greeks called them the wandering stars — *planetos* — because they move across the sky and change their positions in relation to the stars and constellations.

The five brightest planets of our solar system can be seen with the naked eye:

Sky

A poem by Billy Marshall-Stoneking[3]

The guardians of the circumcision ceremony
live in the constellation of Scorpio, and
turn the sky over every night.
The sky is a shell.
The Milky Way, a creek
of gleaming stones.
The Southern Cross is
the footprint of the wedge-tailed eagle,
and mushrooms are fallen stars.
The sun is a woman,
moving by different paths
between winter and summer.
And Jupiter, the dog,
hunts with Saturn, who brings
bush tucker back to Venus.
There are two moon men —
an old man and his son — who once
lived in the mountains;
the father is so large,
if you saw him, there would be
no room for anything but fear.
The son persuades his father
to stay in camp. Some nights he stays
with him there.
If the father were allowed to rise
his light would blind the world.
And once, after the whitefellas came,
the people from wilarata side
saw Jesus in the clouds.

Mercury, Venus, Mars, Jupiter and Saturn. These five planets, the sun and the moon are the origin of the names of the days of the week, translated from Latin via their Old English equivalents. The three remaining planets Uranus, Neptune and Pluto were not discovered until the invention of the telescope.

Mars can be identified by its red colour. Mercury is easiest to locate just before dawn in the eastern sky and just after sunset in the west, because of its proximity to the sun. Indeed Mercury is easier to locate from the southern hemisphere than from the northern hemisphere. The view of both Jupiter and Saturn is greatly enhanced by the use of binoculars or a telescope. Then the rings of Saturn (formed by its many tiny moons) and the moons of Jupiter become visible.

Because the planets are not fixed in relative positions as the stars are, astronomical societies regularly publish charts to assist with locating the planets.

FIGURE 3.13 The riotious colours of a Central Australian sunset. *M. W. Gillam*

STAR CHARTS

The following three pairs of star charts give a basic guide to some of the more obvious stars and constellations. The views to the north and the south are illustrated for three times of the year: April, July and October. The time of the evening represented on these charts is approximately two hours after sunset. For more detail and for star positions at other times of the year, it is worth purchasing a planisphere designed for latitudes 20–30 degrees south. There are also 'star tours' available at the Ayers Rock Resort.

FIGURE 3.14 Star charts for 9.30 p.m. in mid-April, to the north, top, and to the south, bottom. The colours used for the constellations indicate how bright they are.

Constellations:

Brightest 1   Brightest 2   Brightest 3   The path of the planets

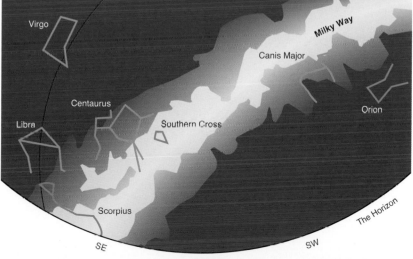

FIGURE 3.15 Star charts for 8.30 p.m. in mid-July, to the north, top, and to the south, bottom.

Constellations:

brightest　　next brightest　　third brightest　　path of the planets

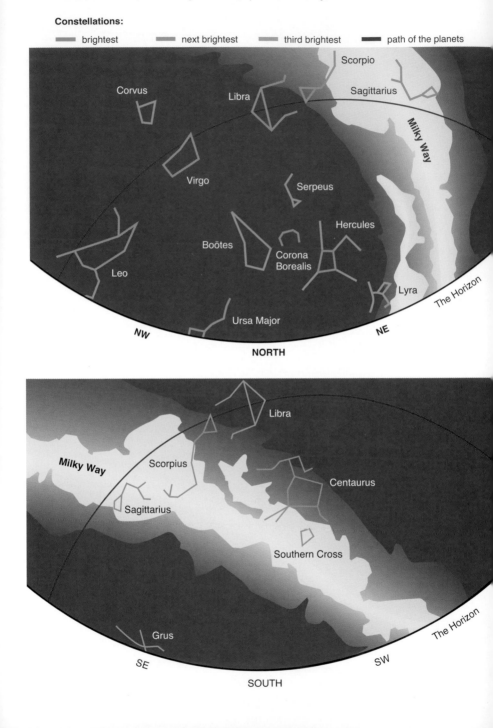

FIGURE 3.16 Star charts for 9.30 p.m. in mid-October, to the north, top, and to the south, bottom.

Constellations:

▬ brightest   ▬ next brightest   ▬ third brightest   ▬ path of the planets

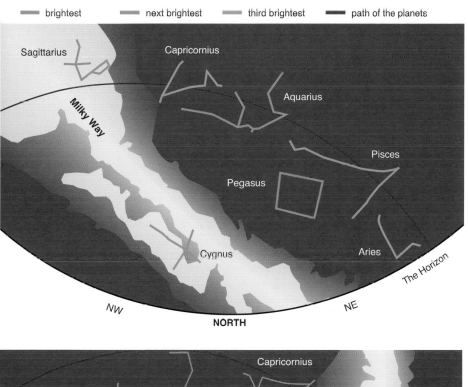

4

THE LAND TODAY
PLANTS AND PLANT
COMMUNITIES

From the sigh of the wind through desert oaks to the cool richness of ferns, shrubs and trees in the gorges, it is very obvious that Central Australia is not a barren desert. Masses of gaudy wildflowers can carpet the ground and cassias and wattles create a yellow haze across the landscape — if there has been enough rain. This lush growth disappears with drought. Then, seeds of ground-cover plants lie in wait for the rain and leaves gradually fall from shrubs and trees. But it is never a barren wilderness.

The variety of plants in Watarrka National Park makes it biologically one of the most important parts of Central Australia. Over 600 plant species have been found there, representing about one-quarter of the total flora of the region. The number of plant species is enhanced by the fact that the park encompasses qualities of the Western Desert, Central Ranges and Simpson Desert. In addition, about 10 per cent of the plant species are special. They are either rare or relict — or both (relict species are those still persisting from a time when the climate was much wetter). Some relict ferns, for example, are found at only one or two sites. Fewer plant species have been recorded at Uluru–Kata Tjuta National Park, but some of the 400 or so that have been found there are also considered to be rare. These species are mostly restricted to the moister areas at the base of the monoliths.

FIGURE 4.1 The major plant communities around Uluru, Kata Tjuta and the George Gill Range. *Christine Bruderlin*

rocky range and outcrops	mulga shrublands	riverbed and riverbanks	sand plain	dunefields	saltla pan or clayp
puli	puti	karu	pila	tali	tjintj

The landscape of the region is not only well clothed, but also very varied. The plant species are broadly arranged in natural associations or communities; that is, groups of species which tend to live together in a particular area or land form. These are partly determined by the land forms described in Chapter 2 and are illustrated in Fig. 4.1. Travelling to Watarrka and Uluru by road will take you through the full spectrum of plant associations found in Central Australia. There are the sand dunes covered with desert oaks and spinifex, thickets of mulga shrubland, dry rivers and creeks lined with majestic river red gums, open woodlands on the floodout fans, tough little shrubs clinging to exposed rock surfaces, vigorous growth in the moist gullies and salty chenopod shrublands.

Aboriginal people also recognise these broad plant associations, and the names they use are included in Fig. 4.1. For them, these communities don't just represent specific groupings of particular plants — they are also the locations or habitats of special plants and animals important for food or for use as implements. The similarity of the Aboriginal and modern ecologically defined plant communities is quite marked. The intimate knowledge of the land, perpetuated in Aboriginal stories and songs, has been vital to the survival of people living in such an unpredictable climate.

FIGURE 4.2 Graceful desert oaks and golden spinifex can be seen on sand dunes and sand plains in both Uluru and Watarrka.
M. W. Gillam

FIGURE 4.3 If there has been enough rain, gaudy wildflowers such as these bluebells will carpet the ground.
M. W. Gillam

The plants themselves have evolved a variety of ways of coping with this unpredictability as listed below:

- Drought-resisting perennial plants that are inactive during a drought but respond quickly when it rains. They include the hardy spinifex and trees such as mulga and desert oak.
- Drought-evading perennial plants (mostly grasses) which seem to die off during a drought but resprout after rain from dormant buds, rootstock or rhizomes.
- Drought-evading ephemeral plants which flower in profusion after rain and die as soon as conditions dry out. They include the daisies and parakeelya. The seeds lie dormant, waiting for the right combination of water and temperature before springing back into life.
- A few species, like the MacDonnell Ranges Cycad, that avoid the extremes of the arid climate altogether by growing in sheltered protected gullies and at the base of the monoliths.

Heavy autumn rains can produce a spectacular wildflower display — in places this profusion can match the flowering of the sand plains of Western Australia. The flowering is controlled by both the quantity and timing of the rainfall — autumn rains can

FIGURE 4.4 Wildflower calendar indicating when certain plants may flower. Some plants such as the silvertails and mistletoes can flower throughout the year. Whether or not plants flower during your visit is entirely dependent on rain; typical weather is shown for each month.

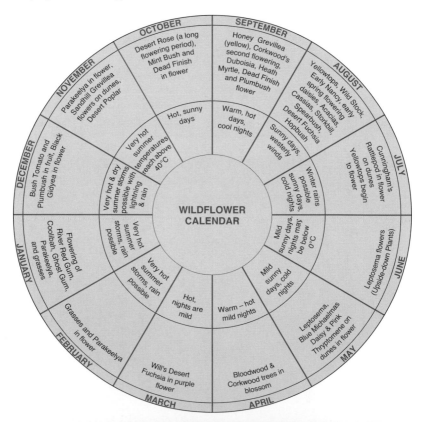

produce annual wildflowers (mostly daisies) in late winter and spring while summer rains mostly promote the growth of perennial grasses. The Pitjantjatjara name for the annual wildflowers is tjulpun-tjulpunpa.

Like drought, fire is another destructive force in the desert. The arid plants have developed survival strategies for this too, and a variety of mechanisms have emerged. Some species, such as the mulga, are usually killed by fire but will recolonise from the seed supply in the ground. Others, including the desert oak and grevilleas may appear dead but will burst forth with new shoots soon after the fire. Some plants can recolonize quickly from windblown seed but, with time, they are replaced by a succession of other species.

The patchiness created by fire within the plant communities is also an important factor in determining which animals will live there. For example, some species such as the Beaked Gecko *Rhynchoedura ornata* prefer the openness of recently burnt sand plain but some of the skinks (*Ctenotus* species) are more common in mature spinifex.

Aboriginal people have long exploited fire to enhance the patchiness of plant communities. Traditionally, they are extremely skilled in their control of fire. The very patchiness of the habitats produces the broadest possible food supply — both plant and animal. Their detailed knowledge of desert plants has been the basis of their subsistence hunting and gathering lifestyle. Plants provide flowers, fruits, seeds and fleshy leaves for food; they can have water-bearing roots and act as hosts for insect foods; they are used for making hunting and gathering implements; they are the source of many vital medicines and chewing tobacco; and they provide firewood and building materials.

The many native plant species in these two national parks have been joined by a few species that have been introduced since the first Europeans came to Central Australia. Some, like Buffel Grass *Cenchrus ciliaris* were introduced to rehabilitate areas damaged by stock and vehicles and to curb erosion. It has since spread widely through Central Australia, outcompeting several native grass species. Couch Grass *Cynodon dactylon* is another invasive weed. It mostly grows on the banks of creeks and stabilises the sand a change from the natural sand mobility which is a feature of these rivers.

FIGURE 4.5 These resprouting hakeas have survived a wildfire; the mulga trees in the background are dead and will regenerate from seeds. *M. W. Gillam*

Another very obvious introduced plant is Rosy Dock or Wild Hops *Rumex vesicarius*. After a good winter rainfall the lush growth of this species can cover the countryside in a blaze of red. It is especially colourful in the light of the setting sun — but it is a weed. It is a native of northern Africa and western Asia which escaped from a garden in Alice Springs. The claim that it originated from seed in the stuffing used in camel saddles does not appear to be true.

Each of the major plant communities or habitats of the two national parks is described in detail in this chapter. Distinctive features of the communities, plants of importance to Aboriginal people and the effects of fire are discussed. Some individual plant species are described.

SAND PLAINS AND DUNES — TALI AND PILA

Of the larger trees of the sand areas, undoubtedly the most characteristic is the desert oak, the finest of all the casuarinas. It grows to a height of forty feet or more, usually in open groves destitute of any other growth save spinifex. In a melancholy way it is a most beautiful tree with dark drooping plumes of 'foliage' and a stem which appears jet black against the bare red sand. *H. H. Finlayson*[1]

The sand plains and dunes are the most widespread of the land forms in Uluru–Kata Tjuta National Park and to the south of the George Gill Range at Watarrka. Known as tali and pila to the local Aboriginal people, they comprise about 82 per cent of Uluru and 35 per cent of Watarrka. The greatest variety of plant foods can grow in this, the driest of the communities. The Desert Oak *Allocasuarina decaisneana* (p.68) is a magnificent feature of this landscape (Fig. 4.2). Patches of other vegetation (e.g. Desert Heath Myrtle and *Acacia* shrublands) regularly occur in between, especially on the dune slopes and crests. And always there is spinifex.

The desert oaks occur as scattered trees or as distinct groves on the lower slopes of the sand dunes. Other tall shrub species are the Ironwood *Acacia estrophiolata* and the Corkwood *Hakea suberea* (Fig. 4.49). Sometimes scattered mulga or mallees are present but these species are much more important in other plant communities.

The spinifex (p.66) mostly covers the swales (low lying areas between dunes) and on the dunes is mixed with the shrubs. The type of spinifex, or hummock grass, in this sandy country varies. Around Yulara and Uluru it is Soft Spinifex *Triodia pungens*; in the north of Uluru National Park it is Hard Spinifex *T. basedowii*; in Watarrka, Feathertop Spinifex *Plectrachne schinzii* is most common.

Shrubs which commonly occur on the dune slopes and crests are Umbrella Bush *Acacia ligulata* and Sandhill Wattle *A. dictyophleba*, Honey Grevilleas *Grevillea eriostachya* (Fig. 4.6) and *G. juncifolia*, Desert Hop-bush *Dodonaea viscosa*, Cassia *Senna artemisioides* and Long-leafed Desert Fuchsias *Eremophila longifolia* and *E. willsii*. The Parrot Pea *Crotolaria cunninghamii* is especially spectacular when it is in flower.

FIGURE 4.6 The delicious nectar in honey grevillea flowers is sought after by a variety of animals, including people. *J. A. Kerle*

On the ground, spinifex survives all but the worst droughts. After rain other grasses and a wide variety of annual plants fill the bare spaces. The purple parakeelyas (*Calandrinia* species), fanflowers (*Scaevola*), pussytails (*Ptilotus*), daisies (*Helipterum*) and the Upside-down Plant *Leptosema chambersii* (Fig. 4.7) grow in splendid profusion. The Upside-down Plant, which grows around the Kata Tjuta lookout car park is a most unusual plant. The large, bright red flowers cluster around the base of the plant, often lying on the sand. The flowers produce lots of nectar, and while the ground-feeding birds are harvesting the nectar they pollinate the flowers. Aboriginal people also collect this nectar.

In some localities the desert oaks are replaced by a tall open shrubland, with umbrella bush and Rattlepod Grevillea *Grevillea stenobotrya* (Fig. 4.8) being most common. Other taller species include the Desert Kurrajong *Brachychiton gregorii*, Desert Poplar *Codonocarpus cotinifolius* and Camel Poison Bush *Gyrostemon ramulosus*. The Desert Heath Myrtle *Thryptomene maisoneuvii* can be seen covering the slopes of the dunes as a mass of densely growing bright green shrubs, less than one metre high. *Rulingia loxophylla* on the other hand is a low, spreading shrub which prefers the flatter swales and disturbed areas such as road verges. It colonises quickly after fire. The Desert Raisin *Solanum centrale*, along with other bush tomato (*Solanum*) species, can also be found.

Mallees — multistemmed eucalypts — are another important plant species growing in the sandy country. The Blue Mallee *Eucalyptus gammophylla* (Fig. 4.11) is the most common. Like the desert oak woodland and tall open shrubland, mallee habitat can be seen along the road from the Ayers Rock Resort to Kata Tjuta. Other mallee communities occur in remote parts of the parks. In these the three species *E. oxymitra*, *E. mannensis* and *E. trivalvis* are often all present.

One very special and rare sand dune plant community in Uluru National Park is dominated by Sandhill Mulga *Acacia ammobia* (Fig. 4.9). It is found in the east of the park but it is not accessible to visitors. This tall slender wattle grows on the dune slopes in association with various other shrubs and spinifex. Because the wide swales have clayey soils Sandhill Mulga is interspersed with groves of Common Mulga *Acacia aneura*. Sandhill Mulga is particularly good for building the yuu (windbreaks) and wilytja (shelters) used by Aboriginal people.

FIGURE 4.7 Bright red flowers of the upside-down plant produce a rich nectar supply which is collected by a variety of birds, from crows to woodswallows. *J. A. Kerle*

FIGURE 4.8 Rattlepod grevilleas mostly grow in the tall open shrubland on dunes. *J. A. Kerle*

FIGURE 4.9 The rare sandhill mulga plant community occurs in Uluru National Park. *J. A. Kerle*

SPINIFEX — TJANPI

> Riding on all day long we kept mounting one sandhill after another, all covered with porcupine grass... *Baldwin Spencer*[2]

Spinifex is a very common and widespread desert grass found mostly in Central and Western Australia — these hummock grasslands cover some 22 per cent of the continent. There are many different species of spinifex, all of which have very tough curled leaf blades ending in a spear-pointed tip. This feature, in association with their hummock shape, gave rise to the name of porcupine grass used by the early European travellers in Central Australia. Most early explorers were not impressed by travelling through spinifex for countless hours. It was viewed as useless for fodder — and painful! Charles Chewings reported in 1930 that 'The whole area is covered, and in most places densely so, with spinifex, which for the most part is of a very poor quality and useless for stock.[3]

The explorer Chewings may not have attached any value to spinifex but it is a vital component of this desert ecosystem. The hummocks or clumps have extensive root systems which penetrate deeply and consolidate the desert sands. Some species, like Hard Spinifex *Triodia basedowii* grow out from the centre of the clump, developing into desert 'fairy rings'. As the outer branches come in contact with the sand they take root and grow afresh. A circle of growing spinifex is left surrounding the original, dead parts of the plant (Fig. 4.11).

This function of anchoring the sand is further enhanced by the fact that spinifex can survive extreme droughts and flourish on infertile soils. It provides shelter for many animals — lizards, mice and insects — even during the worst conditions. These animals can climb or slide through the hummocks with ease or slip into the dense base and hide. They often prefer to dig their burrows at the base of the hummocks.

Spinifex is highly flammable. It is resinous and the dead parts of the plant accumulate rather than degenerate —despite the efforts of spinifex-eating termites! After a

FIGURE 4.10 Spinifex — a vital component of the Central Australian desert. *M. W. Gillam*

fire the ground surface can be left bare but the roots remain to hold the sand and to resprout. Spinifex can resprout in response to regular heavy dew but the rate of growth of the clumps is enhanced by rain.

Not only does the spinifex readily regrow after a fire but so do many other plant species. Indeed the plant diversity soon after a fire is much higher than in mature spinifex grasslands. With time, many of these species are outgrown by the spinifex, which ultimately dominates the landscape.

Aboriginal people also look favourably upon the tjanpi. Clumps of the more resinous species (especially Soft Spinifex) are threshed to extract the resin crystals. These are skilfully separated from the chaff by being yandied in a wira (bowl) (Fig. 4.13). This is almost always done by the women who also separate grass seeds from the husk by the same shaking process of yandying. The resin crystals are then heated under a burning stick until they congeal into a mouldable, black tar-like gum. While it is warm and soft it can be moulded to glue stone edges to hunting and working implements and to mend a variety of implements. It sets very hard. This fascinating process is demonstrated by the Mutitjulu people who conduct the Liru Walk at Uluru.

FIGURE 4.11 Spinifex rings and blue mallee. *M. W. Gillam*

FIGURE 4.12 Spinifex is important to many animals. Spinifex ants build protective tunnels, visible here, between clumps using spinifex resin, and they feed from sap-sucking scale insects on the spiky leaves *J. A. Kerle*

FIGURE 4.13 Yandying the spinifex chaff to make spinifex resin. *Christine Bruderlin*

DESERT OAK — KURKARA

The presence of large, elegant desert oaks in the spinifex grasslands gives illusion of open parkland. These long-lived trees belong to the casuarina family and are its only representative in Central Australia. Like other casuarinas the drooping 'foliage' is made up of green branchlets — the leaves are the tiny spiky brown scales which ring the branchlets at regular intervals. The insignificant male and female flowers are separate but are both on the same tree. Conversely, the cone is large — a beautiful piece of bush sculpture which produces many wind-dispersed seeds (Fig. 4.14). The seedlings first emerge from the ground as a very spiky clump of branchlets — too spiky to be grazed by kangaroos or rabbits. They then grow into a poplar-shaped tree before the main trunk divides and develops a canopy. It is thought that this change in shape might be triggered by the deep-growing taproot striking subterranean water.

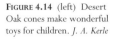

FIGURE 4.14 (left) Desert Oak cones make wonderful toys for children. *J. A. Kerle*

FIGURE 4.15 (bottom left) Young, poplar-shaped desert oaks. *J. A. Kerle*

FIGURE 4.16 (below) Desert poplar. *J. A. Kerle*

The picnic area outside the ranger station in Uluru–Kata Tjuta National Park (map p.vi) is set amongst desert oaks. The shade of kurkara can provide a wonderful respite during a hot day out in the bush. Aboriginal people also value kurkara as firestick material. Once it is alight the dense resinous timber does not easily go out.

DESERT POPLAR — KANTURANGU

This tall poplar-shaped tree, with its pale grey, pink or green bark and bright green leaves (Fig. 4.16), stands out in recently burnt spinifex grasslands. After a fire the seeds sprout and grow quickly, reaching about three metres. Unlike the Desert Oak it has a short lifespan. All Desert Poplars in an area are about the same age, having responded to the stimulus of the same fire or drought-breaking rains. They also grow along road verges, where the disturbance of road building has mimicked the distur bance caused by fire. They are not related to English poplars.

The flowers and fruits are quite small but prolific. Because the tree has a short life — generally less than ten years — it needs to leave a substantial seed supply in the soil, waiting for the next fire. It generally falls over at the end of its life, partly as a result of the weight of the fruits and the impact of edible beetle larvae in the lower trunk and roots. The Aboriginal people collect these grubs by snapping the tree off at the base.

OTHER SAND DUNE TREES AND SHRUBS

Wattles (*Acacia*), Grevilleas, corkwoods (*Hakea*), native fuschias (*Eremophila*) and desert heath myrtles (*Thryptomene*), are all scattered over the sandy country. Many of them provide food and medicines for Aboriginal people. The grevillea flowers, especially those of the yellow and green Honey Grevillea, produce lots of delicious, sweet nectar. The flowers are either eaten, sucked or soaked in water to provide a sweet drink (Fig. 4.17). Some of the Native Fuschia flowers and the Desert Heath Myrtle also produce sweet nectar.

The wattles have a variety of uses. Their seeds, especially those of the Umbrella Bush and Colony Wattle, are collected, roasted and ground. This paste is then eaten without further preparation. Umbrella bush seeds are especially important during droughts. Edible grubs are found at the base of the stem of this wattle. The boiled bark of the umbrella bush provides a cough medicine and the leaves are smoked to give a vapour bath.

The Quandong, or Bush Peach, was once a very important food source for the local people. The trees were quite common and widespread in the sand dunes and plains and when they fruited they could be absolutely loaded with bright red fruits. People feasted on them — either eating the fruit raw or grinding the dried fruit into a paste. They also took advantage of emus which gathered to feast on these nutritious fruits as well. The kernel of the hard seed was used medicinally to treat aches and pains. Unfortunately quandongs are now uncommon, possibly as a result of grazing by feral camels and rabbits.

Mallees are another valuable plant. The nectar and seeds of the Blue Mallee have been used for food with the fine seeds being ground into a flour. The trees are good for making big spinifex fires too — the burning leaves, carried up in the smoke, spread

FIGURE 4.17 Aboriginal children enjoy sucking the sweet nectar from the honey grevillea.
Christine Bruderlin

the fire when they land some distance away. Importantly, the trees can also provide water from water-bearing roots. The long sub-surface roots are broken off and tied vertically over a vessel to drain. The Desert Kurrajong *Brachychiton gregorii*, also has water-bearing roots.

SMALL SHRUBS AND HERBS

Bush Tomatoes (Fig. 4.18) are mostly low straggly plants which can bloom prolifically, producing a mass of purple flowers with yellow stamens. Some produce an edible fruit. They belong to the family Solanaceae which includes not only tomatoes and potatoes, but also deadly nightshade. Some of the bush tomatoes are highly poisonous too. Of the edible species, the Desert Raisin *Solanum centrale*, is especially valuable because the yellow fruit dries, turns brown and stays hanging on the bush. They may be harvested when the need for food is greatest or they can be eaten fresh. The Western Nightshade *Solanum coactiliferum*, is only eaten when ripe and yellow. The fruits contain bitter juice and seeds, both of which are removed before eating. They may be eaten raw or baked. A variety of *Solanum* species can be seen growing on the road verges — but beware, some must definitely not be eaten!

FIGURE 4.18 Bush tomatoes have a purple flower and often grow along road verges. *J. A. Kerle*

Both the Desert Rattlepod *Crotolaria eremaea* and Parrot Pea *Crotolaria cunninghamii* are used for medicinal purposes. The desert rattlepod is pounded, mashed and either rubbed into the head and chest or tied on as a poultice to cure general illness. The parrot pea is boiled to produce a decoction which can be used on burns, wounds, sores, boils and cuts and as an eyelid wash. The boiled juice of the Sticky Hop-bush *Dodonaea viscosa* is used for curing toothache.

The two succulent herb species, Munyeroo *Portulacca oleracea* and Parakeelya *Calandrinia balonensis* (Fig. 4.19) occur sporadically after rain. The yellow-flowered Munyeroo, which grows only after non-winter rains, produces vast quantities of seed. To collect this the plant is picked when the pods are ripe and left in a wira to dry out. The seed is extracted by threshing and then cleaned by winnowing and yandying. The clean seed is ground to a paste and small cakes are baked in the ashes and hot sand. Alternatively, both the munyeroo and parakeelya roots may be cooked and eaten. The fleshy leaves of parakeelya have the added value of providing moisture — the leaves being broken open and sucked. Kangaroos and cattle also eat parakeelya for its moisture in this dry environment.

FIGURE 4.19 The succulent parakeelya readily grows and flowers after rain; it is a valuable bush food. *J. A. Kerle*

MULGA SHRUBLANDS — PUTI

> In this virgin country the mulga, both in its bushy and arborescent forms, is an attractive symmetrical plant... Like most plants of the Centre, it blooms after any heavy rain, apparently largely independent of the season of the year. The flower is a little golden-yellow bottle-brush, deliciously scented, and when a rain-storm has raised new life in hundreds of square miles of mulga parks, the expanse of blossom and its perfume are not easily forgotten. *H. H. Finlayson*[4]

Away from the sands, on heavier soils known as red earths, the Desert Oak and spinifex are replaced by Common Mulga *Acacia aneura*. Some 20 per cent of the Australian continent is occupied by mulga shrublands — a large and fragile part of the arid and semi-arid regions (Fig. 4.20). Mulga is another unique part of the landscape, unusual in that these large shrubs are dominant in such a dry and infertile environment. In Central Australia mulga shrublands can cover extensive areas or can be interdigitated with other major plant communities, especially the spinifex dunes. This distribution is controlled by soil type.

In the 'hundreds of square miles' of mulga described by Finlayson, including the area around Uluru and Watarrka, the trees are not always spread evenly across the landscape. Instead, they grow in large patches or groves with open grassy patches in between. In the groves the mulga is almost always the only tall species present. Occasionally the Bloodwood *Corymbia opaca*, Corkwood *Hakea suberea* and tall Witchetty Bushes *Acacia kempeana* occur and emerge above the mulga. The plant diversity within mulga shrublands is found amongst the understorey shrubs and grasses.

There, spinifex is replaced by a variety of perennial and annual grasses, especially the Woolly-butt *Eragrostis eriopoda*. The particular species found amongst the ground cover plants varies in response to the season, timing of rainfall, fire history and the history of grazing. Of the grasses, Kerosene Grass *Aristida contorta*, Nine Awn *Enneapogon polyphyllus*, Cotton Grass *Digitaria brownii* and Umbrella Grass *Enteropogon acicularis* are common. The Prickly Wild Tomato *Solanum quadriloculatum*, Caustic Bush *Euphorbia tannensis*, the bushes of Silvertail *Ptilotus obovatus*, Green Longtail *P. polystachys* and several daisies are also present at times.

Probably the most frequent understorey shrub is the Witchetty Bush — an erect shrub with broad leaf-like phyllodes (p.76). There will also be some young mulga trees, native fuchsias *(Eremophila gilesii* and *E. latrobei)*, Native Currant *Canthium latifolium* (p.77) and Cassia *Senna artemisioides* scattered under the mature mulga and in the spaces between the mulga groves.

FIGURE 4.20 Mulga shrubland, resplendent with flowering annuals. *J. A. Kerle*

In the area from the Uluru Ranger Station to the ring road around the monolith, there is a sparse mulga shrubland — regenerating after being burnt by vast bushfires which swept through the park in 1976. In general the shrubby understorey and grasses in a fully developed mulga shrubland are too sparse to carry a wildfire — unless there has been a succession of good rainy seasons. On the other hand the immature mulga communities have more shrubs and grasses and can carry a fire more readily. If these fires recur in quick succession, and if the trees are too young to have set seed, the mulga community can be wiped out. So fire is not used as a management tool by Aboriginal people for mulga — unlike the spinifex grasslands.

FIGURE 4.21 The Orange Immortelle *Waitzia accuminata* can be found amongst the mulga after a good winter rainfall. *J. A. Kerle*

Protection of the mulga shrublands — or puti — by Aboriginal people has been vital because they provide a range of foods, medicines and materials. Foods can be harvested directly from the plants — seeds, bush bananas, native currants — or from animals that prefer to live amongst the mulga. The animal foods include honey ants, goannas, witchetty grubs, lerps, galls and echidnas. Materials for building yuu (windbreaks) and wilytja (shelters), for making functional tools and for firewood are all available within this plant community. A truly productive place in the desert.

Despite the infertility of the red earths where the mulga grows, and the capricious rainfall regime, this community is remarkably stable. Strategies have evolved which ameliorate these conditions and stretch the periods of productivity. A key to this process is the interaction between plants and animals — especially the invertebrates.

Mulga trees draw nutrients from deep below the soil surface and return it in leaf fall. The diagram on page 75 illustrates the process. Ants are attracted to the rich food supply which they find in the tree: they harvest the seeds and take them into their nests, eating only the aril, a little attachment rich in carbohydrates; they collect nectar from special secreting glands on the phyllodes called extra-floral nectaries; they feed on the sweet fluid exuded by sap-sucking insects. In turn, the soil in ant mounds can contain three times the amount of phosphorus and up to 200 times the amount of nitrogen found in surrounding soils. These conditions enhance seed germination.

The dense mulga grove communities generally occur on gently sloping land. With the massive stormy downpours which typically occur, water flows in sheets rather than being channelled. The flow carries debris and disperses seeds and animals through the community. This gentle flow of water and nutrients also enhances the growth of a fragile algal crust on the soil surface — another means by which nutrients are built up in the mulga groves. And water can penetrate more deeply into the soil through disused ant nests, although most of the active nests avoid flooding by having mounds or turrets around their openings (Fig. 5.44).

While the most extensive and best developed mulga shrublands grow on deep red earthy soils they also grow on rocky hill slopes. In these places the mulga is generally shorter and shrubbier and mixed with cassias *(Senna* species), native fuchsias *(Eremophila)*, Dead Finish *Acacia tetragonophylla* and Mint Bush *Prostanthera striatiflora*.

Rocky mulga shrublands are found around the parking areas for the Kata Tjuta Walk (p.171) and on the low hills and valleys (Carmichael Sandstone) of Watarrka National Park (p.vii).

MULGA — WANARI

Mulgas are a wonderfully variable group of species of *Acacia*. As with almost all *Acacia* species, the 'leaves' are really flattened leaf stalks which perform the same function as leaves. They are properly called phyllodes and can vary from one to 12 millimetres in width, one to 25 centimetres in length. They may be green, grey or silvery blue. The plant itself may grow as an erect low shrub or attain a height of 15 metres.

Within Uluru–Kata Tjuta National Park, the mature common mulga mostly grows as a branching tree with a broad canopy, but there is also a 'Christmas tree' form (Fig. 7.19). Some of these most attractive trees can be seen on the walk through the Valley of the Winds (p.81). Uluru Mulga *Acacia ayersiana* and Horse Mulga *A. ramulosa* both look similar to common mulga and they can all be found together. Uluru mulga grows only at the base of Uluru but horse mulga is more widespread occurring in both national parks.

Although mulga will flower in response to any substantial rainfall the main flowering is seasonal, occurring in spring and summer. Seed production is variable but is most successful with good rains in late summer. The pods drop and are ripe about nine months later. Germination of these seeds will not happen unless there is sufficient rainfall or they are cracked and stimulated by the heat of a fire.

The mulga has evolved some remarkable adaptations to this infertile and drought-prone environment. The trees actually collect water. This is particularly important during the light gentle rainfalls. Most of the phyllodes point upwards, the rain drops dribble down the phyllodes on to the branches and then down the trunk. This stem flow significantly increases the water available to the roots; 25mm of rainfall can be concentrated into 140mm within the root zone of the tree, making small showers more effective. Moisture loss is further reduced by the phyllode structure and alignment. The vertical phyllodes are mostly small with a waxy cuticle, sunken stomates, a hairy surface and a high oil content.

The roots of mature mulga trees penetrate deeply into the soils, drawing nutrients to the surface. But it is not a one-way path (Fig. 4.22). Nutrients return to the soil surface through leaf fall. The quantity of this can range from 40kg per hectare to a massive 6000kg per hectare in good seasons. This return of nutrients into the tree is enhanced by nodules of symbiotic bacteria on the surface of the roots which convert atmospheric nitrogen into a form which can be used.

This nutrient flow also becomes a direct food source for a range of invertebrates. Nestling at the base of each phyllode are tiny specialised glands. These extra-floral nectaries exude a sugary sap which is harvested by a variety of ants — it is especially favoured by honey ants (Fig. 5.45). Mulga sap is also sucked out by scale insects. These tiny insects excrete a sugary liquid which, in turn, is harvested by ants, birds and people.

For Aboriginal people, a mulga community provides significant resources and many of these come directly from the mulga tree itself. The hard, mature seeds are a staple food source. They are collected by breaking branches from a tree, leaving them to dry out and then threshing to collect the pods. The seeds are separated from the pods by rubbing and tapping, collected in a wira and cleaned by yandying. Back at camp, they are parched and cracked in hot ashes, winnowed and yandied again, ground and finally moistened to produce an edible paste. Branches are broken off to collect the sweet

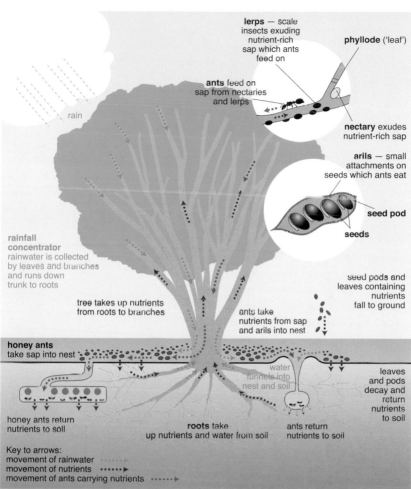

lerps — scale insects exuding nutrient-rich sap which ants feed on

phyllode ('leaf')

ants feed on sap from nectaries and lerps

nectary exudes nutrient-rich sap

arils — small attachments on seeds which ants eat

seed pod

seeds

rain

rainfall concentrator
rainwater is collected by leaves and branches and runs down trunk to roots

tree takes up nutrients from roots to branches

seed pods and leaves containing nutrients fall to ground

ants take nutrients from sap and arils into nest

honey ants take sap into nest

water funnels into nest and soil

leaves and pods decay and return nutrients to soil

honey ants return nutrients to soil

roots take up nutrients and water from soil

ants return nutrients to soil

Key to arrows:
movement of rainwater
movement of nutrients
movement of ants carrying nutrients

FIGURE 4.22 As part of their desert survival strategy, mulga trees concentrate moisture and nutrients around their roots and have a mutually beneficial relationship with some species of ants. This diagram shows how the mulga tree and ant nests channel rainwater to the roots, and how the roots draw up water and nutrients from the soil and carry them to the branches. Nutrients are returned from there to the soil by ants feeding on sap from nectaries and scale insects, and on arils from seedpods, and by the decay of fallen leaves etc. In addition symbiotic bacteria on the surface roots re-cycle nutrients to the tree.

FIGURE 4.23 Sweet sticky lerps or lac scales which live on mulga and witchetty bushes.
J. A. Kerle

sticky lerps. Lerps (Fig. 4.23) are often detected by observing flocks of birds feeding in and flying above a group of trees. The people collect branches, strip off the leaves and carry the bundled branches back to camp. There the branches are soaked in water, producing a mulga honey.

Kurku, a clear sweet gum exuded by the tree in response to attack by insects, is another food — it is treated as a lolly! Tarulka (mulga 'apples') are a more substantial food source. These are insect galls which grow to about one centimetre in diameter and are collected and eaten when they are reddish in colour. Lastly, mulga trees frequently have parasitic mistletoes growing in the branches which don't necessarily kill the mulga. They produce small, sweet but sticky edible berries. They are thought of as children's food and the sticky seed is discarded.

The dense hard mulga wood has a multitude of uses. Spearthrowers (miru), barbs (mukulpa), spearheads (wata), boomerangs (kali) and digging sticks (wana) are all made from the bigger branches and the trunk. Many of the carved wooden artefacts for sale from the Maruku Arts and Crafts Centre at Uluru demonstrate the qualities of this wonderful timber. But one of its greatest values is as firewood, producing good hot coals.

WITCHETTY BUSH — ILYKUWARA

Witchetty grubs — the larvae of a cossid moth — are a favourite and nutritious food. They live in the lateral roots of witchetty bushes. Not all of these witchetty bushes are infested by the grubs: their presence is detected by looking for swellings in the roots or listening for a hollow sound when the ground is tapped at the base of a shrub. Several grubs can be extracted from one root. Witchetty bushes can also carry the red scale insect (lerp) that is found on mulga, and the ground-up seeds are eaten.

The Witchetty Bush *Acacia kempeana* mostly grows in association with mulga. It is a little like a shrubby low mulga but has broad phyllodes, rounded at the tip. It was once common around Uluru but did not regenerate vigorously after the 1976 bushfire; there are healthy stands growing west of Kata Tjuta.

While the witchetty bush does have some medicinal properties, zebra finches which build roosting nests in this and other shrubs are probably more useful. Their droppings are used as a poultice for headaches, the droppings being caked thickly on to aching heads!

FIGURE 4.24 Children digging for witchetty grubs under a witchetty bush. *J. A. Kerle*

FIGURE 4.25 Delicious witchetty grubs and the root in which they were living. *J. A. Kerle*

NATIVE CURRANT

This species (*Canthium latifolium*) can be a shrub or small tree up to four metres in height. It has very distinctive broad leathery lime-green leaves and white flowers which grow in clusters. It can grow in a variety of plant communities but is most often found amongst mulga and along watercourses. The black juicy 'currants' are a prized food of Aboriginal people — being eaten raw or pulped with water.

MOUNTAIN RANGES AND REMNANT ROCKY OUTCROPS — PULI

For the desert Aboriginal people the Central Australian mountain ranges and rocky outcrops were true oases. During extended droughts these were the places where water could be found most reliably and where wildlife and food plants continued to survive. Rainfall around the ranges

FIGURE 4.26 Native currants, which are eaten raw or pulped with water. *J. A. Kerle*

and outcrops is higher than in the vast surrounding sand dune deserts and runoff is high, quickly replenishing the rock holes. Seepage of water from within the porous Mereenie Sandstone of the George Gill Range made that area an even more important drought refuge.

White explorers also found these places to be a welcome relief in their travels through Central Australia, especially in the George Gill Range. In 1873 Ernest Giles wrote of this range:

> The country round its foot is by far the best I have seen in this region; and it could be transported to any civilized land, its springs, glens, gorges, ferns, Zamias and flowers would charm the eyes and hearts of toil-worn men who are condemned to live and die in crowded towns.[5]

And, of course, Uluru and Kata Tjuta had their own appeal both as dramatic scenery and as oases.

The Central Australian ranges are unique. They are geographically isolated from the moister edges of the continent but represent a moist microenvironment within the arid centre. They are dominated by bare rockfaces or steep stony slopes, creating the impression of barrenness. But this is a false impression. Tucked out of sight are crevices, gullies and valleys with almost permanent waterholes and a wealth of plant life. This contrast is nowhere more obvious than at the first glimpse of the Garden of Eden from on top of the 'beehives' on the Kings Canyon Walk (p.171).

The most remarkable feature of the Central Australian ranges is not that they are bare or lush, but that they are incredibly varied. Even the rockfaces vary, depending on aspect, shading and the amount of soil accumulated in the crevices (Fig. 4.28). The boundaries between plant communities are often quite abrupt, the plants responding to changes in moisture availability caused by changes in the topography. The creeks are different from each other. Their precise characteristics are controlled by the size and structure of their catchment and by the irregularity of the channel gradients, which produces a linear sequence of moist and dry microhabitats.

FIGURE 4.27 The rugged mountain ranges in Central Australia are oases in a sea of sand. *M. W. Gillam*

FIGURE 4.28 Steep stony slopes of the George Gill Range; subtle variation in aspect influences the density of plant growth. *J. A. Kerle*

The differences in geological structure between the George Gill Range and the monoliths only serves to enhance the variety of habitats and plant species that grow in each of these places. In Watarrka National Park, the rocky habitats fall into two broad types — the sandstone hills and the low hills and valleys. These are divided into nine vegetation communities, some of which can be further subdivided. The unique topography of the George Gill Range has a reduced fire frequency, allowing many fire-sensitive species to flourish. The rock formations of Uluru, Kata Tjuta, the foothills around Kata Tjuta and the Sedimentaries (just outside the park boundary) represent the full range of rocky habitats for Uluru–Kata Tjuta National Park.

ULURU

The monolith itself has very little vegetation on it. There are perennial grasses and sedges in isolated depressions and fig thickets in some high rocky gullies. In contrast, the plants around the base of the rock tend to form dense thickets in protected valleys, especially along the southern face. Aspect has an obvious influence over the plant growth around Uluru. Along the drier northern face is a very sparse shrubland with Bloodwood *Corymbia opaca*, mulga and a variety of cassias, wattles and native fuchsias. Occasionally, in places with a more channelled runoff, there is a denser mulga shrubland with scattered bloodwoods.

FIGURE 4.29 Plumbushes grow prolifically in the moister valleys around Uluru. *J. A. Kerle*

FIGURE 4.30 Sticky hopbushes with their white or red flowers are generally found growing with plumbushes. *J. A. Kerle*

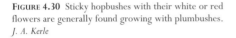

The western and southern faces of Uluru are flanked by much more varied vegetation. In general the growth of mulga and bloodwoods is not as sparse and in some places can be quite dense. In the protected valleys, such as Kantju and Mutitjulu, there can be a forest of bloodwoods up to seven metres in height covering dense thickets of Plumbush *Santalum lanceolatum* (Fig. 4.29), Sticky Hopbush *Dodonaea viscosa* (Fig. 4.30) and perennial grasses. Five wattle species, including the Uluru mulga, and two grevilleas are also scattered through these thickets. Only one such thicket occurs on the northern face. The death of the bloodwoods around Mutitjulu has mostly been caused by disruption to water flow as a result of erosion.

The dramatic and subtle variation in the vegetation surrounding Uluru can be seen while walking the Uluru circuit track — valley thickets, big dense clumps of fig trees and changing densities of mulga and bloodwoods. The subtle influences of aspect, runoff and fire on these alluvial plant communities can also be observed.

KATA TJUTA

The rise and fall of the Kata Tjuta domes provides places for a greater variety of plant communities than are found at Uluru, varying from almost bare domes to dense shrub growth in protected valleys. Most of this variety can be seen on the walks into Olga Gorge and through the Valley of the Winds (map, opposite page).

Wandering from the car parks over the lower stony slopes of Kata Tjuta, both walking tracks pass through a low open shrubland. There you will find a variety of wattles such as Black Gidgea *Acacia pruinocarpa*, Dead Finish *A. tetragonophylla*, witchetty bush and mulga, as well as cassias *(Senna artemisioides, S. artemisioides* ssp. *sturtii),* and Long-leafed Desert Fuchsia *Eremophila longifolia*. Occasional Long-leafed Corkwoods *Hakea suberea*, Beefwood *Grevillea striata* and Bloodwood *Corymbia opaca* stand out above the shrubs. On the ground are Silvertails *Ptilotus obovatus*, Crimson Foxtail *P. sessilifolius*, prickle bushes *(Scerolaena* species*), Swainsona* and perennial grasses.

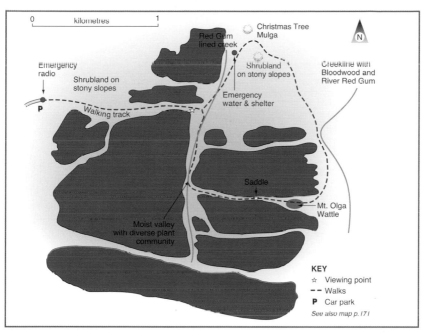

FIGURE 4.31 Plant communities you will see in the Valley of the Winds, Kata Tjuta

FIGURE 4.32 (left) Plant growth is very sparse on the domes of Kata Tjuta but even a small accumulation of soil and moisture enables spinifex and the hummocky grass to grow. *J. A. Kerle*

FIGURE 4.33 (below) The resurrection fern, which nestles in pockets of soil under rocks, will be transformed from this brown, apparently dead, plant into a lush green fern just a few hours after rain. *M. W. Gillam*

As you climb into the domes the plants become more and more sparse, especially on the steepest slopes. Patches of spinifex grow in rubble depressions and scree slopes, but there may be little else. The spinifex growing on Kata Tjuta is different from that encountered in the sand country. Called Porcupine Grass, *Triodia irritans* grows in compact clumps and although it is not resinous, the clumps can have a sticky feeling. The Resurrection Fern *Cheilanthes lasiophylla* is also there, nestling in pockets of soil under the rocks. It is so named because rain can make an apparently dead plant spring back to life.

FIGURE 4.34 Early Nancy, a delicate pink lily, grows amongst sedges and grasses along boggy creek edges in good seasons. J. A. Kerle

Beautiful creek lines run alongside the Olga Gorge track and below the Valley of the Winds lookout. After rain they flow for a short time, cascading and rippling over boulders and into pools. Although they cannot be relied upon as a source of water many of these pools remain for a long time, being replenished even by small showers. The stately River Red Gum *Eucalyptus camaldulensis* (p.93) can find enough moisture to survive, and is surrounded by hopbushes, wattles, corkwoods and plumbushes.

As the walking track continues into Olga Gorge the microenvironment becomes increasingly protected from the desert extremes — extremes of temperature, wind and moisture. In the gorge grow beautiful specimens of Spearbush *Pandorea doratoxalon* (p.88), Fig *Ficus platypoda* (p.87) and thickets of plumbush and Mount Olga wattle *Acacia olgana*.

A similar well-protected plant community grows in the narrow gorge to the south of the lookout over the Valley of the Winds. Turn right on to the circuit track after crossing the bridge. This pretty little rocky creek contains a fascinating variety of low shrubs — indigo (*Indigofera* species), Rock Nightshade *Solanum petrophylum*, Round-leaf Wattle *Acacia strongylophylla*, the rare hummocky grass *Eriachne scleranthoides* (Fig. 7.16), *Seneccio* and others.

To the north (turn left), the circuit track initially follows the creek. After rain the boggy edges can be carpeted by the delicate pink lily Early Nancy *Wurmbea centralis* (Fig. 4.34) growing amongst the sedges and green grasses. Turning away from the creek the track again passes through a low open shrubland. Although this is similar to the outer slopes of the domes, the presence of large desert hopbushes and plumbushes indicates that conditions for plant growth inside the domes are not quite as harsh. As you stand to admire the view to the north of Kata Tjuta on this part of the track, you may also see an attractive Christmas tree-shaped mulga, parasitised by a mistletoe on its lower branches.

From the open shrubland the track turns south between another creek line and an impressive conglomerate dome, and ultimately turns west into a narrow, very sheltered valley. The track winds through a dense thicket of Mount Olga wattle below the saddle connecting the two domes. The breathtaking view from the top of the saddle highlights the dark creek lines winding between the open shrubland and light green patches of porcupine grass and the hummocky grass *Eriachne scleranthoides*.

FOOTHILLS

Gently sloping minor rock outcrops and scree slopes associated with the Kata Tjuta formation can be seen to the west of the domes near the sunset viewing area, and along the Petermann Road towards the western boundary of Uluru National Park (map, p.vi). A similar formation, The Sedimentaries, occurs on Aboriginal land just outside of the national park, to the west of the Yulara village.

Both these rocky areas have patches of low open shrubland, annual grassland with low trees and scattered shrubs and patches of mulga shrubland. The mulga is especially common along the little creek lines which drain these outcrops. Mulga, witchetty bush, cassias, native fuchsias, *Ptilotus* species and a variety of annual grass species are the most abundant plant species.

GEORGE GILL RANGE

The Kings Canyon Walk (p.176) climbs steeply from the sheltered canyon of Kings Creek, up a sparsely vegetated scree slope to a plateau dotted with beehive formations. There the track wanders between the beehives, passing through shrubby vegetation, moist narrow crevices and across creeks and bare rock surfaces. At the first lookout you can look down upon the heavily wooded Kings Creek and along to the mouth of the Garden of Eden. After hiking through the harsh environment amongst the beehive domes, the Garden of Eden transports you to another world. The contrast is stark. From there the second half of this circuit walk continues across the exposed plateau, through and over narrow moist gullies and between the domes.

In this part of the George Gill Range there are six plant associations:

- ◘ spinifex shrubland of scree slopes and foothills
- ◘ shrubland on low hills perched on the plateau
- ◘ sparsely vegetated sandstone domes
- ◘ spinifex shrubland on upper hill slopes and crests with areas of bare rock
- ◘ deep gorges and gullies
- ◘ sand dunes perched on top of the plateau with desert oaks and spinifex

Of these associations, only the perched sand dunes are not encountered on the Kings Canyon Walk. Where they do occur, these dune formations are quite similar to those described for areas away from the ranges.

The scree slope plants are best observed on the climb at the beginning and the descent at the end of the Kings Canyon Walk. Looking at the plants can be a good excuse for a rest stop on the climb! The spinifex there is yet another species, Weeping Spinifex *Triodia clelandii*. The common name describes the way the flower spikes bend over. This is also the most abundant type of spinifex covering the lower hill slopes of the West MacDonnell Ranges. Spinifex isn't the only grass species — there are also some perennial grasses such as Wanderrie Grass *Eriachne mucronata* and Woolly-butt *Eragrostis eriopoda* mixed with silvertails. Amongst the shrubs you will find Dead Finish *Acacia tetrogonophylla*, Umbrella Bush *Acacia ligulata* and the Rock Fuchsia *Eremophila freelingii* with occasional larger plants such as mulga.

FIGURE 4.35 The almost bare domes of the George Gill Range are crisscrossed by deep crevices where an interesing variety of plants grow. *J. A. Kerle*

The shrubland at the top of the climb is representative of the perched low hills. As well as the mulga, rock fuchsia and umbrella bush, there is Blue Mallee *Eucalyptus gammophylla*, Cassias *Senna artemisioides* spp. *filifolia* and *sturtii* and witchetty bushes. In other areas, *Acacia macdonnelliensis* and mulga are more common and the spinifex is *Plectrachne melvillei*, rather than weeping spinifex.

In part, the stunning beauty of the George Gill Range results from the stark, mostly bare domes and slopes. A few plants struggle and survive in these extraordinarily dry and hot places. *Baeckia polystemonea* is one such plant (below). Its normal growth is as an erect shrub up to three metres in height — but not in this hostile place. Here it rises from tiny cracks in the rock in a contorted and twisted and often horizontal form. Some old specimens with thick stems may have only grown 20–50 centimetres. Other larger specimens spread over the rock surface but are less than half a metre in height. *Baeckia* is a rare species but is readily found on the circuit walk. Bonsai Ghost Gums *Corymbia aparrerinja* are another delightful result of the harsh growing conditions. These are best seen on the plateau to the south of the canyon.

FIGURE 4.36 The contorted form of a *Baeckia* struggling to survive on inhospitable bare rock above Kings Canyon. *J. A. Kerle*

FIGURE 4.37 A pool of water in the Garden of Eden reflects the bare domes above and the surrounding gums and cycads. *J. A. Kerle*

Wanderrie grass, Mountain Primrose *Goodenia grandiflora* and *Pomax rupestris* also grow where there is almost no soil. If a little more soil has accumulated, a variety of additional species will grow. Amongst these are the figs, Mint Bush *Prostanthera striatiflora, Acacia macdonnelliensis,* Caustic Vine *Sarcostemma viminale,* spinifex *Plectrachne melvillei* and beautiful specimens of the White Cypress Pine *Callitris glaucophylla.* In some spots, seepage enables rare plants such as the Trigger Plant *Stylidium inaequipetalum,* Sundew *Drosera indica* and *Centrolepis eremica* to survive.

Erosion of the vertical cracks through the Mereenie Sandstone has enabled plant communities to grow which would not survive in the surrounding harsh environment. These communities can be divided into those which grow in wet gorges and those which grow in dry gullies and valleys. They vary greatly in their area and in the plants they contain.

Near the beginning of the circuit walk the track winds between the beehive domes and passes through a narrow protected slot with two large specimens of the cycad *Macrozamia macdonnellii* (p.89). A little further on the track passes through a broad dry gully in which there are small gums,

FIGURE 4.38 Bloodwood tree almost covered by a flowering mistletoe. *J. A. Kerle*

Holly Grevillea *Grevillea wickhamii,* mint bushes, white cypress pines, sticky hopbush and *Acacia macdonnelliensis.* The spinifex *Plectrachne melvillei,* caustic vine and a variety of perennial grasses cover the ground. From other unprotected slots crisscrossing the open plateau, tall shrubs such as beefwood and mulga protrude. In one of these south of the Garden of Eden is the unusual sight of a caustic vine (p.89) almost covering a beefwood.

The Garden of Eden is the other end of the spectrum. It is a large deep valley with permanent waterholes (Fig. 2.24). The river red gums grow tall and straight and are surrounded by cycads and a variety of perennial grasses and sedges. Ghost gums, figs, white cypress pines and spearbushes are also common, mostly on the slopes. The density of the trees and shrubs and shading by the valley itself make this a cool moist place, even on very hot days.

Beautiful deep permanent waterholes are another feature of the George Gill Range. Two of these can readily be visited — one at Kathleen Springs and the other above the main waterfall from the Garden of Eden into Kings Canyon. These are the places where most of the relict water loving plant species are found — but not all of them occur at every waterhole. The Creeping Fern *Cyclosorus interruptus* is a large attractive fern at Kathleen Springs. It is found around several of the waterholes in the George Gill Range — but otherwise occurs only in the Australian tropics! There are others such as the Swamp Lily *Ottelia ovalifolia* (Fig. 7.24) and the water plant *Polygonum plebium.*

Surrounding the Kings Canyon Resort are the low hills and valleys of the darker Carmichael Sandstone. The plant communities there are slightly different from those found on the Mereenie Sandstone. They include shrublands, grasslands and patches of bluebush or saltbush. Mulga and witchetty bush are the most common shrubs, but Latrobe's Desert Fuchsia *Eremophila latrobei,* umbrella bush, dead finish, striped mint bush and various cassias are also there. Large trees include bloodwoods, Whitewood *Atalaya hemiglauca* and Beefwood *Grevillea striata.* On the ground are grasses such as the Nine Awn *Enneapogon polyphyllus,* some weeping spinifex, caustic vine and a variety of forbs.

The landscaping around the Kings Canyon Resort is also worthy of description. Wherever possible the existing vegetation has been retained and enhanced by watering. For the plantings only local native species have been cultivated — except for the Sturt's desert pea (Fig. 7.20). The purple-flowered *Rulingia magniflora* is a rare species within the park which has flourished in parts of the resort. Cassias and wattles have been extensively planted, especially around the reception and commercial buildings, and Sturt's desert rose provides an attractive screen between the verandahs of the units and the road. When flowering, these plantings provide a magnificent display.

SOME PLANTS OF THE ROCKY RANGES AND OUTCROPS

Some of the plants found in these areas are distinctive and have been most important for Aboriginal people.

Bloodwood — Muur-muurpa (Fig. 4.38)

The Bloodwood *Corymbia opaca* is one of the four most common eucalypts in this region. It is common around Uluru and in the Valley of Winds at Kata Tjuta. It also occurs in the woodlands adjacent to the George Gill Range and on the floodplains and floodouts of the watercourses. It is most easily distinguished from other eucalypt trees by its rough, flaky yellow-grey bark. To confirm your identification look for the bell-shaped gum nuts on the ground underneath — they are usually about 1.5–2 centimetres long. You may also find large brown apple-shaped 'fruits' clustered on the branches. These are called 'bloodwood apples' or 'bush coconuts'. They are not the fruits of the tree, but a gall formed by an insect.

This is another plant which has multiple uses for Aboriginal people. The timber is highly valued, being used for making wiras (bowls) and the process is demonstrated by the Mutitjulu Guides on the Liru Walk at Uluru. As firewood, the timber is quite simply the best! It produces hot, lasting coals — ideal for baking bread or cooking a camp oven roast. The bloodwood apples — angura — are an important food. They are collected while the gall is still active, split open, and both the large white grub and the coconut-like lining of the gall are consumed. Native bees may also live in the trunk and water can be obtained from the roots.

The red sap, from which the Bloodwood gets its name, is sometimes found in dried lumps on the bark. It has medicinal value. When the tree is damaged, the sap oozes out and is then available for use. Fresh sticky gum can be rubbed directly and repeatedly on to sores and cuts. Alternatively, lumps of the dried crystalline form can be soaked to make them sticky. A liquid wash can also be made by boiling the crystals in water until they have dissolved. This is used on burns, sores, cuts and aching muscles and even to relieve soreness around the eyes. It is a powerful healer and is still regularly used.

Ghost Gum — Para, Pilpira (Fig. 4.39)

High on the steep sides of rocky gorges you often see a white-trunked tree apparently growing straight out of the rock. This is a Ghost Gum *Corymbia aparrerinja*. In deep soils it can grow to 15 metres. It has dark green drooping foliage. The smooth white bark is powdery and will leave a film on your hand if you rub it. On the Kings Canyon

Walk (pp.176–78) you will notice some unusual looking ghost gums. Some are short-er and have a little rough bark; others grow in a bonsai form.

Figs — Illi (Fig. 4.40) and Plumbush — Arnguli (Fig. 4.29)

These two species are common around all the rocky habitats and are of considerable importance to Aboriginal people as well as to a variety of native animals.

The Native Fig *Ficus platypoda* (Fig. 4.40) is a relative of the well-known cultivated fig and similarly produces edible fruits. These are much smaller and not nearly as tasty but they do represent a valuable food resource. The figs are eaten when ripe, as indi-cated by a change in colour from yellow to a rich red. They are mostly eaten fresh, but the fallen dry fruit can be ground into an edible paste or made into balls for later con-sumption. They have been found to be a good source of protein, some fats and trace elements. The figs are enjoyed not only by people — several bird species including the spotted bowerbird and black-faced cuckoo-shrike, take advantage of this prolific food supply. So did brushtail possums before they disappeared from this country.

The fig itself is not a true fruit. The tiny flowers are contained inside and are fer-tilised as the result of a complex partnership between the fig and a tiny wasp. The wasp struggles her way into the fig through the hole at the top and, while fertilising the fig flowers, lays her eggs in a very protected place. The tiny seeds are the fruits. There are many of these sprawling fig shrubs around Uluru but one of the most obvious is at the bottom of 'the climb'.

The plums from the Plumbush *Santalum lanceolatum* are another desirable food. During summer and autumn — if there has been enough rain — Aboriginal women col-lected them in large quantities, carrying them back to camp in mimpus (bowls) on their heads. The purple-black fruits are small, with a thin fleshy covering around a single large seed. The fleshy skin is eaten raw or mashed with water to provide a tasty drink. The dried fruit can be reconstituted with water and eaten. The plums were considered to be an excellent food in the days when there was no sugar, no flour and no tea.

FIGURE 4.39 (left) The white streak of a ghost gum in the rocky ranges. *M. W. Gillam*

FIGURE 4.40 (above) Sprawling native figs provide a valuable food resource. *J. A. Kerle*

The leaves and fruits of the plumbush are both desirable foods for possums and cattle. They are highly nutritious. The wood is like the related Sandalwood *Santalum spicatum* of South Australia and has been exported for its perfumed wood and oil. This no longer happens.

Spearbush — Urtjanpa (Fig 4.41 and 7.26)

The Spearbush *Pandorea doratoxylon* is a most attractive plant — a climbing, twining shrub of the sheltered rocky gorges. The feathery leaves and clusters of bell-shaped flowers enhance this impression. The creamy flowers have purple-brown markings and a mass of hairs in the throat. The branches grow into long canes which are used by Aboriginal men for making lightweight hunting spears. For this purpose the twisted canes are straightened using the heat from a fire.

Early Nancy (Fig. 4.34)

Early Nancy *Wurmbea centralis* is found only around Kata Tjuta — and only if there has been enough rain. Then the underground bulbs of this lily spring into life and the marshy ground where it grows can become a mass of delicate pink star-shaped flowers.

Wattles

The mountain ranges and remnant rocky outcrops contain a great diversity of wattles. Some, such as mulga, witchetty bush, umbrella bush and black wattle are widespread, and are commonly found growing in sand or on rocks. Others like the Uluru wattle and Mount Olga wattle have a very restricted distribution centred around those two outcrops.

FIGURE 4.41 The spearbush with its bell-shaped flowers, is a climbing twining shrub of sheltered rocky gorges. *J. A. Kerle*

FIGURE 4.42 Dead finish, a wattle with small spiky phyllodes, grows on the rocky slopes of Kata Tjuta. *J. A. Kerle*

Dead finish, kurara (Fig. 4.42), is another wattle which is important as an Aboriginal food source: the seeds are ground and eaten in the same way as the seeds from witchetty bush, mulga and umbrella bush, and the plant has medicinal qualities. It can be used as an antiseptic, an astringent and a wart remover. In order to remove warts, up to six of the spiky phyllodes are inserted into the base of a wart and left there until it starts to bleed. They are then taken out. After four or five days the wart withers and may be removed. This is quite a painful process but very effective! The antiseptic and astringent preparations are made by soaking the root bark.

Caustic Vine — Ipi-ipi (Fig. 4.43)

Caustic Vine *Sarcostemma viminale* is one of the more bizarre plants growing on the George Gill Range and around the Kings Canyon Resort (p.173). It is apparently leafless and the pale green cylindrical stems have obvious joints. Sometimes these jointed stems can be long and trailing. The leaves are not entirely absent, having been reduced to rudimentary scales at each joint — a mechanism by which the plant conserves water.

For Aboriginal people ipi-ipi has several medicinal uses. It can be either burnt and used for smoke treatment or the milky sap used for skin problems. In the smoke treatment, a large quantity of the vine is burnt in a pit to produce a thick smoke. The sick person lies over the pit until they feel better — and perhaps a little numbed! The milky sap flows readily from a broken stem, especially after rain when the sap flow is stronger. The milk is dabbed directly on to irritated skin to control infections such as scabies. Alternatively, a handful of sappy stems are broken up and soaked in hot water. After removal of the stems the liquid can be used as a general wash for skin complaints.

MacDonnell Ranges Cycad (Fig. 4.44)

The fronds of the MacDonnell Ranges Cycad *Macrozamia macdonnellii* look feathery, but are tough and spiky. It is one of only two species of plants in Central Australia which belong to the primitive group called gymnosperms — seed plants with no flowers. They are a remnant of the wetter past. They occur throughout the George Gill and MacDonnell Ranges, mostly growing in the moister gorges and gullies but also in crevices high up on the walls of gorges.

Cycads are extremely slow-growing plants, so those with a large trunk are very old. Male and female cones grow on separate plants; the male cones are

FIGURE 4.43 The caustic vine, with its leafless jointed stems, is one of the more bizarre-looking plants to be seen on the Kings Canyon Walk. *J. A. Kerle*

FIGURE 4.44 The toxic fruits of the primitive MacDonnell Ranges cycad consist of white egg-shaped capsules encased in red flesh; often a capsule can be found amongst the debris along creeks. *J. A. Kerle*

FIGURE 4.45 White cypress pines are most common where fires are uncommon. *J. A. Kerle*

FIGURE 4.46 Red flowers of the holly grevillea attract the nectar-feeding birds. *J. A. Kerle*

longer and narrower than the female cones. When they are fully developed the fruits are large white egg-shaped seeds encased in bright red flesh. There is no record of local Aboriginal people ever soaking these seeds to leach out their toxins in order to eat them, as people have done in other parts of Australia. Rock wallabies eat the outer skin of the fruit and rock rats may have eaten the rich but toxic seed.

White Cypress Pine — Kulilyuru (Fig. 4.45)

With its dense blue-green foliage and almost black trunk, the White Cypress Pine *Callitris glaucophylla* is an atractive tree. It mostly grows on hill slopes or in gullies and gorges and attains a height of only about four metres. It is destroyed by fire and consequently is found only where fires are uncommon. Like the MacDonnell Ranges Cycad, the White Cypress is a gymnosperm but in this case the male and female cones occur on the same plant. The needle-like leaves are strongly scented.

This is one of the most widespread of the native Australian pines, being found in all mainland states. The timber, which repels termite attack, has long been used as a building and fencing timber. While it was never a commercial timber in Central Australia, it was widely used by the white settlers for building dwellings and stockyards. Aboriginal people used it as an antiseptic and decongestant. A concentrated aromatic infusion was made from the leaves and small twigs and then applied to skin rashes or to the chest for colds. Alternatively, people lay in the smoke from burning branches, slept and sweated, and so rid themselves of illness.

Holly Grevillea (Fig. 4.46)

The tall shrub with blue-green holly-shaped leaves and gorgeous bright red flowers is the Holly Grevillea *Grevillea wickhamii*. It is a bright splash of colour in the dry rocky gullies of the George Gill Range and is often the place to see nectar-feeding honeyeaters.

Rock Fuchsia

The Rock Fuchsia *Eremophila freelingii* is far less showy but is a widespread species growing in the dry rocky shrubland around Watarrka. After a dry spell the drooping grey foliage can make these bushes appear almost dead, but they respond dramatically to good rains and soon look vigorous and healthy. They are one to two metres high and have narrow, soft hairy leaves grouped at the ends of the branchlets. The tubular flowers are generally lilac but can be pink, blue or white.

The Rock Fuschia's aromatic resinous leaves have a variety of medicinal uses. A wash is prepared by boiling the leaves in water and then straining them off. This is used to treat cuts, sores and scabies; taken as a drink to relieve colds and diarrhoea; or rubbed on the body or around the head as a decongestant. Even the early European settlers acknowledged the value of this plant and made a medicinal tea from it.

Mint Bush   (Fig. 7.23)

Another very attractive shrub is the Mint Bush *Prostanthera striatiflora*. The name *striatiflora* means striped flowers — the white flower is bell-shaped with purple stripes and yellow spots in the throat. The bush grows to about two metres and the small leaves (20-25mm long) have a strong fragrance when crushed. Like the rock fuchsia, the Mint Bush is valued as an antiseptic, counter-irritant and decongestant. One vital difference is that preparations made from the mint bush must *never* be taken internally nor come in contact with the eyes and must be used sparingly on babies. The plant's toxic properties have been well recognised by Aboriginal people who scattered dried and crushed leaves over waterholes to stupefy emus and make them easier to catch. Branches are left beside the water to warn other people against drinking it.

Emu Poison Bush — Pituri

The shrub *Dubosia hopwoodii* is known by two names: Emu Poison Bush and Pituri. In Central Australia it is used for poisoning game in the same way as the mint bush. It is considered so poisonous in this region that Aboriginal people caution that the plant should not be handled near children. The same species in Queensland is less toxic and has been traded extensively across Australia as a chewing tobacco. The alkaloids nicotine and nor-nicotine are present in the leaves of this shrub; the higher levels of nor-nicotine in Central Australia are the cause of the lethal toxicity.

Native Tobacco   (Fig. 4.47)

In Central Australia, the herb *Nicotiana* — not *Dubosia* — is the widely used native chewing tobacco. There are nine species of *Nicotiana* but only four are commonly used. Some grow in rocky areas, including the beginning of the Kings Canyon Walk near Kings Creek, in the Garden of Eden (p.176) and along the Kathleen Springs track (map, p.vii). All species look similar, having large pointed leaves and a tall stem with a cluster of white tubular flowers at the top. The long narrow flower tubes flare at the end and are open at night. These species belong to the same genus of plants as commercial tobacco. Aboriginal people harvest the whole plant, dry and crush the leaves and then mix this with ash derived from the bloodwood, ghost gum or mulga before they chew it.

FIGURE 4.47 The native tobacco *Nicotiana* grows prolifically around the George Gill Range. *J. A. Kerle*

DRY WATERCOURSES — KARU

The dry rivers of Central Australia are a hallmark of this country. The white sand of the Finke River formed an important early route for people travelling from South Australia to the Centre. But it is necessary to redefine our terms: here the rivers and waterfalls generally have no running water! The rivers are exciting when they flow — often in a raging flood — but for most of the time they are dry. When it does rain the rise of the water can be exceedingly rapid — but so can the fall. A river crossing may become impassable for ten minutes or for several days.

Within Uluru and Watarrka National Parks the watercourses draining the mountain ranges and remnant rocky outcrops are not major watercourses like the Finke, but rather are smaller shorter creeks which flood out into the sand dunes. The major rivers — Finke, Palmer, Hugh and Todd — can be visited when travelling between these parks and Alice Springs (see map on p.vii and also p.138).

The dry rivers and creeks and their associated floodplains have another distinctive plant community. River Red Gums *Eucalyptus camaldulensis* (Fig. 4.48) are the dominant feature of the larger rivers such as the Palmer and the Finke — majestic, with their dappled creamy trunks under a spreading grey-green canopy. As the creek channels become smaller the size and number of river red gums decreases. On Kings Creek scattered river red gums are mixed with Ironwood *Acacia estrophiolata* and Bloodwood *E. opaca*. The riverbank vegetation merges in with the floodplain species.

A variety of small trees and shrubs are regularly associated with the floodplains and floodouts of the watercourses. Prickly Wattle *A. victoriae*, mulga, dead finish and witchetty bush are commonly found, as are the Bush Orange *Capparis mitchelli* and Bush Passionfruit *Capparis spinosa*. The Bush Orange, a small tree with a very dark trunk and dark green foliage, is easily distinguished from the low sprawling bush passionfruit shrub. Cassia *Senna artemisioides,* Desert Fuchsias *Eremophila sturtii* and *E. gilesii* and the Bush Plum *Solanum lanceolatum* are scattered throughout. The Inland Tea-tree *Melaleuca glomerata* is commonly found associated with watercourses in

FIGURE 4.48 The contorted trunks of river red gums shine in the sunlight along a watercourse in Central Australia. *J. A. Kerle*

Central Australia, but surprisingly it does not occur in Watarrka National Park.

The groundcover of the floodplains is the domain of the grasses — both annual and perennial. There are many species and they once provided an important food source for Aboriginal people before they had access to flour and bread. The perennial species include Native Millet *Pannicum decompositum*, Kangaroo Grass *Themeda avenaceae*, Native Oat Grass *Themeda avenacea*, Bandicoot Grass *Monochather paradoxus*, Cotton Grass *Digitaria browniana* and Silky Brown Top *Eulalia aurea*. The introduced Buffel Grass *Cenchrus ciliaris* is also a perennial and is spreading widely throughout Central Australia, especially along the watercourses. The annual grasses grow quickly after rain, seed profusely and die off, leaving lots of seeds to continue the cycle. The Nine Awn *Enneapogon cylindricus*, Kerosene Grass *Aristida contorta* and Pigeon Grass *Pannicum laevinode* are annuals.

Seeds from many of these grasses were once regularly collected and then cleaned by skillfully rubbing, singeing, winnowing and yandying. Grinding stones like those in the caves on the Mala Walk (p.165) were used to grind the seeds into flour. The paste made by mixing the flour with water can be eaten raw or cooked in hot sand, making a traditional damper.

A variety of forbs and vines grow amongst the floodout grasses — they are mostly prickles and introduced species! The Caltrop *Tribulus terrestris*, Lifesaver Burr *Sida platycalyx* and Bogan Flea *Calotis hispidula* all have nasty prickles. The Wild Turnip *Brassica tournefortii*, Rosy Dock *Acetosa vesicaria*, Paddy Melon *Citrullus lanatus* and Couch Grass *Cynodon dactylon* are all introduced species which readily grow on the banks or in the river bed. A few of the native species you might find are Silvertails *Ptilotus obovatus*, Munyeroo *Portulacca oleracea*, Red Soldier *Euphorbia drummondii* and the Desert Rattlepod *Crotalaria eremaea*. The Bush Banana *Marsdenia australis* is an important native vine which produces large edible fruits, unlike the Snake Vine *Mukia maderaspatana* and Tar Vine *Boerhavia coccinea* which do not. The bulb of yalka *Cyperus bulbosa* can grow prolifically on floodprone areas and has been an important Aboriginal food.

River Red Gum — Itara   (Fig. 4.48)

The River Red Gum *Eucalyptus camaldulensis* is a wonderful tree. It can provide shade, shelter, food, medicine and wood for people and an amazing array of animals can live in it. It is the most widespread of Australian eucalypts and varies in trunk colour, leaf shape and colour, and overall size, depending on the local environment. In the heat of a desert day, the shady spreading branches of a river red gum are a most welcome sight. The trees can grow to 35 metres and the blotchy white, grey and red trunk is usually gnarled and twisted. Young straight trees can be easily distinguished from the Ghost Gum *Corymbia aparrerinja* by rubbing your hand on the trunk: the ghost gum will leave a white powdery coating on your hand.

The many scars on the trunks of river red gums tell a lot about their history. There are scars left by the impact of rocks and logs hurtling down a flooding river and there are various wounds caused by insects. Cicadas feed on the roots as nymphs and lay their eggs in the branches; large grubs burrow into the branches; sap-sucking scale-insects live on the leaves. The flaking bark provides shelter for spiders, geckoes and small goannas. The hollows are nests for many parrots and bats and once provided homes for possums.

Food for Aboriginal people comes from many of the animals that live in the trees. The grubs (large beetle larvae) found in the branches and roots and the lerps on the leaves are particular favourites. Lerps are the white sugary scale secreted by sap-sucking coccid insects (Fig. 4.23). People collect the little scales and roll them into a ball, which is eaten later like a lolly. Ash from the burnt bark can be mixed with native tobacco (pituri) and of course the timber produces an excellent cooking fire with good hot coals.

Both the leaves and the bark are used for medicinal purposes. The leaves are a good source of eucalyptus oil —a product which is now readily available commercially for the relief of colds and flu. The oils were extracted by crushing the leaves between rocks and then boiling them. The wash produced was rubbed on to the skin or drunk. A red wash is also obtained by boiling the dark inner bark — this is used as an anti-septic for sores including scabies.

Ironwood   (Fig. 5.12)

The variety of small trees growing on the floodplains also provides a range of bush foods and some medicines. The seeds of the Ironwood *Acacia estriophiolata* are crushed and mixed with water as a sweet for children. The gum which exudes from wounds on the trunk is eaten or used as an ointment; there are two types of gum — one sweet and one medicinal. This dark-barked tree with drooping foliage is quite widespread throughout the region, occurring with desert oaks as well as along watercourses. The bark has sev-eral uses. The inner bark of the younger branches and smaller roots is boiled or crushed in water. The wash prepared from the branches is used on boils, scabies and sore eyes and the dark red preparation made from the roots is used for healing burns and sores.

Corkwood   (Fig. 4.49)

The corky bark from the corkwood trees *Hakea eyereana* and *H. suberea* can also be used to treat burns. The bark is carefully burnt and then crushed with sand to a fine, black, slightly oily powder. This is then blown on to large open sores or small severe burns and covered with a bark bandage — possibly long strips of ironwood root bark. Corkwoods are valued for their large yellow flower clusters as well. The dark sweet nectar is sucked from the flowers or squeezed with water to make a sweet drink. These small gnarled trees with prickly foliage can be heavily covered with flowers in a good season.

Bush Orange, Bush Passionfruit, Bush Banana

The Bush Orange *Capparis mitchelli*, Bush Passionfruit *C. spinosa* and Bush Banana *Marsdenia australis* bear little resemblance to the cultivated fruits they are named after. The two *Capparis* species have large showy white or pale yellow flowers with four petals, four sepals and numerous long stamens. The flowers, which open only for one night, are apparently pollinated by moths. The bush orange has a green fruit about the size of a lemon which is found sporadically in summer. It is a very good source of vitamin C and thiamine. The wild passionfruit contains a seedy pulp and splits open when ripe. The fruit from the bush banana vine is pear-shaped and is another important Aboriginal food.

FIGURE 4.49
Corkwoods, ironwoods and grasses are commonly found along river banks. *J. A. Kerle*

5

THE ABUNDANT
ANIMAL LIFE

A wedge-tailed eagle, soaring in the rich blue sky above the cliffs or struggling to fly from a bloated carcass on the roadside; an occasional kangaroo feeding on the green-pick of the road verge; a flock of red-tailed black cockatoos or brilliant budgerigars: these are the images of wildlife in Central Australia. But they represent just a tiny fraction of the rich and varied wildlife of the Australian deserts.

Where is all this wildlife? While it is abundant and varied, it is not always visible. The animals must survive in the harsh desert conditions of soaring summer daytime temperatures, freezing winter nights and frequent long dry conditions. Often their behaviour is cryptic — they are there but you just can't see them. Many are nocturnal or active only at dawn and dusk. Large animals, including red kangaroos and emus, are uncommon. Small animals — insects, lizards, mice — hide in burrows or live amongst the spinifex and leaf litter in order to conserve body moisture and avoid the extreme temperatures. Most of the wildlife is around your feet! Look for the evidence of tracks in the sand (Figs. 5.2 and 5.3).

FIGURE 5.1 Pink cockatoos stand out against the iron-stained rock and the rich blue sky of Central Australia. *M. W. Gillam*

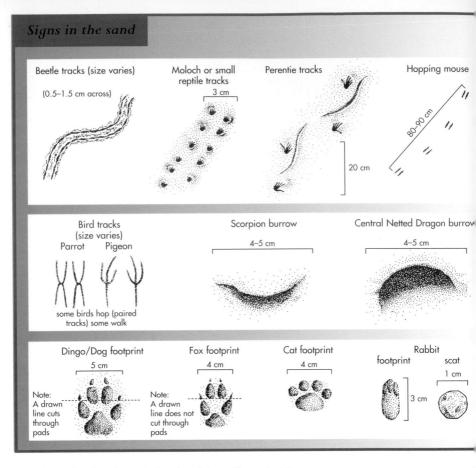

Beetle tracks (size varies)

(0.5–1.5 cm across)

Moloch or small reptile tracks

3 cm

Perentie tracks

20 cm

Hopping mouse

80–90 cm

Bird tracks (size varies)
Parrot   Pigeon

some birds hop (paired tracks) some walk

Scorpion burrow

4–5 cm

Central Netted Dragon burrow

4–5 cm

Dingo/Dog footprint

5 cm

Note: A drawn line cuts through pads

Fox footprint

4 cm

Note: A drawn line does not cut through pads

Cat footprint

4 cm

Rabbit
footprint   scat

1 cm

3 cm

Figure 5.2 A guide to animal tracks and signs. *Christine Bruderlin*
Figure 5.3 (opposite) A beetle and a variety of lizards have traversed this patch of wind-rippled sand. *M. W. Gillam*

Insects and lizards dominate the desert animal life. Ants, termites, grasshoppers, crickets, moths and beetles are extraordinarily varied. Most of the species have never been recorded or formally named. The lizards — skinks, dragons, geckoes — are better known but not always easy to find. They hide under the spinifex and, if disturbed, disappear rapidly. They make Australian deserts special on a world scale because of the great variety to be found. Why? Because of the incredible abundance of their insect foods, especially termites.

These insect foods, like all desert creatures, respond dramatically to rain. Ant and termite queens swarm, moths dim the lights at night and grasshoppers can be seen busily mating. Birds take advantage of the abundance of food following a good soaking rainfall and often produce several clutches of young in quick succession. The response may not be immediate, however. If heavy rains fall in March or April plant growth and insect breeding will not peak until the warmer weather in July or August. Breeding of wildlife is timed, of course, to take advantage of the subsequent abundant food supply rather than the rain itself.

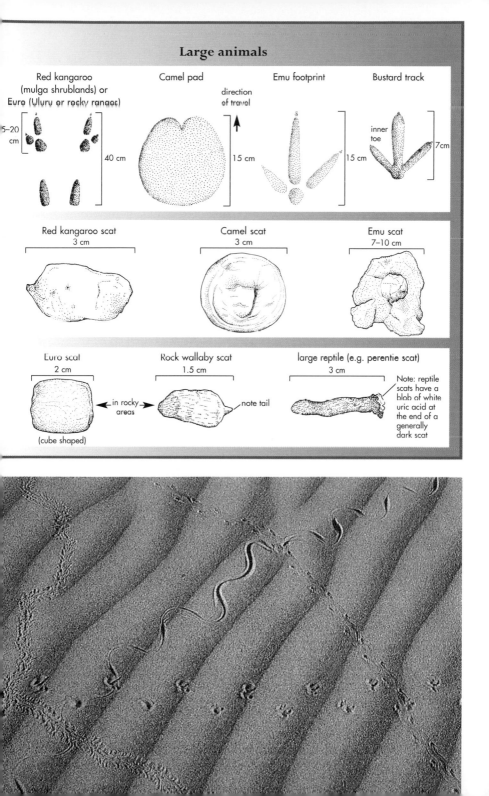

Large animals

Red kangaroo (mulga shrublands) or Euro (Uluru or rocky ranges)

5–20 cm

40 cm

Camel pad

direction of travel

15 cm

Emu footprint

15 cm

Bustard track

inner toe

7cm

Red kangaroo scat
3 cm

Camel scat
3 cm

Emu scat
7–10 cm

Euro scat
2 cm

(cube shaped)

← in rocky areas →

Rock wallaby scat
1.5 cm

note tail

large reptile (e.g. perentie scat)
3 cm

Note: reptile scats have a blob of white uric acid at the end of a generally dark scat

FIGURE 5.4 A Burton's legless lizard slides easily through the spiky spinifex leaves.
M. W. Gillam

FIGURE 5.5 Termites are a vital link in the food chain of Central Australian deserts: they provide a nutrient recycling service and are the primary food supply for many of the lizards, which eat these winged termites as well as the wingless workers.
M. W. Gillam

FIGURE 5.6 Budgerigars and zebra finches share a rock puddle for a drink.
M. W. Gillam

While the brilliant flocks of budgerigars may be seen after good soaking rains, other animals may become less visible. When the country is dry kangaroos often feed along the road verges at dusk and dawn because runoff from the road enhances the growth of soft grasses. But when the country is green they disperse widely and are less often seen. Even then the animals are not evenly distributed across the landscape. Red kangaroos are more likely to be found in and around the mulga country. Euros (Fig. 5.14) prefer rocky hill slopes and mulgaras (p.109) need spinifex.

Within each of the plant communities described in Chapter 4 is a unique suite of animal species. Some of the animals, like perenties, are most common around the ranges but can also be found more widely. Others such as honey ants are restricted entirely to mulga soils. And still others show no particular preference at all — like brown falcons. The most important division of animals is between the sandy country and the rocky ranges and slopes — rock specialists and sand specialists.

In all these habitats birds are the most obvious of the wildlife. They range from the majestic wedge-tailed eagle through to the cryptic and rare grey honeyeater. While no bird species have been lost from the Australian arid lands as a whole, since settlement by people of European heritage, many have declined substantially in numbers. The thick-billed grasswren, for example, was first described from specimens collected in Watarrka National Park, but it is no longer found in the Northern Territory — a loss that can be directly ascribed to the disturbance of the saltbush or chenopod shrublands. The mallee fowl is another species that is no longer present in the region, yet the Aboriginal people knew it well.

Mammals have been much more severely affected with more than 20 species now being either extinct or endangered. Most of the Australian mammal species which have declined over the last 200 years lived in the arid lands and this decline has occurred despite the remote and apparently undeveloped appearance of the country. In fact there have been many disturbances which have contributed to their decline: pastoral grazing; changed burning patterns; feral grazing animals and predators. The mammals most affected are middle-sized species like the burrowing bettong, rufous hare-wallaby (or mala, p.110), bilby and the brushtail possum (p.110). Historical records show that many of these animals were once extremely common. They were important to Aboriginal people both spiritually and for food. Now they eat some of the feral species such as rabbits and cats instead.

Feral animals are a major cause for concern if many of the native species are to survive. Rabbits and camels either compete with the native species for their food or destroy their habitat. Foxes and cats have wiped out the last known populations of some native species. At present there are no known wild populations of feral bird species in the centre but it may not be long before European house sparrows arrive. They have already reached Tennant Creek from the east and Oodnadatta from the south.

So, although there is an abundance of wildlife in the arid land of Central Australia, it is often difficult to find. It is small, cryptic and mostly invertebrate, leaving only tracks in the sand as evidence of the nightly activity. Birds are most likely to be seen and feral mammals are more often observed than the native species are.

BIRDS

While birds may be the most visible wildlife in Central Australia, sightings are dominated by a few groups of species. These include cockatoos and parrots, birds of prey, pigeons and a variety of 'little brown birds'. In broad terms the various species can be classified as: common and regularly seen; visiting vagrants which follow the rainfall; and rare. The 178 species observed in and around Uluru–Kata Tjuta and Watarrka National Parks are named in the Species Lists. Just which of these species can be seen will depend on how dry the country is and on the habitat type you are in.

The bright and noisy cockatoos and parrots loudly advertise their presence. Galahs (Fig. 7.4), budgerigars (Fig. 5.6) and ringneck parrots are always a pleasure to see, as are the less common pink cockatoo (Fig. 5.1), red-tailed black cockatoo and mulga parrot (Fig 5.11). Sitting surveying the scenery or soaring overhead are the brown falcon, whistling kite, nankeen kestrel or wedge-tailed eagle (Fig. 5.9). In the rocky ranges the presence of these and other less common birds of prey such as the peregrine falcon is indicated by the splashes of 'whitewash' below a ledge or crevice.

The presence of some 50 species of waterbirds and wading birds on a bird list for this dry part of Australia, may come as a surprise. But all these species are incredibly mobile, moving vast distances seeking patches of water. When there has been sufficient rain to fill the claypans, salt lakes and waterholes, this apparently hostile country provides a feast of shrimps, aquatic invertebrate larvae and various algae and aquatic plants. When enough rain has fallen to maintain these waters for a while, species such as pied stilts and black-tailed native hen will breed. Even the smallest patch of water will attract a white-faced heron, white-necked heron or black-fronted dotterel.

The perky zebra finch (Fig. 5.6), one of the smallest birds, moves in small flocks. They are frequently seen zipping in and out of the grass tussocks, shrubs and trees, or down to drink at a puddle, calling all the while. A variety of honeyeaters are also generally resident, especially around the Ayers Rock and Kings Canyon Resorts. White-throated miners and white-plumed honeyeaters are the most common, but brown, singing and spiny-cheeked honeyeaters can also be there feeding on the native grevilleas, wattles and gums. The grey crested pigeons (Fig. 7.21) are also found around the resorts and carparks, running and cooing to each other or flying noisily away.

Contrary to expectations, emus are not common in Central Australia. They *can* be found, mostly in small groups of about three, but only rarely. The larger flocks are more commonly encountered in northern South Australia, western Queensland and south-western Australia. For a few years, visitors to Uluru were able to see a lone emu patrolling the base of 'the climb' at Uluru and the Mutitjulu Walk. It could often be seen surrounded by photographers or stealing food. On one occasion visitors were startled to see it sprinting back and forth in front of the climb with its beak wide open; it had swallowed a lighted cigarette butt! It has since moved on.

Figure 5.7 A black kite with its forked tail soars overhead.
M. W. Gillam

A few rare birds occasionally appear in this part of Central Australia. Alexandra's Parrot is one, although it is more likely to be observed in the sandy deserts of Western Australia. Be careful not to confuse the smaller mulga parrot with an Alexandra's parrot when either flashes past; look for the very long tail and the pink on the head of an Alexandra's parrot. The grey falcon and grey honeyeater have also been found in this region. It may be worthwhile checking all the brown falcons to make sure they aren't grey falcons. Spending longer in amongst the mulga will boost your chances of seeing a grey honeyeater.

In order to observe the widest range of birds, time should be spent in each of the major plant communities described in detail in Chapter 4.

MULGA

Mulga is the best place to find the greatest variety of birds. There is a wider range of smaller insectivorous and gleaning birds than in most of the other habitats. Some of these, including the brown, chestnut-rumped and slaty-backed thornbills and the splendid fairy wren, redthroat, southern whiteface and red-capped robin often move around in mixed feeding flocks. Others, such as the rufous whistler, crested bellbird, chiming wedgebill, white browed babbler, grey shrike-thrush and white-fronted honeyeaters, are less gregarious.

ULURU, KATA TJUTA AND THE ROCKY RANGES

The presence of moist gullies with high plant diversity, sparsely vegetated scree slopes, open woodland, caves and exposed rocky cliffs, all within close proximity, enables these places to support an interesting range of birds. Birds also remain longer in these areas, especially in the moist gullies, well into a severe drought. The protected microclimate enhances plant moisture and insect abundance which in turn enables the birds to stay.

Birds of prey, such as the Australian hobby, peregrine falcon and nankeen kestrel, fly in the updraughts and use ledges along the cliff faces for roosting and nesting. Fairy martins build their nests inside the caves and these can usually be seen in Malaku Wilytja on the Mala Walk at Uluru (p.165). The beautiful song of the grey shrike-thrush often resonates around the cliffs. Along the creeks and in the moist valleys, bright painted firetail finches might be found along with zebra finches and singing and grey-headed honeyeaters while birds such as Richards pipit, black-faced cuckoo-shrike, spiny-cheeked honeyeater, willy wagtail (Fig. 2.13), pied butcherbird and tawny frogmouth (Fig. 7.12) prefer the open woodland.

SAND PLAINS AND DUNES

These open desert oak and spinifex habitats are the harshest of all in Central Australia. They also cover a large part of the land. For birds they can be places of feast or famine. This is where bird numbers fluctuate most dramatically. Many species move in after good rains and this is followed by a lot of breeding activity. While some, like zebra finches, can begin to breed one month after the rain falls, most breed in the following spring.

A few of the species can be defined as resident in this habitat, but most demonstrate great mobility. The black-faced woodswallow is a resident, unlike the masked and white-browed woodswallows which regularly move together in large flocks of up to hundreds of individuals, feeding on flushes of insects and nectar after rain. Crimson chats are also mobile but prefer the more open recently burnt spinifex habitat. In good seasons they can

FIGURE 5.8 Sparsely vegetated red sand dune with spinifex grassland in the swale. *J. A. Kerle*

be very abundant and will supplement their preferred insect foods with nectar. They especially enjoy picking up caterpillars which like to feed on the poached egg daisies during some years of plenty. Amongst the honeyeaters the yellow-throated miner and singing honeyeater are resident species, while the pied and black honeyeaters are nomads.

EPHEMERAL WATERS AND SALT LAKES

It doesn't require large rainfalls to fill some of the small soaks and claypans, and these waters are important to a vast range of birds. It is often rewarding to sit beside a patch of water and watch the parade of crested pigeons, zebra finches, honeyeaters, budgerigars and larger parrots coming in for a drink. Some of the small but more permanent waterholes are inhabited by red-kneed and black-fronted dotterels and red-capped plovers. Bourke's parrots may come in for an early morning or late afternoon drink.

Black duck and grey teal are regularly found on Central Australian waterholes, but given the wonderful big rains which can fill all lakes and depressions, many other birds will be present; cormorants, egrets, herons, spoonbills and a variety of ducks including pink-eared, hardhead and freckled ducks. Access to some of these larger natural waters is restricted around Uluru and Watarrka, but the Sewage Ponds in Alice Springs are worth a visit!

OPEN WOODLAND OF CREEKS AND FLOODOUTS

This habitat is especially important for birds nesting in tree hollows, notably parrots. White-plumed honeyeaters, diamond doves, crested pigeons, weebills, varied sitellas and babblers also flourish in the open eucalypt woodlands. It is worth having a break at the crossing of the Finke River or Palmer River when travelling along the Stuart Highway between Alice Springs and Uluru to look for some of these species.

SOME BIRDS OF PARTICULAR INTEREST

There are far too many birds in Central Australia to describe them all in detail. I have included six here all of which have their own special interest.

Wedge-tailed Eagle *Aquilla audax* — Walawuru (Fig. 5.9)

Standing up to one metre in height and having a wingspan of about two metres, the wedge-tailed eagle is a truly majestic sight. It can be seen throughout the region. Walawuru, as the Aboriginal people from Uluru call it, is the largest Australian eagle

FIGURE 5.9 Wedge-tailed eagles feeding on a carcass. *M. W. Gillam*

FIGURE 5.10 The stately mating display of an Australian bustard. *M. W. Gillam*

and the fourth largest of all eagle species. It is the symbol of the Parks and Wildlife Commission of the Northern Territory — an appropriate emblem for the organisation which cares for the Territory's national parks.

Wedge-tailed eagles are regularly observed feeding on the carcass of a road-killed animal, sometimes in groups of four or five individuals. They often seem clumsy and slow to fly from their meal when disturbed, being hampered by a bulging heavy crop. In this landscape where there may be few substantial trees they frequently perch on shrubs, which they dwarf, or simply stand on the crest of a sand dune.

Although several eagles may gather to feed on a carcass it is rare to see more than two together in the air. As they soar above, the wedge-shaped tail is easy to see, as is the colour of the plumage. The young birds have more golden feathers and are a lighter colour under the wing than are the old birds which are almost entirely black.

The wedge-tailed eagle does not entirely rely on carrion for food although this may be very important for the young birds. They prey on a wide range of animals. Rabbits are particularly favoured, but young kangaroos, bustards and snakes are also taken. They hunt mostly in the early morning or late afternoon, observing the scene from a favourite perch or soaring up high. With eyesight three times more acute than a human's, it is estimated that in daylight an eagle can spot a stationary rabbit one and a half kilometres away.

Australian Bustard (Plains Turkey) *Ardeotis australis* — Kipara (Fig. 5.10)

These large stately birds, standing about one metre high, may be seen walking sedately through open country, usually in pairs. They are uncommon in Central Australia but their numbers may have increased recently. They were once common throughout the whole of the arid and tropical parts of Australia, occurring in large flocks. They are now found in larger numbers only in the Kimberleys of Western Australia, the Barkly Tableland of the Northern Territory and Cape York in Queensland.

If you are lucky enough to see bustards they are likely to stop and watch you before walking slowly away. Approach too close and they will take to the air with a heavy laborious flight. Despite their laboured flight they can fly long distances, seeking areas with a good supply of fleshy seeds, fruits and insects such as grasshoppers. They are a favoured food of Aboriginal people.

FIGURE 5.11 Mulga parrots are most often seen in pairs; the male is the brighter of the two. *G. O'Neill*

Mulga Parrot *Psephotus varius* — Tjulily-tjulilypa (Fig. 5.11)

Mulga parrots are found throughout the arid regions of the southern half of Australia but they are not widespread, preferring mulga shrublands and watercourses. One of the best places to see these attractive small parrots is around the Kings Canyon Resort where, when conditions are right, they can appear in small flocks of twenty or so. There, they take advantage of seeds produced by the local native plants grown around the buildings.

It is more usual to see mulga parrots flying or feeding in pairs. They are generally quiet unobtrusive birds which mostly feed on the ground. When disturbed they fly into a nearby tree. Males and females differ in colour. The males are bright green with patches of yellow, red and blue, giving rise to the other name for this species — Many-coloured Parrot. The females are grey-green with some patches of red and blue.

Babblers *Pomatostomus* species — Tjuun-tjuunpa

The incessant chattering of babblers clearly advertises the presence of these medium-size birds (body length 180–290mm). Also known as 'happy families' they live in closely knit family groups of six to ten individuals — feeding, roosting and breeding together. They move noisily from tree to tree or shrub, or on to the ground, tearing the bark or probing crevices to find their insect food, and all the while calling to each other. Their varied calls are described as a 'yahoo', a cat-like meow and 'peeoo peeoo peeoo'.

Their large domed stick nests which can festoon trees, are the most obvious sign of these birds. They are built for roosting and nesting. Nesting is a family activity, with all members helping to build the nests and feed the sitting female and young. There are two species of babbler in Central Australia; the Grey-crowned and the White-browed. The latter, which can be distinguished by its bright white eyebrow and white chest, has been commonly observed in Uluru National Park but both are common in Watarrka National Park.

FIGURE 5.12 The large domed stick-nest of a babbler in an ironwood tree. *J. A. Kerle*

Crested Bellbird *Oreoica gutturalis* — Panpanpalala (Fig. 2.12)

The crested bellbird is a master of ventriloquism. The haunting notes of its call are frequently heard but the bird is not so easily seen. Aboriginal people call it panpanpalala and the bird calls its name. It is a medium-size bird (200–230mm in body length) which hops around on the ground in search of its insect food. At other times it sits quietly calling from a tree or shrub and may be difficult to locate. It can be heard, and sometimes seen in most habitats but is most abundant in mulga shrublands and eucalypt woodlands.

Mistletoe Bird *Dicaeum hirundinaceum*

This diminutive species (100mm in length) has a very special relationship with the parasitic mistletoes growing on many shrubs and trees. The distribution of mistletoe birds is tied to the presence of these parasitic plants because the birds feed on the fruits of mistletoes. But it is not only the bird which benefits from this. The mistletoe berries have quite a large seed, covered in a sticky gelatinous pulp. To grow, they need to be stuck directly onto the branch of a tree and not fall to the ground. The mistletoe bird has a modified digestive tract which passes the sticky seeds through in less than half an hour. The bird wipes the seeds from its vent and leaves them sticking to the branch, ready to germinate. So, in one procedure the bird obtains its food and the plant spreads its seeds.

MAMMALS

Although the mammals of the Central Australian deserts may not be conspicuous there is, none the less, an interesting and varied range of at least 22 species. They are mostly small, cryptic (good at hiding) and nocturnal. They range in size from the tiny wongai ningaui (below) which weighs 8–10 grams, to the imposing one-humped camel. If the weather has been suitable, populations of some species like the spinifex hopping mouse can explode and you see them hopping across the roads at night. In the depths of a drought they seem to disappear completely.

A list of mammals recorded in Uluru–Kata Tjuta and Watarrka National Parks can be found in the Species Lists. Some of those listed are now extinct. This information is obtained from surveys of wildlife within the parks, but of course these surveys have covered only a very small part of the huge parks. As our work continues we may add new and interesting species. It is even possible that species which have never been found before could be discovered.

FIGURE 5.13 The ningaui weighs only 8–10gm but is a voracious carnivore. *K. A. Johnson*

The small mammals living on the ground include carnivorous marsupials, native rats and native mice, all of which are referred to as 'mingkiri' by the local Aboriginal people. The marsupials (pouched mammals) include three species of dunnart and the fat-tailed antechinus (Fig. 5.18). The desert mouse and sandy inland mouse are both native rodents, and of course the introduced house mouse is also there. Other interesting species include marsupial moles (Fig. 5.16) and echidnas which can be found, sparsely, throughout this area.

Bats are also well represented in Uluru and Watarrka; it is fascinating to listen to the high-pitched 'chip chip chip' sounding in the evening air and to wonder how many different types of bats are calling. Bats are not easy to survey and almost every time an effort is made, a new species is found. We know of at least twelve different bats which could occur in this part of Central Australia. Seven of these species are known to still be there; the remainder are known from cave bones but may have missed being caught alive on our recent surveys.

Of the large mammals, the red kangaroo can sometimes be seen, especially along the roadsides, but not in big mobs such as occur in western Queensland. The other larger native mammals in Central Australia are the euro or hill kangaroo (below) and the black-flanked rock wallaby (opposite). The euro prefers the rocky ranges and slopes and can be found around Uluru itself. Rock wallabies occur in patches throughout the rugged ranges. They are in Watarrka National Park and it is possible to find them around the Kings Canyon Resort. They were once common around Uluru and within Kata Tjuta but have become locally extinct.

The rock wallaby is not the only species to have become extinct in this area since non-Aboriginal people first moved into arid Australia. The brushtail possum, rufous hare-wallaby, burrowing bettong, greater bilby, pig-footed bandicoot, golden bandicoot and western quoll are some of the species that have disappeared. Records suggest that at least 20 species, or more than one-third of the mammals, have been lost from the region. Fortunately some still persist on islands or in very small populations in Western Australia.

Biologists have gathered information about the original, pre-European, mammal fauna and their historical abundance from three sources. Firstly, some older Aboriginal people have clear recollections of the animals present and their relative abundance in the early part of the 20th century. Secondly, records of early explorers have added to this information. Often explorers mentioned wildlife in the context of trying to find food. Other expeditions such as the Horn Scientific Expedition to Central Australia (p.141)

FIGURE 5.14 The euro, or hill kangaroo, can be seen around the base of Uluru and at Kings Canyon. *M. W. Gillam*

FIGURE 5.15 The black-flanked rock wallaby is no longer found at Kata Tjuta and is uncommon in the George Gill Range. *M. W. Gillam*

and trips made by H. H. Finlayson of the South Australian Museum were undertaken specifically to study the animal life of the Centre. The third source of information about the original fauna comes from detailed analysis of bones and bone fragments found in caves. Particularly good collections of mammal bones, probably left there by owls, have been found in the caves of Uluru. Analysis of these remains revealed that 34 species of native ground mammals and 12 species of bats once occurred around Uluru.

The reasons why so many mammal species have disappeared are difficult to determine. Central Australia appears to be fairly undisturbed compared with eastern Australia, so why have the native mammals suffered? This is a fragile environment. All the plant and animal species are finely adapted to surviving the harsh effects of low erratic rainfall and long hot summers. It may not take much to tip the scales against their survival in these conditions.

Rabbits first plagued through Central Australia in the late 1890s and again in 1910. New predators — the european fox and feral cats — moved in. Sheep and cattle were brought into many areas. And drought persisted in varying degrees of severity from the 1920s to the 1960s. All these factors have affected mammal populations in different ways. The most obvious decline in mammals was recorded by H. H. Finlayson between 1931–35 and 1957.

Wild populations of mammals introduced to this country, generally known as feral mammals, have had a significant impact. The four species of importance around Uluru and Watarrka are camels, rabbits, cats and foxes. Rabbit plagues have undoubtedly changed the plant communities and in times of drought rabbits compete directly with some native mammals for food. Camel herds are increasing substantially and can be very destructive. Again, their effect becomes critical during the tough conditions of a drought.

Droughts are also the time when predators are most likely to devastate populations of native mammals. Dingoes have been in Australia for several thousand years and have successfully co-existed with native species. The additional pressures of predation imposed by the cat and fox have been devastating for some species. This is even more significant when the populations of native mammals are already reduced by competition from rabbits.

Cattle have been grazing a substantial portion of Central Australia since late in the 19th century. This area includes the pastoral properties of Erldunda, Curtin Springs, Angas Downs and Tempe Downs which are adjacent to the two national parks. The sandy country and foothills surrounding the George Gill Range have been grazed, but not the country west of Curtin Springs including Uluru National Park.

The sandy spinifex habitats have a greater variety of mammals present than do the ranges, monoliths or mulga. In particular there are more of the small carnivorous marsupials as well as the spinifex hopping mouse. For most people, however, the tracks of these animals across the sand are all that can be seen. Look for the tracks especially around the Kata Tjuta lookout. Red kangaroos are generally more common in mulga country although they can be seen in the sandy shrublands as well.

Marsupial Mole *Notoryctes typhlops* — Itjaritjari (Fig. 5.16)

The marsupial mole, is an important character in the Aboriginal stories of Uluru. It is a distinctive small blind animal with dense, short golden fur, tiny holes for ears and large flattened claws with which it 'swims' through the sand. It doesn't dig permanent burrows; the sand fills in behind it as the mole moves along. Moles appear to be quite widespread, preferring spinifex-covered dune fields. Their tracks are regularly observed around Uluru and Yulara and occasionally the animals themselves are seen, most often after rain.

Very little is known about the habits of marsupial moles. They are hard to find in the wild and to catch. They have never been kept successfully in captivity for very long. They appear to be aggressive hunters, voraciously attacking geckoes and large invertebrates such as centipedes. Appropriately for a burrowing marsupial, the female's pouch opening faces backwards; there are two teats in the pouch. Nothing is known about the breeding of moles: how many young they have or how the young survive when they outgrow the pouch.

The Australian mole is not related to the moles of other parts of the world. It is a marsupial which has developed very similar body characteristics because it has a similar sort of lifestyle.

FIGURE 5.16 A marsupial mole leaves its track across a sand dune. *M. W. Gillam*

FIGURE 5.17 A mulgara and her two young. *K. A. Johnson*

Mulgara *Dasycercus cristicauda* — *Murtja* (Fig. 5.17)

This is one of the larger carnivorous marsupials to be found in Uluru National Park, weighing between 60 and 170 grams, about the size of a rat. Mulgaras are found in similar country to that occupied by marsupial moles but, unlike the moles, mulgaras dig defined and often complex burrows. Nests are built, from sticks and debris, in chambers at the end of the main tunnel. Mulgaras have been found throughout a large portion of arid Australia but generally the populations appear to be small and quite restricted. It is likely that they have some very specific habitat requirements which limit their overall abundance.

Fat-tailed Antechinus *Pseudantechinus macdonnellensis* — *Arutju* (Fig. 5.18)

This little rock-dweller was first found by white biologists in the MacDonnell Ranges near Alice Springs. It is called the fat-tailed antechinus because its tail is thick and fat, especially when its insect food is plentiful. It is found at Uluru, Kata Tjuta and in the George Gill Range but is never very common. It has also been found living in termite mounds, further north in the Tanami Desert.

FIGURE 5.18 The rock-dwelling fat-tailed antechinus. *K. A. Johnson*

Common Brushtail Possum *Trichosurus vulpecula* — Wayuta

The Brush-tail Possum in Central Australia? For many people this possum is the nuisance they know from the roofs of their houses in Sydney or Melbourne, or the pest that is taking over and devastating the forests in New Zealand — not a desert animal. Yes, it can also be found in Central Australia, but it is a rare and declining species there. It was once common in the ranges and along some of the rivers lined with large river red gums.

Wayuta the brushtail possum once lived at Uluru and Kata Tjuta. Its disappearance has saddened the local Aboriginal people greatly as it has strong spiritual significance in this area. They also loved to eat it and the sinews and skins were used too. Anangu are very keen to see wayuta return to Uluru and it is possible to reintroduce them. We have found, by examining 50-year-old droppings left by possums in caves around Uluru, that all the plants they like to eat are still present — so the dream of re-establishing possums in the park could become a reality. Brushtails were also once common throughout the George Gill Range and a few may still be found there.

In arid Australia possums behave a little differently from those elsewhere. They don't require hollow trees for their dens but use caves, limestone sinkholes or hollows in termite mounds and sometimes they even build their own nests. Like all desert-dwelling animals they are affected by droughts and survive in special small patches of high quality habitat. During wetter periods they are able to breed successfully and spread out into other, less favoured, country.

Mala (Rufous Hare-wallaby) *Lagorchestes hirsutus* (Fig. 2.3)

The Mala people of the Tjukurpa (p.14), are an integral part of the Aboriginal history describing the north face of Uluru. When the early European explorers travelled through the arid lands of central and western Australia, these diminutive wallabies were an integral part of the spinifex-covered sandy lands. 'Spinifex rats' as the explorers called them, are now found only in one very vulnerable population in the Tanami Desert. There are also two island populations off Western Australia.

Mala use spinifex clumps for shelter. They dig a shallow burrow or trench and use it to shelter in during the cooler winter months but when the heat is intense in summer they dig a burrow some 70 centimetres deep under spinifex or *Melaleuca* bushes. *Lagorchestes,* part of the scientific name for this species means 'dancing hare', and describes the darting, zigzag way in which mala run when disturbed from their spinifex clumps. Aboriginal people used to burn the spinifex to expose the mala and to catch them for food. This left the country covered by a mosaic of spinifex of varying age, providing mature patches for shelter and young vegetation for feeding on. Large destructive fires were most uncommon then, and the increased incidence of such fires more recently is thought to have been a significant factor in the demise of mala.

Lesser Stick-nest Rat *Leporillus apicalis* — Tjuwalpi

Piles of thick sticks on rock ledges, the collapsed remnants of large nests, are the best evidence we have of the existence of lesser stick-nest rats in the rocky ranges of Central Australia. Nest remnants and bone fragments have been found at Uluru and Kata Tjuta and quite commonly in the George Gill Range. Almost nothing is known about these rats apart from some notes made by the collector Gerard Krefft in 1856–57. He found them to be gregarious, social animals and strictly nocturnal.

The large nests support Krefft's comments that they are social animals. So does the presence of 'amberat' or rock tar. This hard, shiny black substance is found on rock ledges throughout the ranges of Central Australia including the George Gill Range. Sometimes it is in strangely inaccessible places as well as being associated with the stick-nest rat nests. It is thought to be the remains of a communal toilet: a buildup of urine and faeces deposited over thousands of years. Some of this material has been scientifically dated as 10,000 years old. It also contains pollens; study of the pollens and droppings found in the amberat may help us understand why so many arid zone mammal species — including the Lesser Stick-nest Rat — have become extinct.

Greater Bilby *Macrotis lagotis* — Ninu   (Fig. 5.19)

Greater bilbies were once common throughout the Australian arid zone — some 70 per cent of Australia. The species is now rare. It has fared a little better than the four other desert-dwelling bandicoot species which all appear to have become extinct. Bilbies differ from all other bandicoots. They construct burrows and they have long rabbit-like ears, silky fur and a long tail. The black and white tail is carried like a banner by a quickly moving bilby.

They are very efficient at digging. Their burrows can be three metres long and up to two metres below the surface. Much of their food is obtained by digging. They particularly relish large insects and their larvae, especially witchetty grubs, but they also eat seeds, bulbs, fleshy fruits and fungi.

Greater bilbies could return to Watarrka National Park. Rangers and scientific staff of the Parks and Wildlife Commission (PWCNT) are working together to re-establish a bilby colony in the park. Bilbies bred in enclosures in Alice Springs are released into large fenced paddocks in a suitable habitat in the park. When the individuals have settled and acclimatised to the environment the fencing can be cut, allowing them to move out and, hopefully, establish a wild population. Feral predators are controlled in order to give the bilbies the best chance of becoming established. This program is only just beginning.

FIGURE 5.19 The greater bilby once occurred across 70 percent of Australia but it is now an endangered species. *K. A. Johnson*

One-humped Camel *Camelus dromedarius* (Fig. 6.13)

The one-humped camels of Central Australia are the only wild population of these camels in the world. All others are domesticated. Indeed, it is believed that until the Australian populations became established no wild populations had existed in anthropological history: evidence of domestication has been found in some of the oldest excavations. The Australian population is presently estimated at more than 100,000 animals and is increasing. Camels are found in both Uluru and Watarrka National Parks and can be seen amongst the sand dunes on the Lasseter Highway through Curtin Springs.

Camels first came to Australia as invaluable beasts of burden — able to carry large loads and not requiring as much water as horses did. Journals of the early explorers provide ample evidence of the value they placed on their camels and of the deep attachment felt between a man and his beast. They were also a primary means of transport for goods and people in the settlement of Central Australia, including Alice Springs. The Afghan cameleers form a colourful and valued part of the history of this part of Australia. As motor vehicle and train transport took over, most of the domesticated stock were released and established the wild populations.

Camels' ability to conserve water and utilise the fat in their hump for nourishment makes them good desert survivors. As feral animals, however, they are damaging the sand dune country they prefer. They are believed to have caused the severe decline of at least one plant, the quandong, and they are severely damaging the salt bush communities around salt lakes. Their feeding can be very destructive, especially when the country is drier than usual.

Harvesting of camels has the potential to become a significant industry for Australia. Already, live camels are being exported for racing in the Middle East, and potential markets for meat, hide, camel hair and other by-products are being investigated.

Spinifex Hopping Mouse *Notomys alexis* — Tarkawara (Fig. 5.20)

This endearing native mouse may be seen at night in sand dunes around Yulara, especially after good rainfall. When the Ayers Rock Resort camping ground was first

FIGURE 5.20 The spinifex hopping mouse is an endearing native rodent which can be seen around the Ayers Rock Resort. *M. W. Gillam*

FIGURE 5.21 The central netted dragon can often be seen; it lives in most habitats, especially mulga, floodouts and the run-on areas beside rocky ranges and outcrops. *M. W. Gillam*

developed spinifex hopping mice would venture into campsites, cheekily collecting crumbs as they hopped around on the sand. Their large eyes and ears, long tufted tail and big strong hind feet all add to their attractiveness. Like all our native rodents they do not have the pungent odour associated with the introduced house mouse.

The spinifex hopping mouse is a social animal, living in family groups. They are most often found amongst the sand dunes and sand plains where they dig burrows; these are cool and moist and may extend a metre underground. They are extraordinarily well adapted to surviving in the desert. They do not need to drink, being able to obtain sufficient moisture from their food   seeds, roots, shoots and some insects. They breed opportunistically, maintaining small populations in their favourite country during harsh conditions. After good rainfall has established a flush of plant growth their numbers seem to explode. Not only are there lots of them about but they also appear in unusual places, such as around the base of Uluru.

LIZARDS, SNAKES AND FROGS

Lizards of the Australian deserts are more abundant and varied than those of any other desert in the world. There are around 125 different kinds, differing greatly in shape, size, habitat preference and lifestyle. The reptiles found in Uluru and Watarrka National Parks reflect this wonderful diversity.

The majority of the 72 species of reptiles and frogs found in Uluru, and the majority of the 59 species in Watarrka, live amongst the sand dunes, but others are also found in the mulga and around the rocks. All known species are listed in the Species Lists with more being found in Uluru than Watarrka. This probably reflects the fact that more time has been spent surveying the fauna there. Indeed, analysis of the habitats in Watarrka, and of the species likely to occur in those habitats, indicates that as many as 76 species could be found in time.

But they won't all be the same species for the two parks. The ring-tailed dragon *Ctenophorus caudicinctus*, for example, can often be seen on the Kings Canyon Walk (pp.176–78) but it is not found in Uluru. The presence of this species is indicative of the more varied rocky habitats found around the George Gill Range — unlike the fairly smooth and restricted rock outcrops in Uluru National Park.

If desert LIZARDS are so common, why aren't they more visible? Most are small and behave secretively. They need to avoid predators — eagles and hawks, goannas, snakes, dingoes and perhaps western quolls. They hide in the spinifex and scoot in and out of open spaces to catch their food or to move elsewhere. We need to tune our perceptions to detect tiny movements — to see a skink sliding through a spinifex clump or a military dragon race out to catch an insect. Desert lizards don't concentrate their activity around the places we frequent. Don't just sit by a waterhole — very few lizards will go there to drink. Instead, the best way to see them is to sit quietly on a sand dune surrounded by spinifex, in the late afternoon or on a hot summer moonless evening.

Their behaviour also assists them to survive the extreme heat, cold and dryness of this climate. They are solar-powered! They can easily regulate their body temperature and available energy by moving between the sun and the shade. But this is not enough. Some dig burrows which insulate them from the extremes of temperature and which have a more humid atmosphere than that outside. In winter some species plug the burrow to increase its thermal effectiveness. The winter cold provides a major physical challenge to desert lizards. Most of the small lizards don't hibernate but alternate between periods of activity and inactivity.

The tough, scaly dry skin of lizards provides a good barrier to moisture loss but this is not its only value. For the thorny devil, for example, the horny armour undoubtedly also acts as a defence against predators. Other species which are not so well protected physically have other means of avoiding predation: central netted dragons (Fig. 5.21) beautifully match their preferred sandy substrate; the tree geckoes (*Gehyra*) can change colour — from dark grey to translucent white depending upon where they are. And of course, being able to disappear down a burrow is an added protection.

Australian lizards are divided into five broad groups: skinks, geckoes, dragons, goannas and legless lizards (Pygopids, see Fig. 5.4). Each of these groups adopts a different strategy for surviving the rigours of the desert and within each group there is a range of lifestyles and behaviours.

The SKINKS are the most abundant group. They tend to be smooth and shiny and are often striped and brightly coloured. They are active during the day. One of the easiest to see is the little Tree Skink *Cryptoblepharus plagiocephalus* — it is active on trees and on the walls of the Ayers Rock and Kings Canyon resorts. Most other skinks forage amongst the leaf litter and some, like the *Lerista,* have almost completely lost their legs and 'swim' through the sand when foraging. The smaller skinks prefer insect foods but the larger species such as the central blue-tongue (Fig. 2.11) also eat flowers and fruits.

FIGURE 5.22 The striped skink, *Ctenotus piankai* camouflaged in a spinifex tussock. *M. W. Gillam*

FIGURE 5.23 The smooth knob-tail gecko is a sand dune dweller. *M. W. Gillam*

FIGURE 5.24 The sand goanna is one of two large goannas in Central Australia; the larger perentie is black with large yellow spots. *M. W. Gillam*

GECKOES, on the other hand, are almost entirely nocturnal and their preferred foods are insects and spiders. They are soft-bodied; the skin is thin and loose and usually feels velvety. Gecko tails have a wonderful variety of shapes and are often important for defence against predators. Some *Diplodactylus* species can exude a nasty fluid from glands in the tail and, like the skinks, they can drop and regrow them. They hibernate in winter.

DRAGONS and GOANNAS are the lizards you will most often see. They hunt actively during the day and are mostly found on the ground. When moving rapidly they run on their hind legs. They have a rough tough skin and do *not* drop or regrow their tails. They are all carnivorous, eating anything from insects to bird's eggs, other lizards, birds and carrion. Dragons tend to be smaller than goannas but even the goannas range in size from the well known Perentie *Varanus giganteus* which can be 2.5m in length to the little 180mm Short-tailed Pygmy Goanna *Varanus brevicauda*. Goannas typically have a deeply forked tongue which they flick in and out, unlike the thick rounded tongue of other lizards.

The LEGLESS LIZARDS or PYGOPIDS are found only in Australia and New Guinea. They are long and thin and often confused with snakes. Unlike snakes, they do have a tiny trace of their back legs — a clawless flap of skin beside the vent. It is an unfortunate reality that many people mistake Pygopids for 'baby snakes' and kill them. One desert species, however, has taken advantage of this similarity. The Western Scaly-foot *Pygopus nigriceps* adopts a snake-like posture and will pretend to strike if threatened, flicking its slightly forked tongue in and out. It is a very convincing pose, even though the species is not poisonous.

SNAKES are much less common, are not as diverse and are observed even less frequently than lizards. Six of the 15 species of snakes included in the Species Lists are poisonous — but they tend to try to avoid human contact. If disturbed they will mostly just slip away unless you harass them. It can be more dangerous to try to kill them than to let them go.

Two large, non-poisonous pythons, the Woma (Fig. 2.7) and Stimson's python might also be seen. The story about Kuniya the python and the Liru (poisonous snake, Fig. 2.8) warriors is a most important part of the Tjukurpa (p.14).

The seven remaining snake species are small and harmless, and some are very beautiful. The Desert Banded Snake *Simoselaps anomalus* has a series of bright orange and black bands and is especially attractive. The worm-like blind snakes are more unusual. They live mostly in the topsoil, ant nests and termite mounds. They have a tiny mouth and feed almost exclusively on termites and ants. They can exude a rather foul secretion. They are most often encountered in swimming pools at Alice Springs and Yulara!

FIGURE 5.25 The brilliantly coloured narrow-banded snake is nocturnal and non-poisonous; it lives in sandy country. *M. W. Gillam*

FIGURE 5.26 The burrowing shoemaker frog comes to the surface to breed only after there has been sufficient rain for the tadpoles to complete their development before the water dries up. *J. A. Kerle*

FROGS in the desert? Of course, but only a few species which have developed remarkable ways of surviving the infrequent and erratic rainfalls. Three species have been found around Uluru and six in Watarrka. They include two tree frogs and four burrowing frogs.

Heavy storms breaking a long drought quickly set off a deafening croaking chorus of the burrowing frogs *Cyclorana maini* and *Neobatrachus sutor*. Water in the pool in Kantju Gorge at Uluru may contain lots of the very large *Cyclorana* tadpoles. These desert frogs have developed both physiological and behavioural mechanisms which enable the adult frogs to survive through droughts but they still require water for breeding and development of tadpoles.

Only the burrowing frogs such as the shoemaker frog (Fig. 5.26) have been found in Uluru. These species burrow underground and can survive for long dry periods so they are not dependent upon the more reliable waterholes such as those in the George Gill Range. They can be found far out into apparently inhospitable country. They survive, entombed by a cocoon which the frog makes

FIGURE 5.27 Desert tree frogs are quick to breed after flooding rains have fallen. *M. W. Gillam*

from the old skin it has shed. This provides such a watertight suit that the frog can remain underground for months and maybe years if there is no rain. As soon as sufficient rain falls and water penetrates to the frog it eats the cocoon and returns to the surface. If conditions are right it will breed immediately, and so allow sufficient time for the tadpoles to metamorphose before the water dries up.

Desert Tree Frogs *Litoria rubella* (above) are more reliant upon the semi-permanent waterholes of the ranges. They survive with the help an unusual behavioural mechanism rather than a physiological mechanism. These tiny frogs can retain more moisture and keep warmer in winter by congregating in narrow rock cracks or crevices or in moist soil under rocks. They cram together but regularly rotate position, so that they all have turns at being on the outside of the cluster and able to feed, and in the middle keeping relatively moist and warm.

■　■　■

The overall abundance of lizards, snakes and frogs found in the region of Uluru and Watarrka is enhanced by the variation in the countryside. This is because many of these animals have quite specific habitat requirements — some need soft sands for burrowing, while others are restricted to harder soils or patches of moisture. Although the region is mostly sand plain and dune field, the harder soils of mulga shrublands, rocky outcrops or ranges, and creek channels or floodouts regularly occur, providing a diversity of habitats.

SAND PLAINS AND DUNES

These areas are the stronghold of the stripey skinks (*Ctenotus* species, Fig. 5.22) with up to 12 different types occurring close together. All these skinks are active during the day, foraging mostly in and around shrubs and spinifex clumps. *Ctenotus calurus* is an especially attractive animal, its bright blue tail giving it the name *calurus* or 'beautiful tail'. Unlike some of the skinks, this species does not race in and out of shelter when feeding. It is continually moving, steadily, all the while lashing its bright blue tail — and occasionally stopping to dig up an insect larva.

Generally, the *Ctenotus* are not fussy about what other animals they eat but invertebrates, especially termites, are mostly preferred. Termites are an exceptionally abundant food source and common species such as *Lerista bipes* and the worm-like blind snakes feed almost exclusively on them. The small harmless Desert Banded Snake *Simoselaps anomalus*, however, much prefers to eat lizards and lizard eggs.

Of the lizards that frequent the sandy spinifex habitats some are more common in the open areas which remain for a few years after a fire, but others prefer the dense vegetation growth found more than five years after a fire. The open space species include the Beaked Gecko *Rhynchoedura ornata*, the small goannas (*Varanus brevicauda* and *V. eremius*) and the sand-swimming skinks, *Lerista*. The two knob-tailed geckoes — *Nephrurus laevissimus* (Fig. 5.23) and *N. levis* are very similar animals, yet one prefers to live on the dune crests and the other in the swales of the unburnt dune habitats.

The Military Dragon *Ctenophorus isolepis* (below) is one of the fastest and most obvious

FIGURE 5.28 The military dragon is one of the most visible of the reptiles of the sand dune lizards; it can often be seen skidding between spinifex tussocks. *M. W. Gillam*

FIGURE 5.29 The narrow-banded sand-swimmer can disappear by quickly submerging into the sand; its colours provide a remarkable camouflage. *J. A. Kerle*

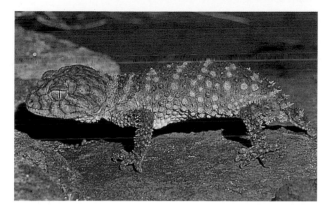

FIGURE 5.30 The large rock knob-tail gecko has rough knobbly skin, and is never in a hurry; despite its size it uses camouflage to avoid predators. *J. A. Kerle*

FIGURE 5.31 The spiny-tailed gecko lives mostly in mulga communities. *J. A. Kerle*

lizards of the spinifex. A small dragon, it runs on its hind legs, snapping up any insects it can find. On hot days, when the sand temperature can be 60°C, it rests only on its heels.

ROCKY AREAS

The abundance and variety of lizards in the rocky parts of these parks is not nearly as great as in the sandy spinifex habitats. The four skinks which prefer the rocks and surrounding harder soils are not as strongly striped or vividly coloured as the sand dwellers. This can change when they are breeding, though — *Carlia triacantha* is generally greyish brown, but a breeding male has a coppery green face and bluish grey back.

The rock-dwelling Ring-tailed Dragon *Ctenophorus caudicinctus* is often seen racing around the domes above Kings Canyon — in contrast to the Earless Dragon *Tympanocryptis lineata* (Fig. 7.17) which hides under rocks and, if exposed, freezes and relies on its camouflaged colouring for protection. Look carefully. It is found around Kata Tjuta and the George Gill Range amongst the rocks and on flat hard ground. Another rock dweller found in Watarrka which relies on camouflage for protection is the Knob-tail Gecko *Nephrurus asper* (Fig. 5.30). This large gecko has an aggressive threat display — hissing with its mouth wide open while doing push-ups! It is harmless.

The Black headed Goanna *Varanus tristis* (Fig. 7.11) and the perentie can both be found around Uluru. The black-headed goanna especially likes the cool rock surfaces in Kantju Gorge and Mutitjulu. It also occurs in the woodlands surrounding Uluru and along the creeklines which flow from Kata Tjuta and the George Gill Range. Tree-dwelling geckoes (*Gehyra* species) hide during the day under the bark of these woodland trees, while long-nosed dragons (*Lophognathus* species) forage amongst the grasses and leaf litter of the creeks in Watarrka.

Frogs are also most common in the rocky country. *Cyclorana maini* and the two *Neobatrachus* species are associated with ephemeral creeks and waterholes, especially around the base of Uluru. The tree frogs (*Litoria caerulea,* and *L. rubella*) prefer the rock pools and waterholes of the ranges.

MULGA SHRUBLANDS

The Spiny-tailed Gecko *Diplodactylus ciliaris* (Fig. 5.31) and Pygmy Mulga Goanna *Varanus gilleni* (below) are two lizards most likely to be found amongst the mulga. The abundance and diversity of reptiles there is, like the rocky habitats, lower than in the sand and spinifex, and the species vary little in abundance. The increase in numbers of lizards which follows good rainfall in the spinifex communities is not matched in the areas with hard soils or rock.

Other reptiles commonly found in the mulga include *Ctenotus leonhardii* and the Desert Skink *Egernia striata,* the tree geckoes, the military dragon, dwarf bearded dragon and the sand goanna (Fig. 5.24), the blind snakes and, of course, the Mulga Snake *Pseudechis australis*. Another common name for the mulga snake is the king brown — it is a large, aggressive and dangerous snake best left alone but, as with most of the venomous snakes, it is rarely seen.

INTERESTING REPTILE SPECIES

Here is some information about a few of the many interesting species of reptiles of the region.

Thorny Devil *Moloch horridus* — Ngiyari (Fig. 5.33)
The unfriendly appearance of the thorny devil belies its inoffensive nature. A slow-moving dragon lizard with a very fast tongue, it is most frequently seen after rain in sandy country, standing and feeding at a trail of black ants. With this sort of behaviour, its armour plating provides valuable protection from predators. Is the fleshy, horny knob behind the head a false head? A predator decoy? There is some evidence to support this possibility. Of about 200 thorny devils observed around Uluru–Kata Tjuta National Park five had either lost or damaged these lumps.

The bizarre skin of this dragon lizard is not just defensive; it is also a water collecting device, a valuable adaptation for a desert dweller. For a long time it was thought that the moisture simply soaked through the moloch's skin. In

FIGURE 5.32 The pygmy mulga goanna is almost always found in mulga trees, where it hides under the bark of dead branches. *J. A. Kerle*

FIGURE 5.33 The fierce-looking thorny devil is only a threat to ants, especially the annoying little black ants. It is slow-moving and harmless: be careful not to run over any on the Lasseter Highway where these animals can regularly be seen. *J. A. Kerle*

fact the spines help to gather droplets of dew which then collect and run along minute channels on the skin to the corners of the mouth. The animal then drinks this water by moving its tongue and jaws.

When they are active, thorny devils can be seen on the roads, especially on the Lasseter Highway. Be careful not to run over them!

Perentie *Varanus giganteus* — Ngintaka

The only goanna in the world which grows larger than the perentie is the komodo dragon of Indonesia. A large adult perentie is an impressive sight, being between two and two and a half metres long and with large yellowish spots on its dark brown or black skin. Perenties are more likely to be seen around Uluru, Kata Tjuta and the George Gill Range than in the sandy country, where the Sand Goanna *Varanus gouldii* is more common. When feeding, perenties can travel long distances, traversing all kinds of country. They eat insects, birds, other reptiles and mammals.

All large goannas can run either on all four legs or just on their hind legs. On open ground they are faster when running on all four, so their running on hind legs has been thought to be more important as a threat, especially between rival males. However, when chased by a sprinting ranger at Uluru, a perentie completely outdistanced him by running on hind legs and tobogganing over fallen branches and grass clumps, rather than dodging around them. There is still a lot to learn about the ecology and behaviour of the perentie!

Dwarf Bearded Dragon *Pogona minor* — Ngapala

As the weather warms up in August and September it is not unusual to see bearded dragons warming themselves on roads or sunbaking in the tops of shrubs. They can be found in a variety of habitats, but especially in the spinifex and mulga shrublands. This dragon would make a more valid emblem for Central Australia than the frill-necked lizard which is often used in tourist promotions. The frill-neck is a tropical species.

The Pitjantjatjara people call the bearded dragon ngapala. According to these people ngapala don't emerge in August just to soak up the sun, they also begin to breed. They lay their eggs at the end of a deep straight burrow. In one such burrow excavated by Aboriginal people near Kata Tjuta there were nine eggs at one metre depth. Sometimes the female digs several trial burrows before laying her eggs. When the eggs are ready to hatch the female returns to the burrow to let the young out. The burrow entrances are semicircular in shape.

Ctenotus septenarius — Muluny mulunypa

The thrill of discovering a new species is still possible in arid Australia. *Ctenotus septenarius* was first recognised as being different from other stripey skinks by ranger Greg Fyfe, when he first saw it at The Sedimentaries, near Uluru National Park, in 1982. As an avid herpetologist new to the area he was carefully identifying everything he found, but this one was unusual. Soon afterwards, he found the same unusual skink with 'too many' black stripes at Kata Tjuta as well. Nothing happened for four years until he discovered yet another population at Henbury Meteorite Craters east of Watarrka. Eventually he collected sufficient information and it was formally described as a new species in 1988.

It is a burrowing species. At this stage it is known from only the three original locations which are on the slopes of rock outcrops and stony hills.

INVERTEBRATES

Little is known about the insects and other invertebrates of Uluru and Watarrka National Parks. There are undoubtedly more kinds of ants, beetles, termites, grasshoppers and spiders there than all the other animals combined! Not just a few more but many, many more. Most of them are very well camouflaged and don't move around in the open (Fig. 5.34). All we see of some are their tracks in the sand. Others may advertise their presence by being brightly coloured, having persistent calls or building obvious identifiable nests. Almost all are unnamed.

Invertebrates in the arid zone take advantage of all the various habitats and micro-habitats. They occur in the very driest of places. There the hard outer skeleton helps reduce water loss; this is further reduced when they hide in burrows or cracks and crevices and are active only at night. Others seem not to care, running about in the middle of the day when sand temperatures are 65°C.

Those that cannot survive without some moisture are confined to damp places, but even they must have some unusual methods of surviving through long droughts and reappearing when it rains. The more permanent waterholes, such as those in the George Gill Range, are usually teeming with invertebrates. But even small puddles are quickly colonised after they are formed. Where do these animals come from? Some are brought in by the wind, while others emerge from dried eggs left by adults in the last puddle.

Rainfall brings life to the desert and this is most obvious in the case of the inverte-brates, especially in the summer. They build up to vast numbers and are of major importance in the cycling of nutrients and functioning of the desert ecosystem. Some, like grasshoppers and termites, chew up huge quantities of plant material. They in turn are eaten by others — ants, spiders, centipedes and vertebrates such as lizards, echid-nas and carnivorous marsupials.

Most species of invertebrates do not occupy a wide range of habitats. Some of the gall wasps occur on only one type of tree; one tiny wasp lives only inside the fruit of native figs; a red scale insect occurs on mulga and witchetty bushes; witchetty grubs are in the roots of only a few species of *Acacia*. Other invertebrates are extremely widespread — small meat ants and bush flies being very obvious examples. Each of the vegetation communities has its own suite of inverte-brates, but not enough is known about them to provide a list of what to look for.

The Common Bush Fly *Musca vetustissima* (Fig. 5.35) occurs throughout Australia but is most abundant in dry open woodland. The flies are greatly affected by temperature and humidity, even disappearing in the cold of winter. A good frost reduces their numbers. Historical evidence, like the comments of Dampier, Pelsaert and Grey when they first landed on Australian shores in the 17th century, indicates that this pestilential fly has always been abundant and widespread.

FIGURE 5.34 (left) The gibber grasshopper is one of the well camou-flaged insects of the desert. *J. A. Kerle*

Insects also cause the unusual lumps and bumps often found on the leaves stems and flowers of many desert plants. These lumps or 'galls' are a growth response by the plant to a chemical injected by an insect when it lays its eggs. The eggs develop into larvae inside a gall, feeding on the sap within its protected home. One of the most obvious galls is the 'bloodwood apple'. This large woody gall, which can be 50mm in diameter, occurs on blood-wood trees around the base of Uluru and at the mouth of Kings Canyon. It is also called a bush coconut. Both the large grub and the white 'flesh' of the gall are good bush tucker.

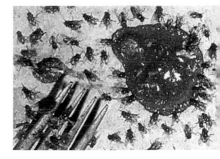

FIGURE 5.35 The common bush fly — perhaps the most easily observed species of our wildlife! Bush flies can occur in distressing numbers in summer and can disappear completely during a cold winter. *M. W. Gillam*

All major groups of insects, arachnids (spiders, scorpions), centipedes and crustaceans (shrimps and others) can be found in Uluru and Watarrka. Amongst the insects there are beetles, cockroaches, grasshoppers and crickets, lacewings, moths and butterflies, and myriads of ants and termites. Most of these animals have a hard external body skeleton which undoubtedly helps to reduce dehydration. Recently a soft bodied animal — an earthworm — was discovered around Uluru. It is remarkable that an animal which usually lives in moist soil has survived in such dry country. The Uluru earthworm is a completely new species. It has never been collected anywhere else and has definitely not been recently transported from elsewhere. The first worm was found, at the base of the southern side of Uluru, after a period of rain. Subsequently more have been found in dense leaf litter under desert oak trees. Almost 100 years ago, earthworms were found at two locations in Central Australia by the Horn Scientific Expedition. Those specimens which differ from the Uluru worm, were described by Professor Baldwin Spencer but none has been found since. There are plenty of surprises in arid Australia and much more to learn!

INVERTEBRATES OF THE WATERHOLES AND PUDDLES

Shield shrimps (Fig. 5.36) are amongst the more obvious of the water dwellers of these parks. They are almost always present in the small rockpools and puddles on top of Uluru. The Mutitjulu people even make carved wooden shield shrimps for sale. These large crustaceans — up to 30mm in length — can withstand high water temperatures and salinity, and their remarkable reproduction enables them to survive the drying up of their pools.

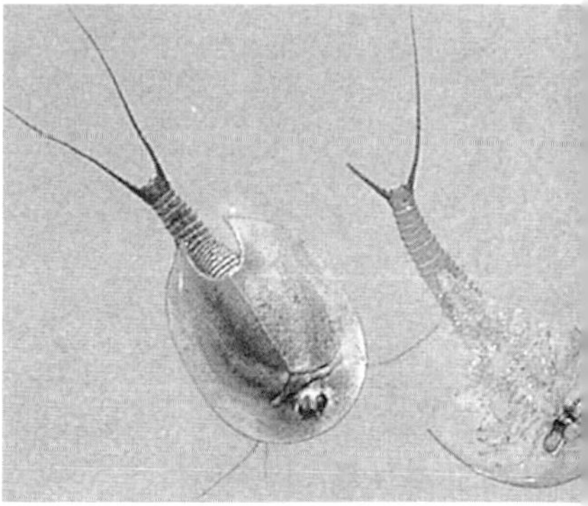

As the pools begin to dry, the shrimp lays fertilised eggs which are not affected by desiccation. They may even *need* to be subjected to drought conditions if they are to develop when the claypan or puddle fills again. The eggs either remain in the dried mud of the depression or are transported elsewhere — by the wind or on the feet of birds. When rain falls again they hatch quickly and the newly developed shrimps lay thousands of *unfertilised*

FIGURE 5.36 Shield shrimps appear in rock pools, puddles and claypans soon after rain has fallen; their eggs can lie dormant and survive long dry periods. *M. W. Gillam*

eggs. These eggs develop into shrimps and continue the cycle until the water is teeming with millions of shield shrimps. It is only the drying up of the puddle which stimulates the development of a few males which, with the surviving females, produce the drought-resistant fertilised eggs. Brine shrimps and fairy shrimps are also present in many of the temporary desert pools.

In contrast with the temporary nature of the pools used by shield shrimps, the George Gill Range contains waterholes which are almost permanent. Although the water flow through the creeks is entirely unpredictable the deep pools persist, being partly replenished by seepage from the porous Mereenie Sandstone. As a consequence the streams and waterholes of the George Gill Range have unique aquatic invertebrate communities — containing unusual species left over from the period when Central Australia was much wetter.

One of the most interesting of these animals is the waterpenny. This water beetle, which has a coin shaped larva, is usually found only in southern Australia. As the adult can hardly fly it is unlikely that it moved through the arid country surrounding the Centre and must therefore be a remnant species. The water scorpion is more likely to be seen in the waterholes. This large predatory beetle lives underwater but breathes by backing up to the surface and exposing its tail like a breathing tube. It feeds on tadpoles, small fish or aquatic insects by grabbing them with its strong front legs, injecting saliva and sucking out the body juices. There are also at least six types of dragonfly or damselfly, including one which is bright red (Fig. 7.27) and another which is pale blue.

TERMITES

Myriads of termites of many species chomp their way through both living and dead desert plants. The most obvious indicator of termites is the presence of mounds — sometimes small, sometimes huge (Fig. 7.5). In the south-western part of the Northern Territory small termite mounds — which are the home of a colony — can be found in areas with firm soils, such as in the mulga shrublands. Mostly, however the termites are hidden from view. In the soft sandy soils both the colonial home and the feeding tunnels are underground, leaving very little aboveground evidence of their presence.

Termites may be condemned as a pest by most people but they form a vital link in the food chain of the deserts —just as large grazing mammals do in the African deserts. Instead of having an abundance of sweet grasses after rain, Australian sandy deserts are mostly covered by spinifex, unpalatable to grazing mammals but extremely palatable to termites. So plant nutrients are converted into termites which are tasty morsels, especially for reptiles. Some of the termite-eating reptiles even live in termite nests and lay their eggs in the chambers. Other animals are more opportunistic, taking full advantage of the nuptial flights of winged termites or alates (Fig. 5.5). This occurs only after summer thunderstorms when vast numbers of alates take to the air, mate and form new colonies. Most don't succeed in this, however, because they are eaten first!

The colonial and nocturnal behaviour of these soft-bodied insects is the key to their survival in the desert. The mounds or termitaria — whether they be above or below ground — provide protection and a warm moist microenvironment. By being able to survive in the desert, the invaluable termite — which is more closely related to cockroaches than to ants — provides a nutrient-recycling service and is a significant factor in the development of the soil and the types of plants that can grow.

PLANT-EATING INSECTS

In addition to termites plants have to contend with an array of other plant-eating insects. These include grasshoppers, crickets, cicadas, beetles and caterpillars. Sometimes a *Thryptomene* bush will look like a Christmas tree, festooned with little jewel beetles. Some of the many varied types of grasshopper can always be seen — but some are highly camouflaged. The gold-spotted black grasshopper (below) is quite obvious and is most likely to be found on the mint bushes (*Prostanthera*) which are common around Kings Canyon and the Kings Canyon Resort. This flightless grasshopper may spend its whole life cycle on a single bush.

In summer after rain the red gum–lined creeks running from the George Gill Range are filled with the shrill penetrating call of cicadas. There are two large types — a black and orange species which is mostly associated with river red gums, and an even larger greyish one which prefers ghost gums. Several small inconspicuous cicadas occur in other plant communities, including those on the sand dunes. At night, the call of the chirruping crickets takes over in sand dunes. This too is a persistent repetitive song, but is not quite so penetrating.

FIGURE 5.37 The two caterpillars on this thryptomene are well disguised and likely to avoid becoming bird food. *M. W. Gillam*

FIGURE 5.38 This grasshopper lives mostly on mint bushes and flashes its little red underwings to deter predators. *J. A. Kerle*

Many of the tracks left in the sand after a busy night of activity belong to beetles (Fig. 5.2). These include the extraordinary pie-dish beetle (Fig. 5.39) and a rhinoceros beetle which leaves cylinders of sand piled on the surface above its burrow (Fig. 5.40). In the mulga are large grey weevils, identifiable by their long snout. While the variety of beetles in the mulga is often hard to see, a species of *Rhytidoponera* ant is helpful because it deposits the remains of weevils and other beetles on the surface of its mound.

Caterpillars and grubs — the various larvae of butterflies and moths — are very obvious after rain. In fact the ground can become a crawling mass of little black, striped or furry caterpillars. Sometimes armies of them may be seen valiantly trying to climb Uluru, constantly climbing and falling down, climbing and falling down. Crimson chats devour these caterpillars in vast numbers.

The itchy grubs or processionary caterpillars build a bag-nest hanging in a tree or shrub which can be mistaken for a bird's nest (Fig. 5.41). The very hairy caterpillars shelter in their hair-impregnated silken bags during the day, leaving at night to feed. By doing this they avoid the heat and some predators. When they travel they move in a long line, or procession, each one following a silken thread left by the leader (Fig. 5.42). These caterpillars and their nests must not be handled. The little hairs have an effect which is much worse than a stinging nettle. At the appropriate time, the caterpillars burrow into the ground to pupate, eventually emerging as a bag moth. Aboriginal people use the cleaned bag as a bandage.

Another caterpillar which spends all its life underground is the witchetty grub of the goat moth. This large grub, which may be 80–100mm in length is an important food source for Aboriginal people. The larvae feed on the roots of *Acacias* and are most often found in the Witchetty Bush *Acacia kempeana* (p.76, Fig. 4.25). They pupate underground and the impressive moths emerge in autumn.

FIGURE 5.39 The pie-dish beetle leaves tracks in the sand during its nightly wanderings. *J. A. Kerle*

FIGURE 5.40 Cylinders of sand piled on the surface are a sign that a rhinoceros beetle has burrowed down below. *J. A. Kerle*

FIGURE 5.41 This bag-nest does not belong to a bird but to processionary caterpillars; be careful of the nest because it contains the nasty stinging hairs from the caterpillar. *J. A. Kerle*

FIGURE 5.42 A procession of processionary caterpillars! *J. A. Kerle*

FIGURE 5.43 The golden bush cockroach lives amongst spinifex.
M. W. Gillam

Bush cockroaches are also well represented in the desert. Some are extremely attractive. A yellow species is common amongst the spinifex (above); others are brown with yellow bands and still others are dark brown. They are wingless and omnivorous, foraging in amongst the leaf litter. The yellow species will often rest in the top of the spinifex, exposed to full sunlight. When disturbed it drops to the ground and disappears.

THE INCREDIBLE WORLD OF THE ANTS

A stream of tourists climbing Uluru is sometimes referred to as minga — the local Aboriginal word for small annoying black ants! Stand back from the climb and watch the line for yourself. You will quickly see the connection. While the little black meat ants might be the most obvious among the ant fauna they are but a small part of this remarkable group of insects in the deserts. By virtue of their numbers and because the majority of them are predators or scavengers they are exceedingly important in the Australian desert ecosystem. They also structure the soil and assist in dispersing seeds — factors which influence the development of plant communities.

There are probably some thousands of ant species in the arid zone, most of which are undescribed and many of which are undiscovered! They are well suited to the arid climate — they respond to the warm, fluctuating temperatures but when conditions become too hot they can escape to the cooler environment deep in the nest. Most species nest in the soil and some have structures protruding above ground level. They also take advantage of an unusual supply of moisture by harvesting the honeydew produced by scale insects (coccids) and by consuming nectar and other exudates from deeply rooted trees and shrubs (Fig. 4.22).

The sandy country probably contains the greatest diversity of ants, but only a very few species have much more than a simple hole to advertise the presence of the nest. The minute *Pheidole* build a ring of refuse around their hole — using the remains of the grass and wildflower seeds they feed on and store in the nest. The minor workers, which are only one millimetre in length, are dwarfed by the seed refuse they carry. The Spinifex Ant *Ochetellus flavipes* also builds an obvious nest. Like the Aboriginal people these little ants have learnt to extract the resin from the spinifex. They then use that to

FIGURE 5.44 Beautiful architecture of mulga ant nests. *J. A. Kerle*

build their underground nest, as well as their foraging tunnels along the sand surface and around the spinifex leaves (Fig. 4.12). In these protected tunnels they feed on the sugary exudate produced by tiny sap-sucking scale insects.

One ant nest best left alone is that of the bulldog or inch ant. The mound around the nest entrance (Fig. 7.22) is large and obvious and any vibration of the ground will bring a force of these 3cm long ants to the surface. They can inflict a painful sting. They especially like to nest under bloodwood trees but can be found in a variety of places, including in mulga and around the Kings Canyon Resort.

More extraordinary nest architecture can be found in the mulga communities (Fig. 5.44). Mulga ants (*Polyrhachis*) have a variety of structures. The most common is a solid soil ring neatly covered with mulga phyllodes. In the centre are two or three large entrance holes. Another version is a cylindrical turret standing up to 200mm in height and 30mm across. The virtue of these elaborate structures is unknown. The large conical nest with a curved slit, made by a species of *Rhytidoponera* ant, is generally covered by remnants of dead beetles, some leaf litter and droppings of an unknown small animal. Do these puzzling droppings come from an animal that has learnt to live inside the ant nest or from one that uses the mound for its territorial display?

The Honey Ant (below) is one of the most unusual of the Australian ants. It is found only in the groves of mulga and has an insignificant nest entrance. This species, *Campanotus inflatus*, is one of only three known species in the world to have developed a living food storage system. When the desert is bountiful, the worker honey ants collect food and feed the replete caste, which are the food stores, until their abdomens become the size of a grape and are filled with delicious musty-flavoured honey. These repletes hang from the roof of the chamber, imprisoned by their size. Their food

FIGURE 5.45 Honey-ants rely on these honey-filled storage ants to sustain the colony during a severe drought. The storage ants taste simply delicious! *M. W. Gillam*

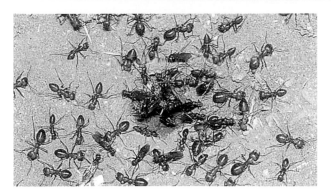

FIGURE 5.46 These red ants are the foraging workers of racehorse ants; the black, winged males are pouring out of the nest in preparation for a nuptial flight. *M. W. Gillam*

comes from honeydew exuded by the scale insects which feed on mulga and witchetty bushes, from 'nectaries' which are little sap-exuding glands on the mulga trees and from the nectar of flowers.

During a drought, when these food sources are unavailable the repletes can feed the colony. The Aboriginal people also like to eat them but it is hard work collecting them; the chambers with repletes may be up to two metres underground in the hard mulga soils.

The Red Racehorse Ant *Melophorus bagoti* (above), which prefers firm soils to sand, also stores food in living ants — but their adaptation is not nearly so extreme. Individuals with swollen abdomens can leave the nest to forage. Racehorse ants forage only during the hottest weather when ground temperatures may be 65°C. They race rapidly around to avoid being burnt, thus earning their common name.

By feeding at this time racehorse ants avoid conflict with the dominant meat ants. Indeed, many ant species avoid attack from meat ants by foraging when the latter are inactive. Although meat ants might be dominant in the ant world they are not immune from attack. Ant lions lie in wait, lurking at the bottom of conical pits! When they detect vibrations they send a shower of sand which makes the unsuspecting ant fall down the pit into their waiting jaws. Ant lions are the larvae of the delicate lacewing.

SMALL BUT VORACIOUS PREDATORS

Spiders, scorpions, centipedes, mole crickets, wasps and some beetles are all very effective predators which occur in many varied forms throughout Central Australia, including Uluru and Watarrka.

The majority of desert-dwelling spiders are large burrowing spiders; the Barking Spiders *Selenocosmia stirlingi*, mouse spiders, wolf spiders (Fig. 5.47), huntsmen and trapdoor spiders (Fig. 5.48). They survive by avoiding the hot dry conditions, sealed in their burrows. They have a big body and thickset legs. They are long-lived (two to eight years) and they can fast for long periods if adverse conditions set in.

These spiders forage at night. They roam across the ground or lie in wait at their burrow entrances for an insect to trip their silken threads. The large eyes of the wolf-spiders shine brightly in a spotlight. They prefer clayey or loamy soils, especially mulga soils, which are easier to build burrows in. At least one species of trapdoor spider has learnt how to build in sand — it builds a silk lined burrow. Some species, like the trapdoors, have a plug over the burrow entrance which can be very well camou-flaged. Others have an open circular hole.

FIGURE 5.47 A spectacular example of a desert wolf spider. *M. W. Gillam*

FIGURE 5.48 Trapdoor spiders cunningly conceal the silken lid of their burrows. *J. A. Kerle*

Other groups of spiders occur in Central Australia but are not so able to cope with the erratic arid climate. They mostly live in the litter but some larger web builders, like the golden orb weaver, can block the way between two mulga trees. While these spiders don't survive dry conditions as well as the burrowing species do, they can recolonise more quickly with windborne spiderlings (juveniles).

Scorpions (below) are also familiar residents of Uluru and Watarrka, with 11 species identified so far. The large desert scorpion is not aggressive, though it reaches 100mm long. It also relies on an elaborate burrow for its survival. A narrow slit forms the entrance to a spiral burrow which may be a metre deep. One species prefers to steal a spider burrow by first eating the occupant!

FIGURE 5.49 The scorpion, a nocturnal hunter. *M. W. Gillam*

6
THE HUMAN
EPILOGUE

The tourist resorts at Yulara (Ayers Rock Resort) and Kings Canyon are just tiny spots on the surface of the desert. No matter how you travel to these places, the vast and apparently empty country is impressive. If you fly to Uluru or take a light aircraft or helicopter tour, you find that the natural features overwhelm the built environment. If you drive, the tiresome hours of travel reveal a big country. Remember, too, how much easier it is for us to travel in fast air-conditioned vehicles than it was for Aboriginal people who walked the country or for early white explorers, visitors and settlers travelling on camels or horses.

The stories of the Tjukurpa, the stars and the geology, plants and animals of Central Australia all take us on a journey that began at an unimaginable time. Just as the resorts are only tiny features in the vast landscape of Central Australia, the human history of this country is but a short epilogue to that time line. Nevertheless, the human history spans many thousands of years and has left a permanent mark on the countryside. The Aboriginal people modified the environment as much as they could to enhance their prospects of survival. Many more changes have happened in the last 130 years of interference by white people.

FIGURE 6.1 The vast and apparently empty sand dune deserts *M W Gillam*

The history of human life in Central Australia can be divided into two parts: the Aboriginal perspective; and the movement of people from other countries on to the land. The story of the Aboriginal people includes their relationship with the land and the disruption of their lifestyle from the time of exploration and occupation by non-Aboriginal people. More recently there has been political recognition of the importance of land to the Aboriginal people and the need to re-establish their rights to it. The non-Aboriginal history is one of exploration, settlement and many changes to the natural environment.

ANANGU — THE PEOPLE OF THE LAND

At the time of the first incursions by people of European origin through Central Australia Aboriginal people were regularly encountered, especially around the rocky ranges and along the watercourses. Despite the arid nature of the country it apparently supported many people. In the area of Uluru, Kata Tjuta and the George Gill Range there were the Yankunytjatjara, Pitjantjatjara and Luritja people. They had close affinities with people throughout the Great Victoria and Great Sandy deserts of South Australia and Western Australia — a cultural network linked by language and kinship, use of the land and spiritual relationship to it (see map p.vi).

In order to survive the rigours of the Central Australian desert climate they needed to travel widely. This allowed them to take advantage of localised rainfalls while other parts of the country remained dry and unproductive. They had a very detailed knowledge of the land: the location of all water sources, including tiny soaks and water-bearing mallee roots; the sources and seasons of seeding and fruiting plants; the preferred habitats and behaviour of many different animals. In most cases the women collected the staple plants and small animal foods while the men hunted the larger game species.

Although the Yankunytjatjara, Pitjantjatjara and Luritja people had strong long-distance contacts with others throughout the western and southern deserts, most of their movements were concentrated in much smaller areas. Within these areas were well-defined living and hunting places as well as sites with special significance for the Tjukurpa (p.14). Some, such as the very reliable springs in the George Gill Range, were apparently deliberately protected from overuse. At times when the drier country had had rain and provided adequate food and water, Anangu (as the local Aboriginal people call themselves) did not remain within the ranges. They moved away, enabling the more reliable supplies to recover. The ranges were refuges — a form of insurance — against the next drought.

FIGURE 6.2 This limestone sinkhole contains a vital water supply in the Great Sandy Desert.
J. A. Kerle

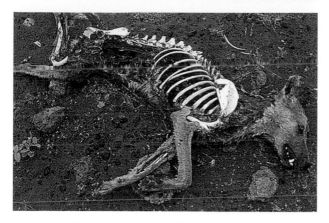

FIGURE 6.3 Droughts take their toll on all life in the desert. *M. W. Gillam*

Droughts have taken their toll on Anangu over the years, causing many deaths and hardships. At least two of these times, in the 1920s and 1960s, are vividly remembered by people living today, who still acutely feel the loss of their relatives. Until recently anthropologists believed that the central deserts could not have been inhabited any earlier than the last ten or twelve thousand years. Prior to that time the country was gripped by extraordinary dryness. It seemed impossible that anyone could live in such conditions.

We now know that the central part of the Australian arid zone was settled by people at least 22,000 years and possibly 30,000 years ago, in the mid-Pleistocene era. This fact has been determined from an excavation of soil under a rock shelter in the Cleland Hills to the west of the George Gill Range. Charcoal remnants were radiocarbon-dated and the stone artefacts and bone material analysed. The rock shelter was used continuously but between 12,000 and 22,000 years ago usage appears to have been quite low with relatively few artefacts being found. From around 6000 years ago the shelter appears to have been used more frequently; it was most regularly inhabited during the last 1900 years.

FIGURE 6.4 The rock shelter in the Cleland Hills in the Western Desert which has been occupied by Aboriginal people for at least 22,000 years. *J. A. Kerle*

EARLY CONTACTS WITH NEWCOMERS

Some Anangu remember when the country was not in drought and they were able to travel freely in small family groups, abiding by their law and knowing where to find water and reliable food resources. This changed when other people, predominately Europeans, began to move into Central Australia. Initially contact was intermittent and irregular, but gradually it increased in frequency. Not only were these new people travelling through the land themselves but they also brought their stock. Many a dependable waterhole was left severely depleted after an explorer had watered his horses or drovers had passed through with a herd of cattle. Rabbits spread through the Centre around the turn of the century, severely damaging many plant species and directly competing with the wildlife.

The level of contact between Anangu and the newcomers varied. In the south-western corner of the Northern Territory, including Uluru and Kata Tjuta, contact was quite limited until about the 1940s. Prior to that time there were a few explorers, occasional doggers (collecting dingo scalps), prospectors and adventurers. They included Harold Lasseter, renowned for his questionable and ultimately fatal expeditions searching for a reef of gold. The infrequency of contact in this area was primarily because the country was not considered suitable for grazing. It was west of the designated pastoral land.

Further east, and especially along the Finke River, construction of the Overland Telegraph Line, establishment of pastoral stations and construction of the railway line resulted in earlier frequent contact with Aboriginal people (Fig. 6.8). Such contact was undoubtedly frightening for the Aboriginal people and often quite violent. They were actively discouraged from their traditional burning practices and had to compete for the use of their waters.

One tragic incident occurred in 1934 at Uluru itself. Several Aboriginal men were arrested for carrying out their own law and killing another Aboriginal man. They managed to escape from police custody and returned to Uluru, but the police eventually tracked them down with the help of Aboriginal trackers. One man was shot and killed in a cave near Mutitjulu. This was a clear and frightening case of conflict between the two systems of justice.

Evidence from visitors to Uluru just before this time clearly indicates that Uluru was being well used by Anangu. For example, H. H. Finlayson saw fresh paintings and stores of dried native tobacco and emu poison bush in 1931. Tragic incidents such as the 1934 shooting, however, increased the fear felt by Anangu and they moved away.

The Luritja people around the George Gill Range had earlier frequent contact with white people than the people from around Uluru. The Finke River was an important thoroughfare to Hermannsburg Mission and pastoral stations were established in the region in the 1880s (Fig. 6.8). Tempe Downs, which incorporates the country now covered by Watarrka National Park was leased at that time.

Cattle spearing by Anangu was a not uncommon practice throughout the Centre and one which incurred the full wrath of struggling pastoralists. Police were frequently called in to deliver retribution. Indeed, police stations were built east of the George Gill Range at Illamurta Springs (1892) and at Boggy Hole further north on the Finke (1889–1892) in order to 'disperse' the Aboriginal people and 'control' their activities. It has been estimated that 500 to 1000 Aboriginal people were killed

FIGURE 6.5 The Finke River meanders its way towards Hermannsburg.
J. A. Kerle

between 1881 and 1891 in the Alice Springs Pastoral District, while only 16 Europeans died in the same period as a result of Aboriginal actions. Although spearing of cattle made the running of a cattle station difficult for the pastoralists most Anangu undoubtedly perceived the cattle as a new source of food in their country.

The cultural integrity of these people was also severely undermined by the removal of many sacred objects or tjurungas from the 1890s onwards. Apart from the 'curiosity value' of these objects, some museum curators firmly believed that the Aboriginal culture was about to die out and so they had a duty to 'preserve' the artefacts. They were not averse to using trickery to locate the tjurungas, even if it subsequently led to the death of their informant. They had very little understanding of the extremely deep cultural significance of these objects. They left meaningless trinkets, tea and sugar, tomahawks and knives as an 'equitable exchange' — but could not interpret the meaning of the tjurungas back home at the museum.

MOVEMENT AWAY FROM THE LAND

As a result of drought, fear, introduced diseases, loss of food supplies and some breakdown of their culture, many people moved away from their land. Certainly the huge South-West Reserve (Fig. 6.6), declared by the government in 1920 to protect the 'desert nomads', was not serving its intended purpose as a refuge. After World War II the government established welfare settlements with schools, medical services and some food supplies. This was in addition to services provided by the well-established mission stations at Hermannsburg and Ernabella. Those in authority generally believed that Aboriginal society was collapsing and the best solution was to assimilate the people, to educate them in the ways of European society.

The Aboriginal culture, however, proved remarkably resilient. Although many people moved into the settlements or lived and worked on cattle stations, they still visited their kin, performed their ceremonies and taught their children about bush foods and the ancient law. Anangu were also curious about European ways — their clothing, food and faster ways of travelling — and some came in from the bush to investigate. The drought that occurred from 1958 to 1965, however, was especially severe and many of the remaining bush people were brought or voluntarily came into settlements for their own survival.

Tourism to Uluru began to gather momentum in the 1950s. At that time Anangu also had become more mobile, using donkeys, camels and occasionally cars for travel. People from the south-west quickly learnt that there was money to be made from tourists and began to sell artefacts at Uluru, Curtin Springs and Angas Downs. Some women were employed as housemaids in one of the lodges. Slowly the people began to establish their own communities in their country.

The growth of tourism, though, brought with it an especially worrying problem for Anangu. Visitors generally had no knowledge of, or respect for, the importance of the sacred sites around Uluru and Kata Tjuta. They did not realise that by entering these sites they were breaking the Law of the Tjukurpa. Much later, in the late 1970s some of the areas were fenced off.

In the late 1960s more people began to move back into their own communities 'out bush'. It was, of course, not a return to live the life of their ancestors. While much of their culture was still alive, they had taken on many of the habits and products of European society. Some of these have been of practical value, such as the use of motor vehicles. Others, like alcohol, have proven disastrous.

RE-ESTABLISHMENT ON TRADITIONAL LAND

The re-establishment of Anangu on their lands did not happen easily or overnight. There were, and still are, many new demands which needed to be reconciled with their lifestyle — pastoral and mining interests and tourism. The growth of the land rights movement and many political battles occurred during the 1970s and 1980s. Yami Lester, the first Chairman of the Uluru–Kata Tjuta Board of Management, has written of his experiences of these years. The many meetings with politicians, the need to confer with elders and give them time to consider proposals before decisions could be made, the dealings with competing mining interests, and the great jubilation that occurred when land titles were returned to the traditional owners — all have been detailed.[1]

The establishment of the more permanent Docker River settlement near the Western Australian border in 1968–69 provided a base for people of the south-west region of the Northern Territory. Docker River Social Club established the Ininti Store and garage at Uluru. This enterprise was used by visitors and locals alike until the Ayers Rock Resort was built. It provided essential fuel and supplies for people travelling through the western deserts, especially for those living in small remote communities or outstations.

More Aboriginal people became resident at Uluru too. In 1975 the community was registered as an incorporated body and later adopted the name of the nearby water-hole, becoming the Mutitjulu Community Incorporated. Many of the traditional owners are still resident in that community and are directly involved as members of the Uluru–Kata Tjuta Board of Management or in the day-to-day running of the park.

For people in the south-west of the Northern Territory and north-western South Australia, the first success in the land rights struggle came in the 1980s (Fig. 6.6). Freehold title to the entire north-west corner of South Australia was granted in 1981. Meanwhile the traditional owners of Uluru were also keen to own their land again. They had been undertaking exhaustive negotiations and participating in extensive legal hearings. In 1979 the Land Commissioner's ruling was that the traditional owners could not claim the national park because it was alienated crown land. Petitions to Prime Minister Malcolm Frazer and negotiations with the Northern Territory Government were unsuccessful. Finally in 1983 Prime Minister Bob Hawke took steps to enable freehold title to be granted to people who had been identified as the traditional owners.

The offer from the Commonwealth Government was conditional upon a lease-back of the park to the Australian National Conservation Agency (ANCA) and the continuation of visitor access. A 99-year lease was arranged, with provision for a review of terms every five years. The negotiations and legislative changes required almost two years to complete. The title was granted to the Uluru–Kata Tjuta Land Trust and the deeds were presented by the Governor General Sir Ninian Stephen on 26 October 1985, at Uluru. This formal occasion and the following celebrations were an acknowledgement of both the importance of this land for Anangu and its importance internationally as a national park. The park is surrounded by Aboriginal freehold land.

Since 1985 Uluru–Kata Tjuta National Park has been managed by the Uluru–Kata Tjuta Board of Management. The board has a majority of Aboriginal members. The Director of ANCA is also a member of the Board, which is actively involved in all aspects of park management. Not only are the Aboriginal people owners of the land but they have a direct control over management decisions as well and some are

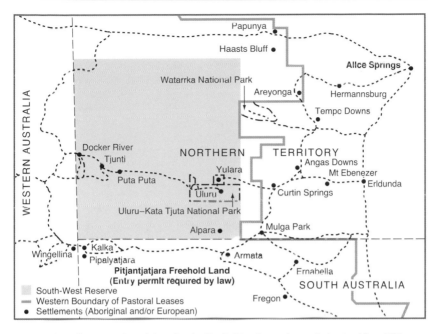

FIGURE 6.6 Land tenure in Central Australia; the 'South-West Reserve' as marked, existed from 1920 to 1940. Land west of the boundary of pastoral leases is Aboriginal freehold land, for which visitors require a permit to visit, except for Uluru–Kata Tjuta National Park.

employed as rangers. While conservation is the primary objective of the park, Anangu are able to continue hunting and foraging on their land.

The Liru Walk (p.169), conducted by Anangu using their own language, is an excellent example of Aboriginal involvement with visitors to Uluru. Maruku Arts is another. This is a display of crafts made by people from the desert communities. This enterprise is owned and managed by the Aboriginal people and the craftwork is sold in the park and interstate. Other commercial ventures such as camel safaris are being investigated as possible Aboriginal enterprises.

Watarrka National Park is run by a Park Management Committee which has several Luritja members. These people do not have freehold title to the land, which instead is

FIGURE 6.7 Presentation of title deeds to the Uluru–Kata Tjuta Land Trust was a formal acknowledgement of the importance of this land to Anangu. *Mutitjulu Community*

vested in the Northern Territory Government. The Luritja people have, however, been granted three living areas within the park near places which are of traditional significance to them. They work with the rangers of the Conservation Commission of the Northern Territory in the management and protection of the park, and have established Kurkara Tours as a way of introducing their culture to visitors.

THE NEWCOMERS TO CENTRAL AUSTRALIA — EARLY EXPLORATION AND DEVELOPMENT

Much of the early European exploration of Central Australia occurred as a bonus from expeditions staged for other reasons. John McDouall Stuart, for example, was intent upon his mission to cross the Australian continent form south to north when he travelled through the Centre between 1860 and 1862. Ernest Giles and William Gosse were part of the race to find an overland route from Alice Springs to the Western Australian coast in the 1870s. There was a strong competitive spirit behind these expeditions and meetings between explorers were carefully avoided.

THE OVERLAND TELEGRAPH LINE

Stuart, the first of the explorers to pass through Central Australia, came into the region a little to the east of the present Stuart Highway. Because his prime objective was to reach the north coast he pursued a northerly bearing as much as possible. His explorations succeeded in establishing a route from south to north across the centre of the continent. He assessed the possible pastoral value of the land and paved the way for the installation of the Overland Telegraph Line, shown in the map below.

The construction of the Overland Telegraph Line in 1871–72 completely changed Australia's ability to communicate with the rest of the world. A message could be sent to Britain in only a few hours instead of taking three months by ship. It was also of critical importance in the opening up of Central Australia by European people. Building it was a remarkable feat. In extremely harsh conditions 3000 kilometres of line and 11 repeater stations were constructed in the year between August 1871 and August 1872. The route passed through isolated and often waterless country. Supplies and materials

FIGURE 6.8 Exploration routes of Stuart, Giles and Gosse and the approximate location of roads, the telegraph line and the railway around 1958 when Bill Harney travelled the country.

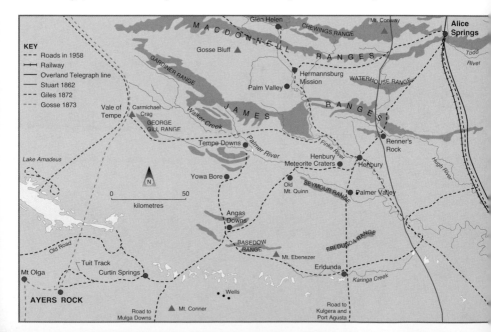

had to be carted in over vast distances, although whenever possible local materials such as stone and timber were used.

The Alice Springs Telegraph Station, now part of an Historical Reserve, was one of the manned repeater stations built along the line. Another, at Charlotte Waters in northern South Australia, is now only a pile of rubble, the stone having been removed from the deserted buildings to construct the nearby New Crown homestead. The Alice Springs Telegraph Station became a focal point for the activities of white people in the Centre and the town grew nearby. The line itself also encouraged other development. Wells sunk along this route were often the only reliable source of water known to the newcomers, and by 1890 all the country along the line thought to be suitable for grazing had been taken up.

For others the Telegraph Line served as a point of departure. Pastoral boundaries were extended west and east and many expeditions started and finished at points along the line. The Finke River, named by Stuart, was a corridor for movement of the newcomers through the Centre, as it had long been for the Aboriginal people. Hermannsburg Mission, established in 1877 on the Finke 130 kilometres west of Alice Springs, became another focal point in the recent human history of Central Australia. Supplies and people came to the mission from Oodnadatta along the Telegraph Line and then followed the river.

FIGURE 6.9 (above right) 'Up the pole for nuts'. Mr Bill Wutke, a telegraphist from the Alice Springs Telegraph Station in the 1920s, is climbing one of the poles of the Old Telegraph Line. These metal poles replaced the original timber poles which were eaten out by termites. *Parks and Wildlife Commission of the Northern Territory*

FIGURE 6.10 Four of the seven Bradshaw children and their Aboriginal servants at the Alice Springs Telegraph Station in about 1900, where their father Thomas Bradshaw, was postmaster from 1899 to 1908. *Parks and Wildlife Commission of the Northern Territory*

FIGURE 6.11 Restored
buildings of the old
Hermannsburg
Mission. *J. A. Kerle*

ERNEST GILES, WILLIAM GOSSE AND THEIR DISCOVERIES

The Telegraph Line and Finke River were basic points of reference for Ernest Giles and William Gosse in 1872 and 1873 in their separate efforts to find a route through to the west — to explore the western part of the continent which was still a mystery to Europeans (Fig. 6.8). Neither of these explorers succeeded in his mission at that time, but both collected a substantial amount of information about the western part of the central ranges and other parts Central Australia.

Ernest Giles left the line just north of the Charlotte Waters Telegraph Station in August 1872 and began his explorations by following the Finke River through to its headwaters. From there he turned west but the desperate scarcity of water in the desert at the beginning of summer forced him to turn south again. This move led to Giles' discovery of the George Gill Range and his sighting of Mount Olga. It also led him to the shores of Lake Amadeus which thwarted his endeavours to reach Mount Olga and to continue his westward expedition. It also undoubtedly prevented him from discovering Uluru.

The George Gill Range appeared to be extremely favourable land to Giles, especially after crossing vast tracts of apparently waterless country covered by spinifex. The foothills were green and grassy, the spinifex was 'fortunately absent', and there was water. Giles passed through this country in October and November of 1872; in the process, he named not only the range but many other features including Carmichael Crag and all the major creeks. The crag was named after Mr Samuel Carmichael who had volunteered to accompany Giles on the expedition at his own expense. Mr Fielder King, whom Giles honoured by the naming of Kings Creek, was a property owner in South Australia and 'an old and kind friend of mine'.

It was during his second expedition in 1873 that Giles finally reached his cherished goal of Mount Olga. But it was not without anguish, for it was then that he discovered that William Gosse had been there first, after visiting Uluru. We can only imagine the extreme disappointment Giles must have felt since he believed his was the only exploring expedition in that vast country. He considered it to be his duty to traverse 'entirely new country', but instead had crossed Gosse's tracks which, he said,

> ... have upset all my ideas. I thought I was the monarch of all I surveyed, and the lord of the fowl and the brute; but lo! a greater than I is here. So I must depart to some remoter spot where none shall dispute my sway.[2]

The expedition led by William Christie Gosse in 1873 was sponsored by the South Australian Government which, buoyed by its successful construction of the Overland Telegraph Line, wanted to pursue further exploration of the inland. Gosse and his party first travelled north from Alice Springs before turning west. They soon confronted the same problems that Giles had faced — lack of water and feed. Gosse too turned south, passing to the west of the MacDonnell Ranges and through country traversed by Giles to Kings Creek. By swinging on to a south-easterly route after leaving Kings Creek Gosse managed to bypass Lake Amadeus. The route also took him to Mount Conner and thence west to Ayers Rock and Mount Olga.

THE 1894 HORN SCIENTIFIC EXPEDITION

The next major expedition to visit the region was not an exploration party but a scientific team. It was the Horn Expedition of 1894, financed by W. A. Horn, a wealthy South Australian pastoralist and businessman. In four months, this expedition travelled more than 3000 kilometres by camel from Oodnadatta to Alice Springs via the George Gill Range, Uluru and the West MacDonnell Ranges and then back to the railhead at Oodnadatta. It was specifically designed to examine the geology, mineral resources, plants, animals and Aboriginal culture of Central Australia, and included scientists with experience in each of these fields. Most prominent were Professor Baldwin Spencer of the University of Melbourne and Professors Edward Stirling and Ralph Tate of the University of Adelaide.

This scientific expedition made an extraordinarily valuable contribution to our knowledge of the natural history of the region. The information collected remains a firm foundation for our knowledge of desert plants and animals. Without this, and without the information collected by H. H. Finlayson of the South Australian Museum in 1931 and 1956, we would have a much poorer understanding of the distribution and abundance of desert animals, especially those now known to be rare or endangered. Finlayson was Honorary Curator of Mammals at the museum, but his incredibly valuable collecting trips to the Centre were undertaken at his own expense and in his own time. The assistance of the Aboriginal people, whom he greatly respected, made a highly significant contribution to the success of his collecting trips.

FIGURE 6.12 Members of the Horn Scientific Expedition found sheltered pools of the George Gill Range to contain many interesting plants. *J. A. Kerle*

Of course, many other people travelled through this country, looking for good pastoral land or minerals, or scalping dingoes. Alan Breaden went to the Centre as a pioneer of the pastoral industry in 1875. In 1897 he led a small exploration party west to Uluru and beyond. The doggers also covered vast areas, often on their own. Their job was to keep the dingoes under control and reduce the number of attacks they made on sheep or cattle. Dingoes had been declared a pest by the South Australian Government and the doggers were paid a bounty for every dingo scalp they collected. But these people did not consider their feats of travelling very extraordinary and rarely left any records. Many fascinating stories remain untold.

TRANSPORT AND COMMUNICATION

FROM CAMELS TO ROAD TRAINS

The first explorers through Central Australia were carried on horseback. A little later the 'ships of the desert', dromedary camels, were introduced to the task. This was the beginning of their highly significant influence on European exploration and settlement of the vast Australian interior. Although Burke and Wills had used camels during their fateful expedition across the continent in 1860, the first major shipment of camels to Australia — from the general region of Afghanistan — was in 1866. And with them came the Afghan cameleers.

Camels were certainly not a fast mode of transport but they were reliable, could carry very large loads and did not require nearly as much water as horses did. In addition to their role in expeditions, camels were the primary means of carting supplies to the remote settlements, goldfields and pastoral properties for over 50 years. Their loads, often weighing up to nine hundredweight (or 460 kilograms) on a large male, included food (e.g. 70kg bags of flour), building materials and even windmills or large and unwieldy extraction equipment for the Arltunga goldfield east of Alice Springs. The greatest numbers of camels were imported during the 1880s and 1890s. Marree, Oodnadatta and Alice Springs all became focal points of the camel cartage businesses.

FIGURE 6.13 Cameleers with their camel train carrying wool south to the markets in Adelaide. *D. D. Smith, National Trust of the Northern Territory*

FIGURE 6.14 A restored Muslim shrine built by cameleers in Maree, South Australia. *J. A Kerle*

FIGURE 6.15 Date palms growing amongst the ruins of Dalhousie Springs Station, South Australia. *J. A. Kerle*

The cameleers themselves form a fascinating and colourful part of the history of Central Australia. They mostly came from a number of nomadic tribes of the Afghanistan (hence the name 'ghan') and Baluchistan region, bringing with them their faith, culture, traditions and food. As a consequence of this, and racial prejudice, they rarely mixed with other people, living in 'ghantowns' which they built on the outskirts of the desert settlements. As devout Muslims they adhered strictly to their faith. Many small mosques were built wherever they lived and they refused to transport either alcohol or pork. They were tough and hardworking — rising at 'Afghan daylight', hours before dawn and on their way by sunup. More often than not they walked the desert beside their string of camels.

While travelling through the bush in this way, they came to know and use a lot of native plant foods, adapting them to the cuisine of their own traditions. They also grew their own foods, most notably date palms. Date palms were planted widely throughout the Centre, ensuring a good fruit supply, especially for use during the fasting month of Ramadan. Indeed their date palms led to the development of date farms in the Centre and some of the original palms are still growing at the Mecca Date Farm near Alice Springs.

The railway from Oodnadatta to Alice Springs was finally completed in 1929 (Fig. 6.8). This heralded a new phase of growth in the development of the Centre and, at the same time, sounded the death knell for most of the camel cartage businesses. There was no road construction away from the main north–south routes, until the 1950s so animals (camels, horses, donkeys) continued to be the main mode of transport in the more isolated areas. In addition to the descendants of the cameleers, who still live in the Centre, there is a lasting reminder of this history in the feral camel herds which roam the desert and are now the basis of a camel export industry!

Today, goods are transported in and out of the Centre by rail or truck. A high standard highway has been built from Adelaide to Darwin and the original railway from Adelaide to Alice Springs has been completely reconstructed, much of it following a different route. As a reminder of the Afghan cameleers the passenger train service to the centre has been called 'The Ghan'. The proposed extension of the railway line, from Alice Springs to Darwin is an ongoing political saga, promised at each election and forgotten soon after. The Centre is also well-serviced by air.

JOHN FLYNN AND THE 'MANTLE OF SAFETY'

While the Overland Telegraph Line revolutionised Australia's ability to communicate with the rest of the world, it did little to improve communication between people in the outback. Messages could be quickly sent between the repeater stations but could not easily be transferred to people in remote areas. They had a very isolated and often lonely existence. In an emergency someone, often an Aboriginal, was sent to a neighbouring station to get help. This could take days.

A major advance in outback communication came with the 'Mantle of Safety', a scheme developed by the Reverend John Flynn of the Australian Inland Mission. His vision was to combine the provision of medical supplies with radio communication and aeroplanes so that people could have better access to help when they needed it. By 1926 a South Australian engineer, Alf Traeger, had developed the pedal radio, a cheap lightweight transceiver which was simple to operate. Power was obtained by pedalling a dynamo while the message was being transmitted. A morse code key was used to begin with, but this was soon replaced by the morse typewriter. The pedal radio could transmit signals over a distance of about 480 kilometres.

The Aerial Medical Service, or Royal Flying Doctor Service as it is now known, followed in 1928. Its first base was at Cloncurry in Queensland. This system of long distance medical consultations was a world first and is still a fundamental service for people in the outback. When people were given a radio, they were also supplied with a comprehensive box of medicines. Consultations could then be carried out over the radio, but if this was not sufficient the flying doctor was called in.

Although the 'Mantle of Safety' was introduced in the late 1920s, it took a long time to become generally available. Even in the 1940s, the de Conlays at Mount Conner were still extremely isolated. Paddy de Conlay was often away for many days working on their own station (as pastoral properties are called), or for Sid Staines at Erldunda Station, leaving Phyllis de Conlay with no other white people nearby. Every fortnight she would send a 'lad' to meet Connellan's mail plane from Alice Springs at Angas Downs. He would leave on Sunday and, hopefully, be back by Tuesday. On some occasions the plane would not arrive or could not land, wasting his whole trip.

At Tempe Downs communication was provided until 1932 by the monthly 'camel mail' service which came with the station supplies. Sending a telegram could take anything up to two weeks, so it was nearly as quick to wait for the mail — or so it seemed. Contact by telegram involved sending an Aboriginal boy by horse to Horseshoe Bend — four days each way — and his waiting there a day or two for a reply. In 1932, when Hermannsburg Mission joined the Flying Doctor network, a telegram could be sent via radio in two days.

It was inevitable that people working with cattle were injured occasionally, and there was sickness. Most of these people, though, had some idea of first aid and the missionaries set broken bones and pulled out bad teeth!

Even in the 1960s, Joe O'Brien, the manager at Tempe Downs, had very little contact with the outside world. O'Brien had been in the Centre for many years and was happy with his isolated lifestyle. He had no vehicle and only a small motor strong enough to power the radio. Occasionally, when he did need to go to town, he would call a taxi in Alice Springs by radio. The taxi driver would take a day to get out there and stay the night. He would return to town the next day with O'Brien. After three days in town the procedure would be reversed.

FROM TWO-WAY RADIO TO THE DIGITAL CONCENTRATOR NETWORK

The old transmitters with a morse typewriter were eventually replaced by hand-held microphones on battery-powered two-way radios. Even with these improvements communication remained a challenge. For Elsie Cotterill at Wallara Ranch in the 1960s, ordering supplies was rarely straightforward. After working out the order she sent it to the suppliers in town by telegram through the Flying Doctor Service. This could be done only at specific times of the day and she had to wait her turn before sending at least two or three telegrams, one to each supplier. It could then take until late afternoon to find out if the required supplies were available.

The radiophone which arrived 20 years later was a wonderful improvement. Mardi Cotterill could ring the supplier directly but only if no one else was transmitting. She had to wait until the red light on the radio went off and then quickly hit the white button and lift the receiver at once to beat any other callers. Several illegal schemes were devised by these practical bush people in order to be the quickest onto the line.

The radio network is still widely used throughout the Centre, although everyone now has access to the standard phone ststem via the digital concentrator network. Radio is a cheap form of communication between stations and is carried for emergency contact by people travelling or working in very remote locations. It is also used by the outback School of the Air through which children in isolated locations receive their primary education from teachers in town centres like Alice Springs. Unfortunately some outback four-wheel-drive tourists do not understand the rules and can abuse the privilege by monopolising the airwaves. Of course, no message sent by radio is private and if reception is poor because of static or bad atmospheric conditions, messages can become very confused. The 'galah session', when the airwaves were open and everyone could have a chat without formality, was often a source of outback amusement — and gossip!

STOCKMEN AND PROSPECTORS

THE STRUGGLE TO ESTABLISH CATTLE STATIONS IN THE DESERT

Expansion of the Australian pastoral industry and the search for routes to take cattle to market drove much of the early European exploration of the Centre. Pastoral leases were quickly taken up on suitable land after construction of the Overland Telegraph Line, and then new leases were established to the east and west.

It was not an easy existence. The early pastoralists and their families struggled against many difficulties: enduring the climate; bringing in and maintaining stock; coping with poison plants; riding out depressed markets. Some leases had a succession of owners, especially during the 1930s and 1940s as they struggled against drought and the poor markets. Some owners, managers and workers succumbed to alcoholism and wasted the hard effort they had given to the land. Raising sheep or cattle in Central Australia has always been a desperate struggle against the climate.

Ernest Giles, excited by the potential of the country he found around the George Gill Range, was one of the first to apply for pastoral leases in the area of Watarrka National Park. His applications were approved in 1875 but he made no effort to stock the land, ultimately selling out in 1883 to the Tempe Downs Pastoral Company. This company immediately began stocking the land and by 1889 there were some 6000 head of cattle there.

Although Tempe Downs was well endowed with natural waters it struggled to survive as a pastoral property, changing ownership and management often. Bryan Bowman, who managed the lease from 1930 to 1938, found that the ruggedness of the country made it very difficult to control the stock and prevent them from 'going wild'. In the 50 to 60 years before the lease was acquired for the national park most stock were run along the southern edge of the range, utilising the waters draining from the Mereenie Sandstone.

Angas Downs Pastoral Lease to the south of Tempe Downs was not established until 1930. It was taken up by Billy Liddle, who first stocked it with sheep. The station remained in the Liddle family until recently and has been a very important transit point in opening up both Uluru and Kings Canyon to tourism.

Further south again is Erldunda Station. This property was divided into two leases, Erldunda and Lyndavale, in recent years. Erldunda Station was first established in 1877 by Richard Warburton, son of the explorer Colonel P. E. Warburton, and Alan Breaden. It was purchased in about 1915 by Sid Staines, whose family still own Lyndavale. Fresh waters associated with the ancestral drainage of the Lake Amadeus system into the Finke River provide some reliable water, but further west the land becomes more 'marginal' for pastoral use.

In 1943 a lease was taken up near Mount Conner by Paddy and Phyllis de Conlay, whom we met earlier. They had very little with which to start their venture, not even building materials, so they excavated a room in the ground and roofed it with mulga saplings, grass and clay. Droughts, very limited water and lack of capital forced the de Conlays to give up and the lease became a part of Curtin Springs Station. This station, established in 1941, was named after the Prime Minister of the time, John Curtin. It was originally owned by the Andrews brothers and since the late 1950s it has been owned by the Severin family.

FIGURE 6.16 Ruins of McNamara's Hut, Tempe Downs Station. *G. Allen, National Trust of the Northern Territory*

FIGURE 6.17 Goldminers during the early 1900s in the Harts Ranges, east of Alice Springs. *Parks and Wildlife Commission of the Northern Territory*

LURE OF GOLD

The mineral potential of the Centre has excited interest since European exploration of the country began. Many prospecting parties have crisscrossed the country seeking their elusive prize. Most of the early interest was in gold and the discovery of the goldfield at Arltunga, for example, kept this interest alive. The exploits of Harold Lasseter, who claimed to have discovered a reef of gold of untold wealth, represent one of the more colourful episodes of prospecting in Central Australia. While it is doubtful that he ever did discover gold, the mystery of his exploits lingers on and continues to entice prospectors seeking their fortune. Hopefully they will not be as foolish as he was. Lasseter became lost and died of starvation, having refused the assistance of the local Aboriginal people.

The mineral potential of Central Australia is still actively being assessed by mining companies — not only for gold, but also for oil and gas. Large fossil fuel reserves have already been located at Moomba in South Australia and Mereenie west of Alice Springs.

VISITORS TO A 'LUMP OF ROCK' — TOURISM

If you travel from Alice Springs to Uluru by road today it will take about five hours. It is even possible, but not advisable, to go there and back in a day. Imagine, then, being on one of the first tours in the 1950s when it took two days to get there, if all went well. The bus was packed with supplies, passengers were collected and off you went. Tours were available only during the six months of cooler weather and the bus was usually airconditioned as there were no windows! The first night was spent at the Mount Quinn homestead north of Angas Downs. Between there and Uluru were several difficult creek crossings and a rough bush track most of the way. Getting flat tyres or bogged in sand were constant threats and causes of delay. Rain could see you stuck in the middle of nowhere for days.

While regular visits to Uluru were not a reality until the 1950s, a few intrepid adventurers did make the trek before then. In 1936 Vic Foy, described as a millionaire globetrotter, organised an expedition into 'Lasseter Country', including Ayers Rock. The expedition was taken by Kurt Johannsen, a remarkable Central Australian bush mechanic who built his own truck, 'The Mulga Express', for the trip. Imagine the panic that came over the group when the truck broke down about 65 kilometres from the Rock, in the middle of nowhere! Johannsen repaired the problem and they had no further trouble in 1600 kilometres of bush-bashing.

There were other visitors. Some recorded their visit; some didn't. Bottles and metal matchboxes were left on top of the Rock with names in them: 1931/32 McKinnon; 1933 Fuller; 1939 Dumas, Clune and Bails; 1940 anthropologist Charles Mountford; 1947 Arthur Groom, who wrote a detailed chronicle of his visit. Most of these visitors travelled from the north. In 1930 the adventurer and prospector Michael Terry pushed the first vehicle track through from the east, travelling from Erldunda to Mount Conner and Uluru, not far from the present Lasseter Highway. He was followed by Sid Staines of Erldunda Station, in 1944. Those who *didn't* record their visits undoubtedly included doggers and station people who had not obtained the required permit from the government's Aboriginal Welfare Branch.

And then there were those who didn't quite make it. In the 1930s a young man, Ellis Bankin, attempted to reach the Rock by motorbike. He did this against the advice of locals and was found, dead, on Lyndavale Station. His bike was sound and had plenty of fuel but it was hot and he was lost. In 1947 a group of schoolboys and masters from Geelong Grammar School travelled in four-wheel-drive trucks from Erldunda, but retreated after reaching Mount Conner. They had been bogged 27 times between Erldunda and Mount Conner and had used up too much of their precious petrol supply.

After a tour in 1950 with a party from Sydney's Knox Grammar School, Len Tuit recognised the tourist potential of Uluru and began to offer regular tours. At that time the Administrator of the Northern Territory was not supportive because he believed there was 'no future for tourism in the Territory'. Nor were southern travel agents convinced that they

FIGURE 6.18 The remains of Mount Quinn homestead, where Len Tuit and his tour parties camped on the first night of his Ayers Rock tours. *Jim Cotterill*

FIGURE 6.19 Connellan Airways in Alice Springs 1963 — where ancient and modern modes of transport met. *National Trust of the Northern Territory*

could market a 'lump of rock'. How wrong they all were! By 1958 there had been 2296 visitors and today Uluru is one of Australia's premier tourist destinations.

Similarly, the Cotterill family found it hard to get support for their venture to open up Kings Canyon for tourism in 1960. Unlike Uluru, Kings Canyon was a well-kept secret, visited rarely by station people and a few interested people from Alice Springs. In 1960 Arthur Liddle of Angas Downs showed Jack and Jim Cotterill the canyon. Jack Cotterill, who was already operating at Ayers Rock, immediately saw the potential but, like Tuit, found it difficult to get support for 'so-called tourist ventures', as his partner called it.

Despite grading of tracks and gradual improvement of roads the trip to Uluru remained potentially hazardous until the sealed Lasseter Highway was completed in 1982. My first visit to Uluru was just before this. It had been raining and the slippery road was often covered by deep sheets of water. It was a slow trip but we did see molochs (thorny devils), processionary caterpillars and other wildlife emerging in the sunny weather after the rain. The road into Watarrka is still not completely sealed and rain can delay travel.

Since 1958 it has been possible to completely avoid the rough tracks and long journey by flying to Uluru. The first formal airstrip was constructed near Taputji on the northern side of the Rock and flights there were made by Eddie Connellan, the pioneer aviator of the Northern Territory. Connellan had been taking flights over the area prior to this and is known to have landed on a nearby saltpan in 1938. Connellan also combined with Alice Springs Tours Ltd, owned by Jack Cotterill and Daisy Underdown, offering fly-in/fly-out tours and later, a fly-in/drive-out option. While this mode of touring to Uluru has steadily expanded, roads remain the only access to Watarrka. An airstrip was built near Carmichael Crag by Ansett–Pioneer in the 1960s for fly-in/fly-out tours but it was not replaced after being washed out a couple of years later.

Recognition of the importance of the tourist industry in Central Australia culminated in 1984 with the construction of the Ayers Rock Resort, or Yulara Tourist Village as it was first called. This enabled extensive expansion and upgrading of facilities to occur without spoiling the marvellous natural attractions of Uluru. The Frontier Kings Canyon Hotel and a new camping ground were built in 1992.

And yet, despite the ease of travel and all the modern conveniences, a sense of mystery still surrounds these places, especially Uluru. The most notorious event in recent history was undoubtedly the strange disappearance in 1980 of the nine-week-old baby, Azaria Chamberlain, from the old camping ground close to Uluru. This mystery has never been completely resolved. Tragic events such as this can happen anywhere, but somehow Uluru creates a different aura.

LEN TUIT

Len Tuit believed in the value of Uluru as a tourist destination long before tourism was recognised as a significant industry in the Northern Territory. His first regular tours to Uluru began in 1955. Prior to this, Tuit had been running tours to Palm Valley west of Alice Springs, occasional visits to Uluru and a coach and mail run between Adelaide and Darwin. He didn't wait for roads to be built for him or for water supplies to be found. He got in and, with the help of other locals, established supplies and facilities.

The earliest trips from Alice Springs to Ayers Rock were rough. They could carry about 20 passengers and their luggage and supplies. It certainly wasn't all plain sailing. On one occasion, so the story goes, Len hit a bump and the food behind the back seat flew into the air. This included a carton of eggs which broke all over the passengers at the back. Len stopped, brushed them down and, with a 'she'll be right', set off again. With the realignment and improvement of the tracks, the original two-day trip was cut to 12–14 hours.

The first accommodation at the Rock was a tent camp. People slept in 'little beach-tents', and ex-army marquees served as a store and a dining room. By 1958 Len had constructed a galvanised iron shed, but visitors still slept in tents. Len's wife Pearl was of course one of the mainstays of this operation — provisioning, cooking and clean-ing. These were five-day tours, with three days spent around Uluru and Kata Tjuta.

At first, water was a constant source of worry for Tuit. He began his Ayers Rock tourist venture when the Centre was experiencing severe drought and Maggie Springs (Mutitjulu) is not permanent or reliable. To begin with he carted water from Curtin Springs and then he set about finding his own water supply. He arranged for a drilling rig to be brought in from Curtin Springs and used his 'bush knowledge' to decide on where to drill. This happened to be where the drilling rig got bogged in a rabbit war-ren — or so one story goes! Good fresh water was struck at a depth of 26 metres with a flow of 84 gallons (380 litres) per hour. An assured supply. These bushmen didn't have much patience with water diviners!

The ever-practical, rough and ready Tuit sold his tourist interests in 1959 to Pioneer Tours, bringing to a close his dynamic role as a pioneer of tourism in the Centre. He operated at a time when the authorities had no faith in this industry and the tourists themselves were his best advertisement.

THE COTTERILL FAMILY

On the Stuart Highway 90 kilometres south of Alice Springs is Jim's Place. In front of this pleasant Wayside Inn are the remains of an old Dodge weapon carrier and an A-shape frame made from steel railway sleepers. These were the vehicle and blade used by Jim Cotterill and his father Jack to cut the first track through to Kings Canyon. The cutting of over 100 kilometres of road through sandhills and dense bush was an extremely difficult operation which took four months to complete. But it was only then that the Cotterills' newly formed Kings Canyon Tours company could begin to operate.

Kings Canyon Tours was not Jack Cotterill's first involvement with tourism in Central Australia. Jack and his family migrated from England in 1952 and soon after-wards, Jack began to work for Len Tuit. In the mid 1950s he began his own tours to Palm Valley and in 1958 turned his interests to Ayers Rock. One of Jack's prime con-cerns was to reduce wear and tear on vehicles and people, so he instigated the fly-in/fly-out tours with Connellan Airways. The Cotterills did the vehicle maintenance and repair work. Their partners, the Underdowns of the Alice Springs Hotel, arranged town accommodation and provisions and the lodge at Ayers Rock was managed by Lance Rust.

The first lodge at the Rock was built by Alice Springs Tours Ltd. It was a corrugated iron building with a dining room, six bedrooms and two bathrooms. There are many funny tales told of life at the lodge — like the use of a human thermometer in operat-ing the showers. Water for the showers was hand-pumped into a drum on the roof and the temperature was controlled by alternately pumping from drums of hot and cold water. Sometimes the person pumping would get talking to someone and forget to switch between drums. A scream from the shower would raise the alarm; persistent screaming would indicate that the water was being pumped from the wrong bucket!

In 1960, when Arthur Liddle took Jack and Jim Cotterill to Kings Canyon, they took a day and a half to do the trip from Angas Downs. There was no road for the last 100 kilometres and they followed creeks, gullies and ranges across country. When they arrived it was drizzling with rain and misty. They couldn't believe the beauty of the place — the wonderful colours, both bold and pastel. That visit changed all their plans. They sold out of Alice Springs Tours and began their 30-year association with Kings Canyon.

In addition to blazing the road through, they built Wallara Ranch 100 kilometres from the canyon and took tours in from there. Twenty people could be accommodated at Wallara. A typical tour took three days: one day down, one day into the canyon and back to the lodge and one day back to Alice Springs. The day into the canyon was a long one, even if all went well. Time was allowed to inspect Aboriginal rock art and to climb the canyon rim; then a barbecue while watching the sun set on the entrance to the canyon. Back at Wallara the weary travellers were greeted with fresh scones baked by Jack's wife Elsie.

In all such ventures, the women were vital to the success. From the time Elsie moved from Alice Springs to Wallara she completely ran the lodge. It was a hard, lonely life. Water was heated in a boiler, washing done in a copper, cooking done over a wood stove and communication with the rest of the world was very poor.

A monument recognising Jack Cotterill's foresight and effort in making Kings Canyon accessible has been built near the climb. It is a well-deserved tribute and one which should apply to the whole Cotterill family.

FIGURE 6.20 Len Tuit's camp of 'little beach tents' near Maggie Springs in the late 1950s. *Jim Cotterill*

FIGURE 6.21 The first lodge at Ayers Rock was this corrugated iron shed built by Alice Springs Tours Ltd. *Jim Cotterill*

BILL HARNEY

A true Australian bushman, Bill Harney was also a wonderful storyteller who thoroughly enjoyed talking to people at the base of the climb at Ayers Rock. He was a gentle, amiable character who cared equally for all people, black and white; a man eminently suited for his job as the first curator–ranger at Uluru. It was in 1957 that he was offered this job over 'the usual cup of tea'. The appointment was prompted by local Aboriginal people's concern for the protection of their important sites. Some artwork had already been defaced by the time of his arrival.

Harney's appointment was for six months a year, during the tourist season from April to September. There were no facilities so he was issued with a tent for his office and living quarters, some pots and pans and a list of instructions! As well as protection of Aboriginal sites, his tasks included caring for the country and issuing of permits and entry tickets after the national park was declared in 1958. Then, as now, some people who had made the often difficult trek to Uluru were most unhappy at having to pay. Why should a visitor have to pay to see an age-old natural wonder? Rarely do these people consider how costly it is to provide even the most basic of services in the desert.

There is no doubt that Bill Harney thoroughly enjoyed his time as ranger at Uluru, learning from the Aboriginal people, talking, posing for photos and sitting around campfires. He was a keen observer of human behaviour and, in his writings, clearly expresses his great affection and admiration for his Aboriginal friends. He also gently chides many of the visitors he met for their arrogance and paternalistic attitude towards himself and the Aboriginal people. He was particularly distressed by inconsiderate tourists who did not understand the value of water in the desert and who fouled the water supply by swimming or washing in it. He loved the country, too, and for him there was no greater pleasure than seeing rain on the Rock, or smelling the rain on the ground and waiting for the change it would bring to the country.

The number of visitors to Uluru increased from about 100 in 1956 to over 4000 in 1961, Harney's last year. In 1963 Bob Gregory, a 'local' from Oodnadatta, was appointed as the first full-time curator, not just for the tourist season. Since that time tourism at Uluru has become a multimillion dollar exercise with millions of visitors coming from all over the world. It is expected that by the year 2000, visits will have to be limited to half a million per year to contain the damage caused by tourism to the natural environment.

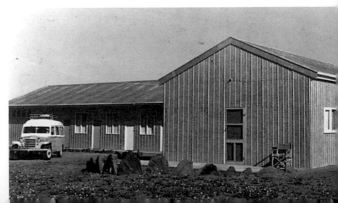

FIGURE 6.22 (below) The original Wallara Lodge and tour bus in May 1961, at the time of the first tour taken by the Cotterill family to Kings Canyon. *Jim Cotterill*

FIGURE 6.23 (left) Bill Harney talking to visitors at Uluru. *Jim Cotterill*

7
ENJOYING YOUR VISIT

With so much to see and do in Central Australia it is most important to plan carefully and to be thoroughly prepared for the local conditions. Where you travel and what you can see and do will depend on how long you are able to spend in the region and on your chosen mode of travel. Various options are available for getting to the Centre: taking one of the many bus tours; flying in or travelling by train and hiring a vehicle; or driving your own car and following your own itinerary. A quick visit will enable you to enjoy the spectacular sights, while a more leisurely trip will allow you to absorb much more about the country and its natural and cultural history.

WHEN TO VISIT

You can visit Central Australia at any time of the year but it is probably best to avoid the hottest months — December, January and February. Even during these months the weather is not constantly scorching but, if it is hot, it is much more likely to stay hot. Rain can fall in any month but is less likely from April to August — of course there is no guarantee. After 32 years of conducting the famous 'Henley-on-Todd' riverbed boat race in dry, hot weather, the Alice Springs Rotary Club organising the event was confronted by a flowing river in October 1993 and had to cancel the race. This a race where boats are carried by people running along the dry riverbed, and not rowed!

In general terms the weather you can expect is as follows (see also Fig. 4.4, p.62):

- December–February: Days generally hot (more than 35°C), often for extended periods; the monsoonal weather in northern Australia can bring rain or hot humid conditions.
- March–April: Persistent hot weather can occur in March but temperatures are generally cooler and the nights are cool. Days 25–35°C; March has a higher average rainfall than April.
- May–August: Generally beautiful balmy days with cool to freezing nights. Days 15–25°C, nights 0–10°C. Usually the driest period of the year, and the skies are very clear.
- September–November: Daytime temperatures warming up again. Extended hot periods can occur in November. Days 25–35°C, nights 10–15°C. Thunderstorm activity can make November a wetter month.

More detailed information about the weather is provided in Chapter 3 pp.44–49.

WHAT TO TAKE FOR WALKING

At all times of the year it is essential to carry plenty of water, wear a shady hat and sunscreen, and have comfortable sturdy shoes for all your walks. Carry everything you will need on walks in a comfortable, small back pack which will leave your hands free for climbing.

WATER

When walking in hot weather you will need to drink *one litre per hour* of water. Fizzy drinks and beer are *not* suitable substitutes as they enhance dehydration and make you feel hotter. This is even more important if you are visiting the Centre from a cooler moister climate. Dehydration can easily occur, with the first symptoms being irritability and dizziness. Be prepared and carry all you need. Make sure you bring suitable portable water containers. Water is available from the Uluru Ranger Station only in an emergency. Oranges and high energy snack foods are also necessary, especially for longer walks.

CLOTHING AND GEAR

Most of the time, Central Australia is sunny. You will need a wide-brimmed hat, sunscreen (SPF15+) and dark glasses throughout the year. In the heat, loose fitting cotton clothing, including a long-sleeved shirt, is preferable. In winter you may need a sweater and jacket for the first couple of hours in the morning and at night. In cooler weather it is a good idea to carry a sweater if you decide to climb Uluru — the wind blows most of the time and it can be surprisingly cold on top. Sturdy shoes are recommended for your own comfort and safety. Inappropriate footwear such as leather-soled shoes, sandals, thongs, or bare feet can cause you to slip while climbing, and cheap soft shoes may not last the distance on the rough, abrasive surfaces.

SAFETY PRECAUTIONS

By following a few basic rules any visitor to Central Australia can have an enjoyable and safe holiday. Even though travel seems easy and the accommodation very comfortable never forget that it is a desert you are visiting.

FITNESS

'Tis a wise person who knows their own limitations', as the old saying goes.

- Be honest when estimating your fitness. Please don't take the attitude 'I'll climb the Rock even if it kills me' because this could be what happens. Walking through the Valley of the Winds or Kings Canyon, and, especially, climbing Uluru are all physically demanding. Choose other, less strenuous walks if you have any doubts.
- Allow plenty of time for your walk. You can enjoy the scenery more and you won't feel under pressure to maintain too fast a pace.

BASIC RULES

The following points are all important rules and will ensure that you enjoy your visit.

- Walk in cool weather and during cool periods of the day, even if you are fit and healthy. In hot weather, this means before 10 a.m. and after 4 p.m. It will be more pleasant and less stressful.
- Do not climb Uluru when it is wet or very windy. The climb may be closed under these conditions.

- Be sensible and careful while walking. Children need to be closely supervised and anyone behaving recklessly can easily fall, endangering other lives as well.
- Confine your walks to the marked walking trails. This will help you to find the way, reduce environmental damage and avoid any unintentional intrusion into sites of Aboriginal importance.
- Avoid walking alone especially on the longer walks. Tell someone else — preferably a ranger — your planned route and estimated time of return. Watch your companions and be alert to any possible signs of distress.
- If you do become lost stay where you are and wait for help to come to you. Sit in the shade.
- Don't forget to carry plenty of water in winter as well as during summer.
- If you are in any doubt about a walk or have any questions *at all* please talk to a ranger. They will be only too happy to provide advice.

FIRE

There is smoke on the horizon, a fire burning gently beside the road, or you are driving through a patch of blackened bush. Fire has long been used as a management tool in Central Australia, first by the Aboriginal people and now by park managers. Management fires are mostly lit during the cooler months and are planned to be small, gently burning patches. Fierce wildfires can occur during the hot summer months and are often caused by lightning. These fires can burn out vast areas.

- You are not permitted to light fires within the parks except in designated fireplaces. Gas barbecues are available in some picnic areas in Uluru–Kata Tjuta National Park; open fires are not permitted. Where there are fireplaces in Watarrka National Park use the wood provided or collect it *outside* the park.
- Outside the parks, be careful with fires at all times and be aware of declared fire restrictions.
- If you have any concerns about a fire contact the park rangers or the police at the Ayers Rock Resort.

FIGURE 7.1 Park rangers light small management fires in winter, following the traditions of Anangu; this increases habitat diversity and reduces the chances of a summer wildfire burning out vast areas. *M. W. Gillam*

FIGURE 7.2 It is important to show respect for wildlife, especially snakes such as this yellow-faced whip snake.
M. W. Gillam

RESPECT FOR WILDLIFE

Snakes are well respected by most people for good reason. Indeed, the most poisonous snakes in the world live in Australia. The most effective way to deal with a snake is to leave it alone. More people are bitten when trying to kill a snake than in other circumstances. So, for your own safety, retreat and do not attack. Snakes are also part of our protected wildlife.

- ◼ A snake can strike only over a distance of about one-third of its own body length, so it is easy to move out of harm's reach.
- ◼ Processionary caterpillars: These hairy caterpillars can cause a severe burning skin irritation. The hairs which cause the irritation also accumulate in the commonly seen bag nests, so leave the nests alone as well.
- ◼ Some ants and spiders have a nasty sting, although most are harmless. Redback spiders are common around buildings in the Centre, but you are unlikely to be bitten unless you aggravate these animals.

EMERGENCIES

Emergencies are the most important reason for walking with other people.

- ◼ If a member of your party is injured contact a ranger. One person can go for help while another stays with the injured person.
- ◼ If a member of your party is lost, do not conduct the search yourself; contact a ranger as quickly as possible.
- ◼ Emergency radios are located at the base of the climb at Uluru, at the Valley of the Winds car park and along the Kings Canyon circuit walk. There is also an emergency water supply on the Valley of the Winds circuit, but this is to be used only if there is a genuine emergency.

PROTECTING OUR PARKS

The basic objectives of park management are to protect the environment, to preserve it for future generations and to enable visitors to enjoy their stay. Park regulations are developed to achieve these aims.

Please leave pets, firearms and animal traps outside the parks.

- ◼ Pets and wildlife do not mix and pets can often annoy other visitors.
- ◼ Dogs *only* are permitted in Watarrka National Park, but *must* be confined to a vehicle at all times.

- Use of firearms or animal trapping can be carried out *only* under permit; penalties apply if these regulations are broken.

Destruction of the natural environment and cultural heritage of the parks must be avoided.

- Firewood must not be collected within any Northern Territory parks.
- Vehicles are not permitted off the main roads or on service roads.
- All natural and cultural features of the parks are fully protected. Any damage to these must be reported to the rangers.
- Do not throw or dislodge rocks from the cliffs — think of the people below.
- Names or drawings must not be carved into the rockfaces.

HOW TO GET THERE (MAP P.VII)

Both National Parks are serviced by good roads, shown on the map of Central Australia. Driving yourself provides the greatest flexibility and will enable you to visit some of the less frequented places. If you have the time, you can drive from anywhere in Australia or if you want to fly to the Centre you can rent a vehicle (including a four-wheel-drive) from Alice Springs and follow your own itinerary.

Regular flights go to Uluru–Kata Tjuta National Park, landing at Connellan Airport, adjacent to the Ayers Rock Resort. Flights via Alice Springs and direct to Ayers Rock are both available. Only air tours, not scheduled air services, are available to Watarrka.

Coach services provide a choice of tours to both parks. They range from large coachlines operating tours of one, two or three days to small 'ecotour' companies offering longer excursions.

Information about these options can be obtained from travel agencies.

In the rest of this chapter, plants, animals and features to look out for are emphasised in capitals. Looking their names up in the index will also guide you to descriptions and illustrations earlier in the book.

ALICE SPRINGS TO ULURU–KATA TJUTA NATIONAL PARK

You can drive the 447 kilometres from Alice Springs to the Ayers Rock Resort in about five hours, via the Stuart Highway south to Erldunda Roadhouse and then west along the Lasseter Highway. There is no need to use a 4WD (four-wheel-drive) vehicle since these highways and the park roads are sealed, all-weather roads. Keep your eye open for BEARDED DRAGONS on the roads, especially around August.

Along this section of the Stuart Highway to Erldunda, you will drive through some beautiful ranges, as well as MULGA and MALLEE shrublands. Around the Watarrka turnoff near Henbury the country opens out into flat plains with remnant rock outcrops. The sandy desert oak communities begin to appear around Erldunda.

Points of Interest

Distances are given in kilometres from Alice Springs, unless indicated otherwise.

Alice Springs Nestled amongst the MACDONNELL RANGES and bisected by the usually dry TODD RIVER.

20km Roe Creek The first of the major dry creeks south of Alice Springs. Further upstream this creek cuts through the MacDonnell Ranges creating Simpsons Gap. The Roe Creek borefield is the source of the town water supply.

40km Waterhouse Range This range extends west towards Hermannsburg.

50km blue mallees An extensive stand of these attractive mallees interspersed with mulga.

70km James Range The highway winds through this rugged range which is incorporated in the Finke Gorge National Park to the west. This range was an important corridor for the movement of Aboriginal people across this country. Note the GHOST GUMS growing on the range.

75km An unmarked dirt track turning east (left) 200 metres south of the cattle grid is the turnoff to Rainbow Valley Conservation Reserve. Obtain information from the Parks and Wildlife Commission of the Northern Territory (p.184) or at Jim's Place.

93km Jim's Place, Wayside Inn established by Jim Cotterill (p.150). Contains an excellent display of photos and stories about Kings Canyon and Wallara Ranch. Fuel is available adjacent to the VIRGINIA CAMEL FARM and the HUGH RIVER.

120km Maloney Creek This creek cuts through the HORN VALLEY SILTSTONE, a rich source of 485 million year old fossils, including brachiopods, cephalopods and gastropods.

126km Finke River A raging torrent when in flood which may cut the highway but usually recedes within a few hours. A worthwhile stop if you want to see some of the riverine birds such as the DIAMOND DOVE, PORT LINCOLN PARROT, RAINBOW BEE-EATER, SACRED KINGFISHER, BLACK FALCON, WEEBILL and various HONEYEATERS.

FIGURE 7.3 The Finke River crossing on the Stuart Highway; floods like this can disrupt travel plans but generally it is only a few hours before the water recedes. *M. W. Gillam*

130km turn off (Ernest Giles Road) to Watarrka National Park and Henbury Meteorite Craters An alternative route to Uluru.

150km Palmer River A tributary of the Finke River. Also a memorable sight when in flood.

200km Erldunda Roadhouse (Desert Oaks Resort), Lasseter Highway intersection Refreshments, accommodation and fuel are available. Turn west onto the Lasseter Highway. It is 247 km to the Ayers Rock Resort. Drive carefully when there are cross winds over the highway, especially if you are towing.

258km (58km west of Erldunda) Mount Ebenezer Artefacts, refreshments, accommodation and fuel are available.

309km (109km west) Luritja Road Runs north to Kings Canyon (Watarrka) and Alice Springs.

340km (140km west) Roadside stop to view Mount Conner This spectacular flat-topped mesa (p.29) will appear to the south of the Lasseter Highway after you pass the Luritja Road intersection. Take time to stop here and walk over the sand dune on the north side of the road where you will see part of the LAKE AMADEUS salt lake system (p.38).

350km (150km west) Mulga Park Road intersection This is an alternative route back to the Stuart Highway which it joins at the South Australian border.

362km (162km west) Curtin Springs Roadhouse Run by the Severin family of Curtin Springs Station. Tours and permission to visit Mount Conner can be arranged from here. Accommodation, camping facilities, refreshments, fuel and aerial tours of Uluru are available.

447 km and 247 km west of Erldunda, Ayers Rock Resort Yulara Village From Curtin Springs the Lasseter Highway mostly passes through sand dune country in which DESERT POPLARS and DESERT OAKS are distinctive features of the vegetation. You may be lucky enough to see a mob of CAMELS along this stretch of the road or perhaps a THORNY DEVIL.

TO ULURU–KATA TJUTA FROM THE SOUTH (MAP, P.VII)

Two kilometres north of the Northern Territory border on the Stuart Highway from South Australia, you have a choice of two routes to Uluru–Kata Tjuta. They are almost the same distance, but one includes 234 kilometres of rough dirt road.

Via Mulga Park — 333 kilometres

Turn west (left) off the Stuart Highway, 2km north of the border at Mt Cavenagh.

Mount Cavenagh to Mulga Park 167km of rough dirt road through dense 'GROVE MULGA', with occasional glimpses of the EVERARD RANGES along the South Australia/Northern Territory border.

Mulga Park to Curtin Springs 79km running north, 67km of which is dirt. Fine views of MOUNT CONNER, which presents a different face from this perspective. It has a dip in it — a drainage channel which breaks the symmetry of the mesa.

Curtin Springs to Ayers Rock Resort 85km.

Via Erldunda — 339 kilometres (all sealed)

Continue north along the Stuart Highway from the South Australian border to ERLDUNDA ROADHOUSE, 90 kilometres.

Kulgera Roadhouse and Police Station 22 km north of the border on the Stuart Highway. Fuel and refreshments are sold and camping facilities are provided. The original KULGERA HOMESTEAD is part of an historical display adjacent to the roadhouse.

Erldunda Roadhouse 92km north of the border. Turn west (left) to Ayers Rock Resort via Lasseter Highway, 247km.

TO ULURU–KATA TJUTA FROM THE WEST

Visitors travelling to the Centre from Western Australia can go via Warburton and Docker River. This can include the Gunbarrel Highway, built by Len Beadel, and the Giles Weather Station. You require a permit to transit Aboriginal land, from the WA Aboriginal Land Trust in Perth or the Central Land Council in Alice Springs (p.180) before travelling this route.

On this road your entry into the Northern Territory is along the beautiful PETERMANN RANGES. You will see the western face of Kata Tjuta first — a most attractive sight, especially in the late afternoon.

ALICE SPRINGS TO KINGS CANYON (WATARRKA) (MAP, P.VII)

The total distance is 331km. Once you leave the Stuart Highway, 130km south of Alice Springs, and turn west (right) onto the Ernest Giles Road to Watarrka, you will also leave the bitumen sealed road. The dirt road is generally well maintained but can become corrugated. If it rains the road becomes slippery and may be cut by flash flooding in the small creeks or the Palmer River. Kings Canyon is 201km from the Stuart Highway. You can also travel this way to Uluru. Yulara is 308km from the Ernest Giles Road–Stuart Highway intersection, via Luritja Road, and 438km from Alice Springs by the same route.

Points of Interest

(Distances are given in kilometres from the Stuart Highway.)

12km Henbury Meteorite Craters turnoff There are twelve craters, the largest being 180 metres wide and 15 metres deep (Fig. 3.2). They are within a Parks and Wildlife Commission reserve.

35km (approximately) The stark landscape is dominated by sparsely vegetated flat-topped hills which are remnants of ancient land surfaces. The fresh erosional surfaces in this area are especially colourful. MULGA shrublands dominate the hill slopes. From the Stuart Highway to the Luritja Road the Ernest Giles Highway passes through Henbury Station.

51km Palmer River crossing.

57km BLUEBUSH shrubland on the north side of the road. This plant community is common in South Australia but also occurs throughout the southern part of the Northern Territory.

66km Illamurta Springs and Finke River 4WD track turnoff to the north.

81km you are passing through DESERT OAK woodland with dense stands of the young, poplar-like trees (p.68).

102km Luritja Road Turnoff (south) This road is the connection through to Uluru and Erldunda. The Giles Highway is sealed from here to Kings Canyon.

166km Kings Creek Station Camping facilities, fuel and refreshments are available. This station is at the centre of the development of the CAMEL industry in Central Australia. Camels are exported live to the Middle East. For the next 15km to the canyon, you travel through desert oak woodland alongside the GEORGE GILL RANGE to the north.

FIGURE 7.4 Flocks of galahs are a common sight as you travel to Uluru and Watarrka. *M. W. Gillam*

179km Park Headquarters Information, water, toilets and emergency services are provided by the friendly ranger staff.

181.5km Kathleen Springs 2.5km from the Park Headquarters. Water, toilets, walking track (disabled person's standard), picnic and barbecue facilities are provided.

201km Kings Canyon The turnoff is 18km west of the Park Headquarters, then 4km north on a sealed road. Water, toilets, walking track, picnic and barbecue facilities are provided. No special access for people with disabilities.

203km Kings Canyon Resort This is 6km west of the canyon turnoff and 10km from Kings Canyon car park, in a picturesque setting, and overlooks CARMICHAEL CRAG.

FIGURE 7.5 Termite mounds in desert oak woodland on the Mereenie Loop Road. *J. A. Kerle*

WATARRKA TO ULURU–KATA TJUTA (MAP, P.VII)

Total distance 305km. Turning south 101km from Kings Canyon Resort, the Luritja Road runs from the Ernest Giles Road to the Lasseter Highway. It is a high standard sealed road which passes through some very attractive DESERT OAK woodland. The roadside stop 20km south of the Giles Road is an especially pleasant place to look more closely at this plant community. Another 10km further on the road crosses some LIMESTONE RIDGES. If you stop along this road listen for the call of the CRESTED BELL-BIRD, 'panpanpalala' (p.104). The Luritja Road–Lasseter Highway intersection is 167km from the Kings Canyon Resort.

WATARRKA TO GLEN HELEN (MAP, P.VII)

Total distance about 290km. The Mereenie Loop Road follows the GEORGE GILL RANGE to the north-west of Watarrka National Park, climbs over the range and continues north-east and then east, joining the Areyonga road which continues almost to Hermannsberg. This road passes through Aboriginal land so you must obtain a souvenir permit from the Kings Canyon Resort. It is a good quality unsealed road but may be corrugated or slippery depending on the weather conditions. Use of a 4WD vehicle is advisable.

This route passes through some beautiful scenery. As you drive north along the George Gill Range you cross creeks containing rocks riddled with SCOLITHUS WORM casts and pass through desert oak wooded valleys. The views from the top of the range are spectacular. Continuing north, the country varies but is dominated by desert oak woodland with small TERMITE MOUNDS and scattered DESERT KURRAJONGS. You might also see a mob of feral DONKEYS. The multitude of side tracks are evidence of prospecting, primarily for oil and gas throughout this area. Please keep to the main track.

Further north the road swings to the east and follows the GARDINER RANGE. When you reach the Hermannsburg road you have two options.

■ Turn west and visit the GOSSE BLUFF comet impact crater (Fig.3.3), then continue north through TYLERS PASS and join the Haasts Bluff–Alice Springs road. This

FIGURE 7.6 The track in the bed of the Finke River between Running Waters and Boggy Hole. Other sections of the track are much more challenging than this. *M. W. Gillam*

will take you back to Alice Springs through the WEST MACDONNELL NATIONAL PARK, via GLEN HELEN LODGE.

- Turn east and visit the Aboriginal people at the WALLACE ROCKHOLE or at HERMANNSBURG where the old mission buildings are preserved; and PALM VALLEY (4WD only) within FINKE GORGE NATIONAL PARK before returning to Alice Springs.

WATARRKA TO HERMANNSBURG VIA THE FINKE RIVER (MAP, P.VII)

Total distance 234km. This 4WD route takes you through sand dunes along an old survey line on Henbury Station to the Finke River, and enables you to follow one of the paths of the Aboriginal people and, much later, of white settlers. Details of the track and distances are provided in a pamphlet produced by the Parks and Wildlife Commission of the Northern Territory (p.184) and distributed from head offices in Darwin and Alice Springs, and park headquarters at Watarrka and Finke Gorge National Parks. It is 99 kilometres from the Ernest Giles Road through to Hermannsburg, and the track is mostly through sand.

Allow a full day for this drive and check conditions carefully before departure. You must be fully equipped for four-wheel-driving and capable of digging yourself out of a bog. You must carry shovels and tow ropes. Don't travel alone. Even experienced locals can get bogged along this route.

Points of Interest

The Finke River — 680km in total length. This river bisects Central Australia. Mostly it is dry and is part of remarkably striking scenery.

Illamurta Springs Ruins of a police camp and administrative centre established in 1893 (p.134).

Running Waters One of the largest waterholes to be found on the Finke River. An important wetland which also has a couple of specimens of the palms found at Palm Valley.

Boggy Hole Another large, reliable waterhole and the ruins of the Boggy Hole police camp, established in 1889. At this point the Finke River cuts through the JAMES RANGE.

Palm Valley The largest stand of the rare RED CABBAGE PALM *Livistona mariae*, a relict of a much wetter era in Central Australia.

Hermannsburg The restored mission buildings (p.140) within the Aboriginal community are open to visitors.

ULURU–KATA TJUTA: ACCESS ROADS AND WALKS (MAP, P.VI)

Ayers Rock Resort at Yulara Village is a self-contained tourist village. It was originally called Yulara, and the township is still referred to by this name. The resort can accommodate up to 6000 people and is filled to capacity at times during the peak season between May and October.

The resort is planted with many Australian native species which attract a lot of birds, especially WHITE-THROATED MINERS, SPINY-CHEEKED HONEYEATERS and CRESTED PIGEONS (pp.99–102). In the dunes at the centre of the resort and surrounding it you might see HOPPING MICE, SKINKS and MILITARY DRAGONS, or at least their footprints (chapter 5). The little TREE SKINKS (*Cryptoblepharus*), run all over the walls of the buildings. In the camping ground you may also see DINGOES, TORRESIAN CROWS and WILLY WAGTAILS, as well as the HONEYEATERS.

A detailed description of facilities available, including accommodation, services, information and tours, is given in the Appendix. A full range of accommodation is available at the resort, from four-star hotels to backpacker lodges, overnight vans and a camping ground. This is the only accommodation available for the park as camping is not permitted in the park itself. The town centre has a supermarket, newsagency, souvenirs, bank, the Ernest Giles Tavern, public telephones and postal services. There is also a service station with both fuel and repair services, a police station, the Royal Flying Doctor Service and a medical centre.

The resort Visitors Centre contains an interesting display about the park and a useful reference library. Detailed information about the many tours can also be obtained there.

FIGURE 7.7 Yellow-throated miners feeding on honey grevillea. *M. W. Gillam*

AYERS ROCK RESORT TO ULURU (MAP, P.VI)

There are excellent views of Uluru and Kata Tjuta from the Resort even though it is located six kilometres outside the National Park. The road from the resort (still the Lasseter Highway) passes through sand plain and dunes covered with HONEY GREVILLEAS (p.64), WATTLES (p.88) and SPINIFEX (p.66) amongst the DESERT OAKS (p.68).

Park entry station 5km from the resort. An entry fee is collected at this station (p.183).

Sunset viewing area This is a further 9km and is set amongst the dunes. There are HONEY GREVILLEAS, CASSIAS, WATTLES and NATIVE FUSCHIAS (*Eremophila*, p.64). Take time to look around you while waiting for the sun to set; look at the plants and for lizards and footprints in the sand (p.96).

Cultural Centre, Maruku Arts & Crafts and Ininti Kiosk It is well worth stopping to view the display here, particularly for its explanation of the Anangu view of the land. Desert Aboriginal arts and crafts, souvenirs, books and refreshments can be purchased from here.

Ranger Station, adjacent to the Cultural Centre Rangers will provide assistance, answer questions and take bookings (p.183) for ranger guided tours (Liru and Mala walks).

AYERS ROCK RESORT TO KATA TJUTA (MAP, P.VI)

Four kilometres south of the Park Entry Station, the Kata Tjuta road turns off the Lasseter Highway to the west. The road passes mostly through patches of sand dunes (p.64), MULGA, WITCHETTY BUSH and MALLEE shrubland (p.72) from the turnoff to the Kata Tjuta viewing platform. This road also goes to Docker River and Western Australia.

26km from the Lasseter Highway A viewing platform set on top of a sand dune provides a wonderful panorama of Kata Tjuta and DESERT OAK woodland. The many-headed formation of Kata Tjuta, eroded joints (valleys) and the slope of the MOUNT CURRIE CONGLOMERATE beds (p.28) are clearly visible. A variety of sand dune plants surround the platform and walkway, and some good examples of the UPSIDE-DOWN PLANT (p.65) occur around the parking area. Animal footprints of the HOPPING MOUSE (p.65), the MILITARY DRAGON (p.96) and other lizards, can also be seen in the sand.

After leaving the viewing platform car park you pass dense patches of bright green DESERT HEATH MYRTLE (p.65), stands of slender, young desert oaks, patches of large mature desert oaks (p.68), BLUE MALLEE (p.65), MULGA (p.74) and DESERT POPLARS (p.69). The last 8km section crosses the alluvial edge of the outcrop, with mulga and WITCHETTY BUSH (p.76) shrubland and BLOODWOODS along the creeks (p.85).

42km west of the Lasseter Highway is the Docker River Road turnoff.

FIGURE 7.8 Annual yellowtops flourish after winter rains. *J. A. Kerle*

44km from the Lasseter Highway Picnic area. Sunset on Kata Tjuta can be enjoyed from there set back from the outcrop. There will probably be fewer people there than are watching the setting sun at Uluru, and it can be just as beautiful. Picnic shelters and toilets are provided.

46km from the Lasseter Highway Olga Gorge (pp.80, 169) car park.

47km from the Lasseter Highway Valley of the Winds (pp. 81, 169) car park.

WALKS AT ULURU (MAP BELOW)

Without a doubt, the best way to feel the aura of Uluru is to walk around the base. If you haven't the time or energy to walk the whole circuit, then the Mala and Mutitjulu walks are an excellent substitute. Climbing Uluru does not provide the same feeling. It does provide a magnificent view and a sense of achievement, but is against the wishes of the Aboriginal custodians because it ignores the spiritual importance of Uluru and can be dangerous.

FIGURE 7.9 Walks around Uluru: the Circuit, Mala, Mutitjulu and Liru walks

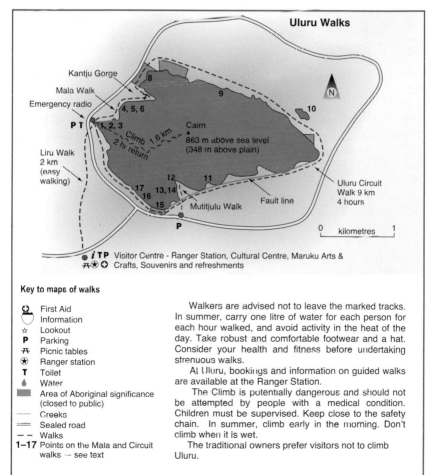

Key to maps of walks

☢	First Aid
◡	Information
☆	Lookout
P	Parking
⛏	Picnic tables
✳	Ranger station
T	Toilet
◖	Water
▬	Area of Aboriginal significance (closed to public)
—	Creeks
═	Sealed road
– –	Walks
1–17	Points on the Mala and Circuit walks — see text

Walkers are advised not to leave the marked tracks. In summer, carry one litre of water for each person for each hour walked, and avoid activity in the heat of the day. Take robust and comfortable footwear and a hat. Consider your health and fitness before undertaking strenuous walks.

At Uluru, bookings and information on guided walks are available at the Ranger Station.

The Climb is potentially dangerous and should not be attempted by people with a medical condition. Children must be supervised. Keep close to the safety chain. In summer, climb early in the morning. Don't climb when it is wet.

The traditional owners prefer visitors not to climb Uluru.

Mala and circuit walks

The full circuit of Uluru is a 9km walk over fairly even ground which can take around three hours. The beginning of the Mala walk is signposted near the climb and this is also a good place to start the circuit walk. The Mala story is told on p. 17.

1 Itjaritjariku Yuu Itjaratjari, the Marsupial Mole, has built herself this shelter and the wedge-shaped stone at the front is the yuu or windbreak.

FIGURE 7.10 Cave art can be seen on the Uluru circuit walk. *J. A. Kerle*

2 Cave paintings (Fig 7.10) These paintings are not a part of the Mala Tjukurpa and, like others you will see around Uluru (such as Fig. 2.10), are difficult to accurately date or interpret. The oldest are probably less than 1000 years old and others have been added within the last 100 years. The meaning of some of the symbols is indicated on the interpretive sign at the cave. The paints used are made from red and yellow ochres, clays stained with iron oxides, white pipeclay and powdered charcoal mixed with water or animal fats.

3 Malaku Wilytja (Figs. 2.16 and 2.17) This cave has been made by Itjaritjari for the Mala women and children waiting for the ceremony. *The women prepare food; the children play happily; they are unaware of Kurpany approaching from the west...*

Malaku Wilytja is also a good place to examine the geological makeup of Uluru (pp.24–27). It is an excellent example of a ground-level cave; the grey surfaces are still being actively weathered. If you look closely at these grey surfaces you can see the very fine sedimentary layers of ULURU ARKOSE as almost vertical stripes in the cave. The older layers are to your left. You can also see the fine grey, green, pink and white grains of the rock. The knobs and ribs projecting from the surface are a slightly harder, more resistant arkose, and should not be confused with the FAIRY MARTIN mudnests which are also on the roof of this cave.

Common plants along the path include PLUMBUSH (p.80) and STICKY HOPBUSH (p.80) and the BLOODWOOD trees. A variety of birds will flit around you, especially in the early morning and late afternoon. You may even see the nocturnal TAWNY FROG-MOUTH (p.167) sitting in a tree.

4 Mala Puta this triangular-shaped cave is the pouch of the female hare-wallaby. It has great spiritual significance and Anangu request that you do not photograph or enter it.

5 Malaku Wilytja This cave is behind a large slab of rock and was made by the Mala women and children. It has long been used by Anangu for sitting and resting in. On the ceiling inside there are marks from the paws of the Mala children. *It is a hive of activity both in and around the cave as everyone excitedly prepares for their ceremony ... no one hears the approach of the devil dingo Kurpany.*

6 Low cave This small, low wilytja is underneath an enormous rock slab. The round holes in the roof have been made by the Mala people to store food for use during the ceremony.

7 Kantju The area around Kantju is especially important to Anangu. They ask that you move quietly and respectfully around here. Kantju is a fairly reliable but not permanent waterhole used by Anangu during their ceremonies. You may see the large tadpoles of the BURROWING FROG swimming in the waterhole or a BLACK-HEADED GOANNA clinging to the rock. There is a vertical fracture in the rock at Kantju Gorge which may have promoted the formation of the gorge.

As you follow the track back out to the road you will pass more caves and the first of the fenced-off sacred sites. The flaky weathering pattern of the surface of Uluru can be clearly seen on the sheer walls.

This is the end of the Mala walk. You can follow the track around the fence to continue the circuit walk.

8 Ngaltawata The ceremonial pole of the Mala men. It has been formed by a topographic joint (p.27).

Along this northern drier side of Uluru the vegetation is more sparse than it is along the southern side. A variety of caves are visible along the northern face. Some, just above ground level, are very large and spectacular. EUROS (hill kangaroos, p.106) occur around these lower caves. There are many honeycomb formations high on the rockface.

FIGURE 7.11 This black-headed goanna was clinging to the rock in Kantju Gorge. *J. A. Kerle*

9 Ininti Waterhole *Lunpa, the kingfisher woman screams out to warn the Mala of the approaching Kurpany, but to no avail.*

10 Taputji This is where Kuniya finally arrived at Uluru after her long journey from the east. It is made up of the oldest sedimentary layers. About 200 metres north-west of Taputji the path crosses a flat rock pavement which is an arkose remnant that has been eroded away (p.24). The large blocks of rock lying around Taputji have resulted from erosion after the formation of a topographic joint.

South of Taputji the track turns to follow the southern face of Uluru. Here the environment is more moist and the valleys are densely vegetated with PLUMBUSH, HOPBUSH and BLOODWOOD trees. Geologists believe that a fault runs along this relatively straight side of Uluru, as shown in map on p.165. EUROS may be seen along this part of the circuit.

FIGURE 7.12 Sharp-eyed observers walking around Uluru may see a tawny frogmouth. *K. A. Johnson*

FIGURE 7.13 Boulders strewn at the base of Uluru near the climb. *M. W. Gillam*

11 Ikari The laughing cave. This is where Tjintirtjintirpa, the willy wagtail woman heard the sound of the Mala ceremonies in the distance and laughed to herself.

12 Mutitjulu The home of Wanampi the ancestral water snake. Although it is not permanent, it is the most reliable of the waterholes around Uluru. Like Kantju, it was an important source of drinking water and it supports FROGS and other wildlife. At night BATS can be heard echo-locating as they feed on insects over the pool and drink from it. The pool was also the water supply for early tourists at Uluru.

13 Living cave This is the first large cave you will pass as you return to the track after visiting Mutitjulu. Anangu camped here close to the waterhole and the smoke from their fires has stained the roof of the cave.

14 Rock art cave Like the art in the cave near the climb, this art is not connected with the Tjukurpa stories. Likely meanings of the symbols are indicated on the interpretive sign.

At this point in the track, it is time to look back and observe the battle between Kuniya and Liru (pp.20–21). On the bluff to the east of the waterhole there is the snake-like scar of Kuniya moving in to strike Liru. Closer to Mutitjulu is a larger darker patch which is where Kuniya ritually dropped sand to control the forces of anger.

On the bluff to the west of Mutitjulu are the two wounds sustained by Liru from Kuniya's strikes (Fig.2.9). As you proceed around the bluff you come to the fallen shield of Liru.

To continue on the circuit track turn off the path to the Mutitjulu car park. Just at that turnoff look up to see the dark green SPEARWOOD bushes high on the slope that were poisoned by Kuniya's rage. The dead BLOODWOOD trees in this area were mostly killed as a result of severe erosion during the 1970s.

15 Bush foods In this area there are BLOODWOOD 'APPLES' (p.86), BUSH PLUMS and FIGS (p.87). PIED BUTCHERBIRDS and GREY SHRIKE-THRUSHES can often be heard singing.

16 Emu meat boulders The track passes between some large boulders which are the emu meat dropped by Lungkata, the blue-tongue lizard, when he was being pursued by the two Panpanpalala (crested bellbird) hunters (p.22).

17 Lungkata's camp The two Panpanpalala caught up with Lungkata as he climbed to his camp. They set a bonfire beneath his camp and killed him. The evidence for this, a large patch of LICHEN, is high on the rockface almost opposite the intersection with the road to the Ranger Station. It is not easily visible from the circuit track.

From this point it is a short distance back to the car park at the climb.

Mutitjulu Walk

This short walk begins from the Mutitjulu car park (it is also a part of the circuit walk). It is well worth spending time here around the caves and at the waterhole. This was an important living area for Anangu; you are surrounded by the Kuniya story from the Tjukurpa (p.19). The features of interest are detailed in the description of the circuit walk.

The Climb

From the car park at the base of the climb to the summit of Uluru and back is 1.6 km and can take two hours or more. If you do decide to climb Uluru, take your time and enjoy the experience because there are no rewards for breaking any speed records. There are several features worth noting.

- To the right of the beginning of the climb are a number of plaques set into the rock. These are memorials to those people who have died in their efforts to complete the climb. The plaques form a sobering reminder of the risks (p.13).
- The large shrub amongst the boulders is a NATIVE FIG tree (p.87). The figs are a desirable source of food both for people and for birds.
- Chicken Rock is at the top of a pile of boulders which have been produced by erosion of the rock, after the formation of a topographic joint (p.27). Do not be ashamed if you decide to abandon the climb at Chicken Rock. This is far enough for many people.
- Lightning scars (p.27) are visible between the two sections of chain. Don't climb in stormy weather!
- Across the top the track wanders up and down over the 'ribs' created by the Two Boys (p.18), which are the more resistant layers of arkose (p.24).
- Puddles — look carefully into any puddles; there may be some SHIELD SHRIMPS there (p.123).
- A few plants grow in pockets of soil on top of Uluru. These include native grasses and small mulgas.

Liru Walk

This ranger-guided tour is so named because it crosses the pathway used by the Liru men on their way to Uluru. The tour is conducted by the Traditional Owners of Uluru, who tell their stories in their own language with minimal interpretation. It is important to book a place as numbers are limited on this very popular tour. It takes about two hours, departing from the Ranger Station.

Your guides provide a fascinating insight into the making of tools and implements, food gathering and some aspects of the Tjukurpa. The making of resin from spinifex is especially fascinating (p.67). The track passes through both regenerating and mature stands of MULGA and provides a very clear view of the Kuniya and Lungkata stories around Mutitjulu.

WALKS AT KATA TJUTA (MAPS PP.171, 81)

Mount Olga Gorge Walk

Mount Olga Gorge is the narrow valley on the northern side of Mount Olga. The track goes directly east from the car park into the gorge. It is a well-constructed track, with walkways and a viewing platform. It climbs over the flared conglomerate slopes and then drops down to the creek. The complete walk takes about one hour for the 2km. There are many points of interest .

As you approach the gorge the layering and slope of the MOUNT CURRIE CONGLOMERATE beds is clearly visible. The beds have a slope of about 15 degrees down to the right and towards the west (p.28).

To begin with, the track crosses the rubbly foothills above the creek, passing through a shrubland with WATTLES, DESERT FUSCHIAS, SILVERTAILS and native grasses.

As you climb on to the slopes of Mount Olga the 'pudding stone' composition of the rock becomes apparent (p.27). Mostly it is stained by the reddish brown iron oxide but freshly weathered rock can be seen in the gullies.

Looking out of the gorge to the west from the highest point on the track, you see a vast, seemingly empty country with a series of ridges on the horizon. These ridges are the mountain ranges that were the source of the sediment for the Mount Currie Conglomerate about 550 million years ago (p. 33)!

FIGURE 7.14 Olga Gorge. *J. A. Kerle*

Just as the track begins to descend into the gorge there are two lenses of greenish epidote-rich sandstone (p.27).

The creek below the track is a beautiful, restful scene, especially if a storm has just passed by and water is trickling over the rock. RIVER RED GUMS and creekside shrubs add to the beauty of the scene.

The track descends to the creek and winds through a dense growth of MOUNT OLGA WATTLES, PLUMBUSH and HOPBUSH.

Further into the gorge the track becomes choked by fallen blocks of conglomerate and a tangle of shrubs. FIGS, SPEARBUSH, PLUMBUSH and HOPBUSH all flourish in the moister microenvironment of these narrow protected valleys (p.82).

Return to the car park along the same path.

Valley of the Winds Walk

This is a very beautiful walk which takes you in amongst the domes of Kata Tjuta. At times it is quite strenuous and you should allow about three hours for the 6km. From the car park the track climbs steadily between the domes to a lookout. This short section is well worth doing even if you are not able to go the whole way. Around the

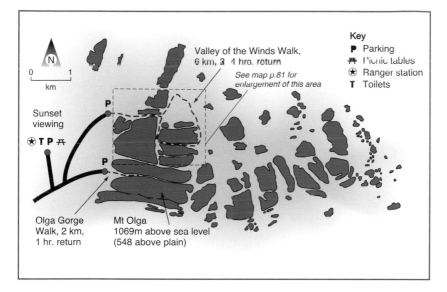

FIGURE 7.15 Walks into Mount Olga Gorge and the Valley of the Winds, Kata Tjuta using the same key as the Uluru Walks, p.165.

circuit there are lots of interesting features (see also the descriptions of the plant communities p.p 80–82).

An emergency radio is located at the beginning of the walk.

From the car park the track wanders over the lower stony slopes of Kata Tjuta through a low open shrubland. This includes DEAD FINISH, BLACK GIDGEA, WITCHETTY BUSHES, MULGA, CASSIAS and NATIVE FUCHSIAS. The taller plants are LONG-LEAFED CORKWOODS, BEEFWOODS and BLOODWOODS, while FOXTAILS, PRICKLE BUSHES and NATIVE GRASSES cover the ground. Look also for the large flat rocks in the conglomerate pavement; these result from the exposed part of the boulder being cracked away (p.28). The EARLESS DRAGON occurs in this habitat but is rarely observed because of its superb camouflage (Fig.7.17).

Further into the domes the vegetation becomes more sparse. There are some large blocks of conglomerate which have fallen from the sides of the domes, and the RESURRECTION FERN grows in pockets of soil tucked under these blocks (p.81).

The lookout is about 1km from the car park and offers a good view to the west of Kata Tjuta and to the east, amongst the domes. The layering of the conglomerate can be clearly seen on the domes to the south of the lookout.

FIGURE 7.16 The Hummocky Grass *Eriachne scleranthoides* on the slopes of Kata Tjuta — a rare species known from only one other location — see p.82. *J. A. Kerle*

FIGURE 7.17 The earless dragon is well camouflaged but it can be seen at Kata Tjuta and Kings Canyon. *J. A. Kerle*

FIGURE 7.18 (below) The perennial yellow-top in the Valley of the Winds. *J. A. Kerle*

FIGURE 7.19 (below) Christmas tree mulga on stony slopes in the Valley of the Winds. *J. A. Kerle*

The track descends steeply from the lookout over a smooth sandstone pavement to a creek lined with RIVER RED GUMS. The sandstone pavement is unusually large for the MOUNT CURRIE CONGLOMERATE. Birds may be specially active along the creek, especially HONEYEATERS.

If there has been enough rain, the EARLY NANCY lilies (p.82) will be flowering along the soggy edges of the creek in spring. In the dry environment on the domes, SPINIFEX and HUMMOCKY GRASS (Fig.7.16) can be seen growing in cracks formed by joints, taking advantage of the accumulation of small amounts of soil and water.

After crossing the creek turn south (right) on to the circuit track and climb the rocky creek. A fascinating variety of low shrubs (for example, INDIGO, ROCK NIGHTSHADE, ROUND-LEAF WATTLE) grow here in the shelter of the domes. PAINTED FIRETAIL FINCHES may come into this creek for a drink.

The track swings to the east (left) and climbs a saddle between two massive domes. The view from the top of the saddle is absolutely spectacular. In front of you are the many heads of Kata Tjuta and behind is the imposing form of the domes, close up.

Below the saddle the track winds through a dense thicket of MOUNT OLGA WATTLE and, possibly, some EARLY NANCY along the creek.

The remainder of the circuit track winds across the footslopes of the domes and is similar to the first section of the track from the car park. Along the northern part of the walk there are some large attractive examples of STICKY HOPBUSHES and PLUMBUSHES (p.80) and some Christmas tree–shaped mulgas.

The circuit track takes you back along the creek and you return to the car park via the lookout.

FIGURE 7.20 Sturt's desert peas are a spectacular part of the wonderful display of local native flowers at the Kings Canyon Resort. *J. A. Kerle*

WATARRKA WALKS (MAP PP.VII AND 176)

All accommodation within Watarrka National Park is restricted to the Kings Canyon Resort. Motel units, a backpacker lodge and an extensive camping ground are available. There is also a tavern, café, restaurant and small supermarket–souvenir shop. Fuel can be purchased (see Appendix).

Information can be obtained from the resort as well as the Park Headquarters at the eastern end of the park.

Some tours are available, including helicopter rides over the canyon and plateau. Kurkara–Kings Canyon Tours, owned and operated by the local Aboriginal community, provides a range of activities including Aboriginal cultural tours, trail rides, sunset viewing, guided walks (including the canyon) and 4WD tours.

The motel units are set between low sandstone ridges and the remainder of the facilities extend into the desert oak woodland. There is a wonderful view of CARMICHAEL CRAG from the camping ground. The resort has been thoughtfully planted with native plants, almost all of which are from the local area. The DESERT PEAS, DESERT ROSES and purple-flowered shrub *Rulingia* are especially attractive when in flower.

MULGA PARROTS and PINK COCKATOOS are frequent visitors and BROWN HONEY-EATERS or MISTLETOE BIRDS are likely to be feeding in the mistletoe-infested mulga trees around the camping ground. PIED BUTCHERBIRDS nest in the desert oaks.

FIGURE 7.21 Crested pigeon, diamond dove and zebra finches coming in to drink; crested pigeons are common around both the Ayers Rock and Kings Canyon Resorts. *K. A. Johnson*

The sandstone around the motel units contains trace fossils of scolithus worms which are 450 million years old (p.40). CAUSTIC VINE, MULGA, WITCHETTY BUSH, UMBRELLA BUSH, DEAD FINISH, MINT BUSH and CASSIAS grow amongst the rocks along with BLOODWOOD, WHITEWOOD and BEEFWOOD trees. DINGOES roam around the resort at night and TREE SKINKS live on the walls of the buildings.

The walks described here are those that have been marked by the Parks and Wildlife Commission. If you wish to explore the beauty of George Gill Range further, the rangers at the Park Headquarters can provide you with advice. You must not, under any circumstances, leave the marked tracks without first obtaining permission from the rangers.

FIGURE 7.22 Bulldog ant nest near the Kings Canyon motel units; these ants have a nasty bite but they generally won't bother you unless you disturb their nests. *J. A. Kerle*

Kathleen Springs Walk (Map p.vii)

This is a very stimulating walk during which you will see a variety of plants, delightful scenery and an interesting interpretation of the Aboriginal and pastoral history of the area. The track is suitable for families and for wheelchairs and takes you to a beautiful rock pool at the base of the range. The return walk of 2.6km takes about one hour, but if you stop to absorb the atmosphere of the waterhole it could take much longer. Water, toilets, picnic tables and gas barbecues are available at the car park.

The car park is set in MULGA shrubland with WITCHETTY BUSH, BLUE MALLEE and ground plants such as PARAKEELYA and SILVERTAILS (p.72).

Kathleen Springs is an important area for Aboriginal people. It is extremely rich in plants and animals which provide a variety of foods, medicines, firewood and materials for implements. This richness is enhanced by the close proximity of the mulga shrubland, rocky ranges and a waterhole. The importance of this area is highlighted by the presence of sacred sites, grinding plates and stones, and rock art. Please show respect.

Quandong Just as the track turns to descend into the creek near the first sign, you can see a QUANDONG tree on the lower side of the track.

Stockyards and watering point The spring was important in the management of cattle in this area (p.145). The signs document the pastoral history. The spring acted as a natural 'trap' for cattle — just as the Aboriginal people had been able to use it for trapping emus and euros.

Sacred ripple rock This is a sign left by the carpet snake ancestor, Inturrkunya, who travelled the gorge, resting at the ripple rock before moving on. The surrounding landscape was modelled by this ancestor.

Along the walk you can see NATIVE TOBACCO, PLUMBUSH, HOPBUSH, RIVER RED GUMS, LEMON-SCENTED GRASS, a huge FIG tree, a variety of birds, euro (hill kangaroo) droppings (p.97) and possibly a EURO itself.

The waterhole supports a lush growth of the rare *Cyclosorus* FERNS amongst the BULRUSHES and PHRAGMITES. There is also a great diversity of invertebrates, the most obvious of these being the blue and red DRAGONFLIES and WATER SCORPIONS. Listen for the calling FROGS. Around the waterhole FIG trees, SPEARBUSHES and WHITE CYPRESS PINES are common.

Kings Creek Walk (Map p.176)

Two walks begin from the Kings Canyon car park. The Kings Creek Walk is the shorter and less strenuous of the two. It follows the creek between the canyon cliffs to a vantage point which has a view of the the cliffs and the dry waterfall at the end of the Garden of Eden. The track winds along the rocky creekbed between shady gums and huge blocks of sandstone that have fallen from the walls of the canyon. Take at least an hour to do the 3km walk (1.5km each way).

There are many interesting plants along this walk, some of importance to Aboriginal people. At the beginning of the track there are BLOODWOOD trees with bloodwood apples, and NATIVE TOBACCO plants on the ground. Further upstream there are tiny purple-flowered PARAKEELYAS, GUINEA FLOWERS, MINTBUSHES with their black and gold grasshoppers, HOLLY GREVILLEAS, CYPRESS PINES and CYCADS amongst the stately RIVER RED GUMS. Up on the cliffs, pencil-like ghost gums hang on to the rocky surface (p.86).

The late afternoon is a good time to sit near the lookout and watch the canyon walls light up as the sun sinks lower in the sky.

FIGURE 7.23 The mint bush is strongly aromatic — this and its distinctively shaped flowers will help you to identify the species. *J. A. Kerle*

FIGURE 7.24 This swamp lily is one of the plant species found in Watarrka National Park which is both rare and a remnant from a much wetter time in the past. *M. W. Gillam*

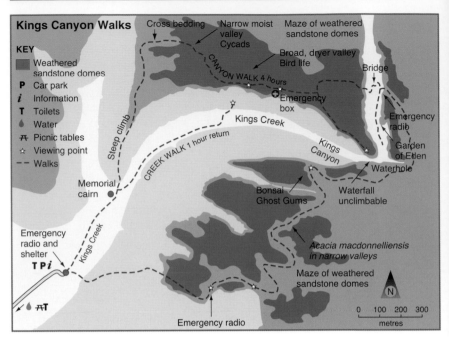

FIGURE 7.25 Walks around the top of Kings Canyon and along Kings Creek, Watarrka National Park

Kings Canyon Walk

This is an absolutely spectacular walk for those who have the time and fitness to do it. The track climbs on to the plateau, wanders between sandstone 'beehive' domes, drops into the Garden of Eden, overlooks the canyon and returns through more bee-hive domes. It is a 6km loop from the Kings Canyon car park and for most enjoyment should take at least three or four hours. It is preferable to walk clockwise around the loop and the track is often rough with some steep, loose rocky sections. Some of the interesting features are highlighted below and the plant commumities are described in more detail on p.83–85.

An emergency radio and a shelter with information panels are located at the beginning of the track.

A memorial cairn to Jack Cotterill who, with his family, was instrumental in enabling tourists to visit Kings Canyon (p.160) is just before the climb on to the range.

The climb A short but steep climb onto the MEREENIE SANDSTONE on top of the range. Stop to admire the view from the MULGA tree halfway up! The surface is quite loose in places so take care while climbing.

The climb takes you on to a spur between two valleys. You might see EUROS on the slopes of the valley to the west in the early morning or late afternoon. Above the climb the shrubs are mostly WATTLES and DESERT FUSCHIAS.

The track is marked with arrows, which are regularly numbered. The numbers run from 1 to 76 and should be used in times of emergency to give an accurate location for an injured person.

Some fine examples of crossbedding (p.31) can be seen to your right soon after the track begins to wind along a narrow 'street' between the beehive domes (near arrows 10 and 12).

The track passes through a narrow cleft where there is enough moisture to support the growth of MACDONNELL RANGES CYCADS (p.89) and GUINEA FLOWERS (near arrow 12).

After passing between more beehives the track enters a broader valley (arrow 17). This contains small branching GUMS, WATTLES (especially *Acacia macdonnelliensis*), CAUSTIC VINE, MINT BUSHES, FIG trees, HOLLY GREVILLEA and SPINIFEX (p.85). It is a good place to stop and look for birds.

The track moves closer to the rim of the canyon about halfway along (arrow 19). There are good views of the redder south wall and of the expanse of country to the south of the George Gill Range.

A second lookout is located near arrow 23. Look carefully at the sandstone pavement in the area for the ripple-marked sandstone and the fast-moving RING-TAILED DRAGON (p.114). The emergency first-aid box is nearby.

Just beyond the emergency box the track forks. Going to the right takes you over a few domes to a lookout above the waterhole and waterfall at the end of the Garden of Eden. You must retrace your steps to continue the circuit walk.

As you walk amongst the dry barren domes, away from the moist cracks and creeklines, you will notice a plant with tiny leaves clinging to the rock. This is Baeckia, one of the few plants that can survive these harsh conditions (p.84).

Close to the top of the Garden of Eden there are a few scattered and stunted WHITE CYPRESS PINES (p.90).

The Garden of Eden An oasis in the desert (p.85). Stairs and a bridge provide access into this valley and reduce environmental damage caused by people scrambling over the rocks. The detour along the valley in the cool moist atmosphere is delightful and well worth the effort. The detour track follows the eastern side of the valley and leaves from the bottom of the stairs.

There is a rich plant life in the Garden of Eden. Along the creek there are the usual RIVER RED GUMS with BOTTLE BRUSHES, WATTLES and FERNS growing at the water's edge. On the sides of the valley there are FIG trees, CYCADS, SPEARBUSES, GHOST GUMS and CYPRESS PINES. This is a plant community which has been protected from fires.

Emergency radio no. 2 is located above the Garden of Eden on the west side.

After climbing back out of the Garden of Eden on to the sandstone plateau the track turns south, crosses a creekline and proceeds to a lookout. This is the best view of the yellowish north wall of the canyon, which looks like butter sliced by a knife.

The 'bonsai' GHOST GUMS are one of the fascinating botanical oddities of the George Gill Range.

FIGURE 7.26 Spearbushes, an important resource for Aboriginal people, grow in Olga Gorge, the Valley of the Winds and the Garden of Eden. *J. A. Kerle*

FIGURE 7.27 A red dragonfly in the Garden of Eden. *M. W. Gillam*

The Ghost Gum(p.86) is a hardy species that grows in quite inhospitable conditions and it is just a low sprawling shrub in this harsh dry environment. You will see some of these gums and also WHITE CYPRESS PINES (p.90) near this last lookout. Keep looking for RING-TAILED DRAGONS.

From the lookout the track wanders amongst the domes and through densely vegetated narrow valleys. Fire-sensitive species such as the CYCAD and the WATTLE *A. macdonnelliensis* are especially abundant.

On some of the beehives you can see the 'whitewash' left by FALCONS and KESTRELS perching and nesting on the ledges (p.101).

Emergency radio no. 3 is located above the final descent.

The descent from the plateau is not as steep as the climb and the track finishes quite close to the car park. Be careful not to slip on the loose stones. Some of the larger blocks have marks left by the paddles of the extinct crab-like cruziana (p.32).

WHERE ELSE TO GO IN CENTRAL AUSTRALIA

Central Australia (see maps on p.vii, 138) contains many more fascinating places which can be visited in addition to Uluru–Kata Tjuta and Watarrka National Parks. In particular, there are the Central Ranges around Alice Springs and the Simpson Desert in the south-east of the Northern Territory.

Alice Springs is now almost surrounded by national parks. To the west is the West MacDonnell Ranges National Park. This contains many magnificent gorges and some spectacular scenery. There is Simpsons Gap, Standley Chasm, Ellery Bighole, Serpentine Gorge, Ormiston Gorge, Glen Helen Gorge and Redbank Gorge. You can visit these places on a day trip from Alice Springs or stay overnight at Ormiston or Glen Helen.

In developing this park the Parks and Wildlife Commission of the Northern Territory has not only provided picnic and camping facilities — there is a bicycle track from Alice Springs to Simpsons Gap and a variety of walking trails have been established. One of the most exciting of these is the Larapinta Trail. Eventually it will extend from the Telegraph Station in Alice Springs to Mount Sonder, about 150 kilometres to the west. It runs along the the top of the MacDonnell Ranges and can be walked in sections.

Finke Gorge National Park also lies to the west of Alice Springs (map, p.vii). This is where you can see the cabbage tree palms which are a remnant from the previous wetter climates of Central Australia. Like the Garden of Eden, Palm Valley is an oasis, which benefits from moisture seeping out of the Mereenie Sandstone. Nearby there is Gosse Bluff and the Aboriginal communities of Ipolera and Hermannsburg which can also be visited.

The East MacDonnell Ranges, to the east of Alice Springs, are different from the West MacDonnells. Geology, topography and vegetation are all a little distinctive. A good way to see this country is to drive the circuit route, but only if it hasn't been raining! This route takes you east to Trephina and N'Dhala Gorges, Ross River, north through the historic Arltunga goldfields, and back to Alice Springs along the south side of the Harts Ranges. Four-wheel-drive enthusiasts can also take the rough detour to the beautiful Ruby Gorge. Although the 'rubies' in this area turned out to be garnets, Arltunga and the Harts Ranges are fantastic for fossicking. You will need to purchase a miner's right beforehand from the NT Department of Mines and Energy.

In Alice Springs itself a huge range of activities are available. These include camel rides and safaris, ballooning, the historical precinct (the Telegraph Station, the original hospital, gaol, courthouse, women's Hall of Fame), museums, a reptile farm and a flora reserve. For anyone interested in the natural environment, a visit to the Desert Wildlife Park is essential. There are also camel rides and safaris.

An easy half-hour drive south of the Alice Springs Airport will take you to the Ewaninga rock carvings. These are a good illustration of the types of Aboriginal petroglyphs found throughout Central Australia. A four-hour drive on the same road will take you through Maryvale Station to Chambers Pillar. (You will need a four-wheel-drive for this trip.) The striking rock formation was important to the Aboriginal people and was a significant landmark for the early white explorers in Central Australia.

Further to the south-east is the Simpson Desert. The 4WD tourist route from Alice Springs to Santa Teresa and Old Andado Station takes you into the sand dunes of this remarkable country. From there you can continue on to Mount Dare, the Dalhousie mound springs and Oodnadatta in northern South Australia.

APPENDIX
BASIC INFORMATION ON ULURU—KATA TJUTA AND WATARRKA

While the information and telephone numbers given are correct at the time of going to press, they are subject to change without notice and no responsibility is taken for any changes. There are many more activities and tour companies than are listed here. Contact Central Australian Tourism, phone 1800 645 199 or (08) 8952 5800, Northern Territory Tourist Commission, phone (08) 8951 8471, or see <www.nttc.com.au> or <www.centralaustraliantourism.com>

ABORIGINAL LAND PERMITS For permits to drive across Aboriginal land, contact the Central Land Council, 31–33 Stuart Highway (PO Box 3321), Alice Springs, NT 0871, phone (08) 8951 6211, <www.clc.org.au>. For Mereenie Loop Road, permits are also available from Information Centre, Alice Springs, (08) 8952 5800 or Kings Canyon, Watarrka National Park, (08) 8956 7442

ACCOMMODATION
Uluru—Kata Tjuta: Ayers Rock Resort, Yulara Village <www.ayersrockresort.com.au>
Central hotel reservations: phone (02) 9339 1040 or 1300 139 889, fax (02) 9332 4555.
Sails in the Desert Hotel ★★★★+
226 rooms, standard twin/double; restaurant, spa/sauna, swimming pool, disabled people's facilities, room service, air-conditioning, private bath/shower.
Desert Gardens Hotel ★★★
100 rooms, standard twin/double; restaurant, guest laundry, swimming pool, disabled people's facilities, room service, air-conditioning, private bath/shower.
Outback Pioneer Hotel ★★★
125 rooms, standard twin/double; restaurant, guest laundry, swimming pool, disabled people's facilities, air-conditioning, some cooking facilities, private bath/shower and communal facilities.
Emu Walk Apartments ★★★+
25 rooms, apartment twin/double, minimum 3 nights stay; guest laundry, air-conditioning, full cooking facilities, private bath/shower.
Lost Camel Hotel ★★★⌐
99 rooms, self-contained; swimming pool; private bath/shower; air-conditioning, some disabled people's facilities.

Watarrka
Kings Canyon Resort ★★★, phone (08) 8956 7442 or 1800 817 622, fax (08) 8956 7426. 70 rooms, twin/double; restaurant, air-conditioning, private bath/shower, tea/coffee facilities.

En route to the Parks
Jim's Place, Stuart's Well, Stuart Highway, 90km south of Alice Springs; phone (08) 8956 0808, fax (08) 8956 0809. Cabins, powered van sites, camping area, fuel, kiosk, public telephone, guest laundry, linen, swimming pool, communal shower/toilet, pets allowed.

Erldunda, Desert Oaks Resort, intersection of Stuart and Lasseter Highways, 200 km south of Alice Springs, 245 kilometres east of Ayers Rock Resort; phone (08) 8956 0984, <www.desertoaksresort.com>. 54 rooms, motel twin/double; air-conditioning, private bath/shower, camping area.

AIRPORTS

Uluru–Kata Tjuta: Connellan Airport: Flight connections with Alice Springs and interstate direct; sightseeing flights, see GUIDED TOURS. Bus connection with Ayers Rock Resort available.

Watarrka: no scheduled flights; some tour flights available, see GUIDED TOURS.

National/International: Alice Springs Airport.

ATTRACTIONS & ACTIVITIES See also GUIDED TOURS
Uluru–Kata Tjuta
Contact the Ayers Rock Resort Tour and Information Centre, phone (08) 8956 2240, fax (08) 8956 2403, for details of attractions, activities and tours. The following is a list of what was available for summer 2001, as a guide only, and all are subject to change without notice. For tours conducted by the park rangers, phone the National Park Cultural Centre (08) 8956 1128.

Watarrka
Local organised tours and activites provided by Kurkara –Kings Canyon Tours.

AUTHORITIES
Uluru–Kata Tjuta
Park authorities/rangers — Parks Australia, PO Box 119, Yulara, NT 0872, phone (08) 8956 2299, fax (08) 8956 2064.
Police — Yulara police station, phone (08) 8956 2166.

Watarrka
Park authorities/rangers — Parks and Wildlife Commission of the Northern Territory, Park Headquarters/Ranger Station, phone (08) 8951 8211, fax (08) 8951 8268. (Postal enquiries to PWCNT Alice Springs regional office — see INFORMATION.)
Police — (08) 8951 8888.

BANKING
Uluru–Kata Tjuta — branch of the ANZ bank is located at Yulara Town Centre with EFT (Electronic Funds Transfer) available for other banks at a fee. The service station in Yulara accepts bank and credit cards.

Watarrka: no banks.

BOOKINGS See Accommodation & camping

BUREAU DE CHANGE Available at Alice Springs Airport, and at banks in Alice Springs and Yulara Town Centre.

BUS & COACH Ayers Rock Resort Shuttle runs a free service between all accommodation sites, Yulara Town Centre and the Visitors Centre at Yulara. There are no other public scheduled services to or from Uluru–Kata Tjuta or Watarrka, though tour companies operate all-inclusive tours from Alice Springs and other national centres.

CAFES

Uluru–Kata Tjuta: located at Yulara Town Centre (takeaway); Ininti Cafe at the Cultural Centre in the Park.

Watarrka: located at Kings Canyon Resort.

CAMPING & CARAVANS

Uluru–Kata Tjuta

Ayers Rock Campground ★★+, phone (08) 8957 7001. On site vans, twin/double; caravans/camping, powered/unpowered sites; kiosk, public telephone, pets allowed. Swimming pool, disabled people's facilities, linen, guest laundry, barbecue facilities. No camping is allowed at any other site within the National Park.

Watarrka

Kings Canyon Resort, phone (08) 8956 7442, or 1800 817 622, fax (08) 8956 7426; powered and unpowered sites; good facilities, guest laundry, swimming pool. No camping is allowed at any other site within the National Park.

Kings Creek Station Camping Ground, phone (08) 8956 7474, fax (08) 8956 7468, <www.kingscreekstation.com.au>, unpowered sites for camping, communal toilet and laundry; fuel, kiosk, public telephone, pets allowed. Powered sites also available.

Along Lasseter Highway

Mount Ebenezer Caravan Park, 58km west of Erldunda, 187km east of Ayers Rock Resort, phone (08) 8956 2904, fax (08) 8956 2801. Eight rooms, powered van sites, camping area; fuel, kiosk, public telephone, restaurant, communal shower/toilet, pets allowed.

Curtin Springs, 85km east of Yulara, phone (08) 8956 2906. Camping area, including rooms and cabins, with communal facilities.

CAR PARKS See maps pp.vi–vii, 166, 171, 176.

CAR RENTAL Companies can be found at Yulara and Alice Springs.

CAR REPAIRS See Motoring Facilities

CLOTHING & EQUIPMENT See chapter 7 pp.154–55.

DISABILITIES See chapter 7. Suitable walks for those confined to wheelchairs are: *Uluru–Kata Tjuta:* Mala Walk, Circuit Walk, Mutitjulu Walk, Liru Walk, Olga Gorge Walk.

Watarrka: Kathleen Springs Walk.

DISTANCES   Alice Springs to Ayers Rock Resort: 447 kilometres; Ayers Rock Resort to Uluru: 19 kilometres; Ayers Rock Resort to Kata Tjuta: 55 kilometres. Alice Springs to Kings Canyon Resort: 331 kilometres; Ayers Rock Resort to Kings Canyon Resort: 305 kilometres; Kings Canyon to Kings Canyon Resort: 10 kilometres. For other distances see the maps on pp.vi–vii.

DOCTOR   See HEALTH SERVICES

EMERGENCIES   Yulara (Uluru–Kata Tjuta) has police, ambulance and fire stations, and a flying doctor base; ring 000 in case of emergencies or see POLICE, FIRE, and HEALTH SERVICES for their direct numbers. Emergency radios are located on the Valley of the Winds Walk at Kata Tjuta and on the Kings Canyon Walks at Watarrka. No other emergency services are located at Watarrka; contact the park rangers or dial 000 in case of emergency.

ENTRY FEE   A park entry fee of $25 per adult (free to children under 16) (covering a period of 3 days) is payable at the Uluru–Kata Tjuta Park Entrance Station, and is correct at the time of going to press.

FIRE   Dial 000 for emergencies, or (08) 8951 6688 for Alice Springs fire service. Yulara fire station telephone number is (08) 8956 2355. Report bush fires to the fire service or to the park rangers.

FUEL   See MOTORING FACILITIES

GAS   Camping gas is available at the service stations at Yulara and Kings Canyon Resort.

GUIDED TOURS   See also ATTRACTIONS & ACTIVITIES. Only details of local operators are given below. Travel agents, tour operators and holiday companies nationwide can also make bookings, or may operate their own tours.

Uluru – Kata Tjuta
The following local tours/tour companies were operational in 2005. Information on bookings is available through the Visitors Centre or through your accommodation.

- Anangu Tours — with experienced Aboriginal guides. <www.ananguwaii.com.au>
- Guide Services — available in English and six other languages. Book through Ayers Rock Resort Visitors Centre.
- Frontier Camel Tours, 1800 806 499 or (08) 8953 0444, fax (08) 8955 5015
- Uluru Motor Cycle Tours.
- Scenic Flights — Ayers Rock Air Services, Rockayer, Air North.
- Helicopter flights — Ayers Rock Helicopters, Professional Helicopter Services.
- Uluru Experience Tours — small group tours and Ayers Rock Observatory.
- AAT King's Tours, Alice Springs; VIP Tours. <www.aatkings.com.au>
- Sunworth Taxi.

Watarrka
- Kurkara–Kings Canyon Tours, 1800 817 622, or (08) 8956 7442. See chapter 7.
- Scenic flights and tours: Ayers Rock Scenic Flights (08) 8956 2345.
- Helicopter flights: Professional Helicopter Services, (08) 8956 2003.

HEALTH SERVICES   A Medical Centre is located at Yulara Village, phone (08) 8956 2286. No other health services are available. In Alice Springs the full range of health services are to be found; Alice Springs Hospital, phone (08) 8951 7777.

INFORMATION

Northern Territory
- ◘   Central Australian Tourism Industry Association (CATIA), Hartley Street, Alice Springs, NT 0870, phone (08) 8952 5800, fax (08) 8953 0295.
- ◘   Parks and Wildlife Commission of the Northern Territory (PWCNT), South Stuart Highway (PO Box 1120), Alice Springs, NT 0871, phone (08) 8951 8250, fax (08) 8951 8290.

Uluru–Kata Tjuta
- ◘   Ayers Rock Resort Tour and Information Centre— see ATTRACTIONS & ACTIVITIES.
- ◘   Ranger Station (Park Headquarters) and Cultural Centre located at Uluru — see AUTHORITIES.

Watarrka
- ◘   Kings Canyon Resort, phone 1800 817 622, (08) 8956 7442.
- ◘   Ranger Station/Park Headquarters, phone (08) 8956 7460, fax (08) 8956 7451.

MOTORING FACILITIES   The Automobile Association of the Northern Territory (AANT) provides roadside assistance to its members and those of affiliated road services — Alice Springs office, phone (08) 8952 1087. For emergency roadside service telephone Alice Springs (08) 8952 1087, Yulara (08) 8956 2188.

Uluru–Kata Tjuta
Ayers Rock Autos (Mobil service station) at Yulara Village, phone (08) 8956 2188. After hours phone (08) 8956 2052 (AANT). Petrol, diesel, LP gas and cooking LP gas are available, with full driveway and repair service and vehicle recovery.

Watarrka
Fuel and LP gas are available at the Kings Canyon Resort service station — no repair service available.

OVERSEAS VISITORS   See also TIME ZONE

Here are some points to keep in mind. First, remember that the seasons are the opposite of those in the northern hemisphere; see chapter 3 pp.42–50 for details.

Remember too that Australians drive on the *left-hand side* of the road (our cars have their steering wheel on the right-hand side). Be very careful, whenever you step on to a road, to look first to your *right*. Also, if you come from a small country you may find our distances are a bit daunting. Don't let this worry you — but ensure, if you are driving here, that you take plenty of rests to break up the trip.

Australia also operates on metric weights and measures. The following *approximations* might prove useful: 1 kilometre is about 0.6 of a mile; 30 centimetres is about one foot; 1 metre (100 centimetres, 1000 millimetres) is 39 inches, i.e. just over one yard; temperatures are quoted in Centigrade not Fahrenheit: 100°F is about 39°C; 32°F is 0°C.

Make sure you read chapter 7 concerning clothing and safety in a harsh environment. And if you do need help in an emergency, remember that on Australian phones the emergency number is 000.

PARK DATA

Uluru–Kata Tjuta

Area of the park: 1325 square kilometres.

Weather: annual average rainfall: 330mm (range 82–935mm); average maximum temperature: 36°C January, 22°C July; average minimum temperature: 21°C January, 4°C July. See also chapter 3 pp.46–48.

Uluru (Ayers Rock) Dimensions: 348 metres above the plain; 867 metres above sea level; 9.4 kilometres in circumference.

Kata Tjuta (Mount Olga) Dimensions: 546 metres above ground level; 36 domes covering 35 square kilometres; 24 kilometres in circumference.

Watarrka

Area of the park: 722 square kilometres

Weather (Tempe Downs): annual average rainfall: 248mm (range 41–980mm); average maximum temperature: 37°C January, 21°C July; average minimum temperature: 21°C January, 2°C July.

Elevation: Carmichael Crag: 908 metres above sea level; Kings Creek: 650 metres above sea level; Canyon walls: 100–150 metres above the creek.

POLICE Police stations are located at Yulara Village, phone (08) 8956 2166 and at Alice Springs, phone (08) 8951 8888, fax (08) 8951 8877.

POST OFFICE A post office is located at Yulara Village. In Watarrka there is a post office at the Kings Canyon Resort. Otherwise Alice Springs is the only location for post offices.

RAINFALL See PARK DATA and chapter 3 pp.46–48.

RANGERS (PARK) See AUTHORITIES

RESTAURANTS See CAFES. Hotels listed under ACCOMMODATION also operate restaurants.

SOUVENIRS

Uluru–Kata Tjuta: Ininti Cafe and Souvenirs: 7.00 a.m. to 5.15 p.m., every day except Christmas Day; phone (08) 8956 2214; Maraku Arts and Crafts Gallery, (08) 8956 2558. Other shops are located at Yulara Town Centre.

Watarrka: A souvenir shop is located at Kings Canyon Resort.

SUPERMARKET Located at Yulara Town Centre and at Kings Canyon Resort.

SWIMMING See ACCOMMODATION and CAMPING.

TAKEAWAY FOOD Available in Yulara Village.

TAXI Ayers Rock Resort (Uluru–Kata Tjuta) only: Uluru Express, shuttle bus for Ayers Rock and the Olgas, phone (08) 8956 2152. <www.uluruexpress.com.au>

TELEPHONE   Public telephones are located at Yulara Town Centre and Camping Ground, and at Kings Canyon Resort Camping Ground.

TEMPERATURES   See PARK DATA

TIME ZONE   Central Standard Time — half an hour later than Eastern Standard Time and 1.5 hours earlier than Western Standard Time. No daylight saving in summer.

TIMING OF VISIT   See p.153.

TOILETS   See maps of the parks and walks.

TOURIST INFORMATION   See INFORMATION and ATTRACTIONS & ACTIVITIES

TOURS   See GUIDED TOURS

TRANSPORT   See BUS & COACH, CAR RENTAL, GUIDED TOURS and TAXI

FURTHER READING

Aboriginal Communities of the Northern Territory of Australia 1988 *Traditional Bush Medicines: An Aboriginal Pharmacopoeia* Greenhouse Publications: Melbourne

Archer, M., Hand, S.J. and Godthelp, H. 1991 *Riversleigh: The Story of Animals in Ancient Rainforests of Inland Australia* Reed: Sydney

Australian National Parks and Wildlife Service 1992 *Uluru National Park: Tour Operator Workbook* published and distributed by ANPWS: Uluru

Baynes, A. and Baird, R F., 1992 'The original mammal fauna and some information on the original bird fauna of Uluru National Park, Northern Territory' *Rangelands Journal* vol. 14 no. 2 pp.92–106

Blackwell, D. and Lockwood, D. 1965 *Alice on the Line* Rigby: Sydney

Brookfield, M. 1970 *Winds of Central Australia* Technical Bulletin 30, CSIRO Division of Land Use Research

Chewings, C. 1930 'A journey from Barrow Creek to Victoria River' *Geographical Journal* (London) vol. 76 pp.316–38

Cogger, H.G. 1992 *Reptiles and Amphibians of Australia* 5th edition, Reed: Sydney

Cogger, H.G. and Cameron, E.E. (eds) 1984 *Arid Australia* Australian Museum and Surrey Beatty & Sons: Sydney

Davey, Keith 1983 *Our Arid Environment: Animals of Australia's Desert Regions* Reed: Sydney

Davis, J.A., Harrington, S.A. and Friend, J.A. (1993) 'Invertebrate communities of relict streams in the arid zone: the George Gill Range, Central Australia' *Australian Journal of Marine and Freshwater Research* vol. 44 pp.483–505

Ellyard, David 1993 *Astronomy of the Southern Sky: A Guide to Observing and Understanding the Wonders of the Southern Sky* Collins Eyewitness Handbooks, Harper Collins: Sydney

Finlayson, H. H. 1936 *The Red Centre. Man and Beast in the Heart of Australia* Angus & Robertson: Sydney

Friedel, M.H., Foran B.D. and Stafford Smith, D.M. 1990 'Where the creeks run dry or ten feet high: pastoral management in arid Australia' *Proceedings of the Ecological Society of Australia* vol. 16 pp.185–94.

Giles, E. 1889 *Australia Twice Traversed: The romance of exploration, being a narrative compiled from the journals of five exploring expeditions into and through Central South Australia and Western Australia from 1872 to 1876* Volumes I (320pp) and II (363pp); Sampson Low, Marston, Searle and Rivington: London, facsimile reprint, Macarthur Press: Sydney

Gosse, F. 1981 *The Gosses: An Anglo-Australian Family* Brian Clouston: Canberra

Greenslade, P.J.M. 1979 *A Guide to the Ants of South Australia* South Australian Museum: Adelaide

Groom, A. 1952 *I Saw a Strange Land* Angus & Robertson: Sydney

Harney, W.F. 1963 *To Ayers Rock and Beyond* Robert Hale: London

Harney, W.F. 1990 *A Bushman's Life: An Autobiography* Viking O'Neil: Melbourne

Institute for Aboriginal Development 1985 *Punu: Yankunytjatjara Plant Use* Angus & Robertson: Sydney

Isaacs, J. 1987 *Bush Food: Aboriginal Food and Herbal Medicine* Weldon: Sydney

Jacobson, G., Calf, G.E., Jankowski, J. and McDonald P.S. 1989 'Groundwater chemistry and palaeodrainage in the Amadeus Basin, Central Australia' *Journal of Hydrology* vol. 109 pp.237–66

Jessop, J. (ed) 1981 *Flora of Central Australia* Reed: Sydney

Johannsen, K. G. 1992 *A Son of 'The Red Centre'* published by K. Johannsen, Morphettville, SA

Johnson, K.A. and Southgate, R.I. 1990 'Present and former status of bandicoots in the Northern Territory' in *Bandicoots and Bilbies* (eds J.H. Seebeck, P. R. Brown, R L. Wallis and C M. Kemper) Surrey Beatty & Sons: Sydney

Kerle, J.A., Foulkes, J.N., Kimber, R.G. and Papenfus, D. 1992 'The decline of the Brushtail Possum Trichosurus vulpecula (Kerr 1798) in arid Australia' *Rangelands Journal* vol. 14 no. 2 pp.107–27.

Kimber, R.G. 1986 *Man from Arltunga: Walter Smith Australian Bushman* Hesperian Press: WA

King, M., Horner, P. and Fyfe, G. 1988 'A new species of Ctenotus (Reptilia: Scincidae) from Central Australia and a key to the Ctenotus leonhardii species group' *The Beagle* (Records of the Northern Territory Museum of Arts and Science) vol. 5 no. 1 pp.147–53

King, Peter 1984 *Plant Identikit: Common Plants of Central Australia* Conservation Commission of the Northern Territory

King, P. and O'Neill, G. 1985 *Wildlife Indentikit: Common Animals of Central and Arid Australia* Conservation Commission of the Northern Territory

Lester, Yami 1993 *Yami: The Autobiography of Yami Lester* Institute for Aboriginal Development Publications: Alice Springs

Low, W.A. et al. 1978 *The physical and biological features of Kunoth Paddock in Central Australia* Division of Land Resources Management, Technical Paper No. 4, CSIRO: Australia

Meredith, P. 1990 'The wedge-tailed eagle: majestic symbol of our inland sky' *Australian Geographic* vol. 17 pp.60–81.

Morton, S.R. 1990 'The impact of European settlement on the vertebrate animals of arid Australia: a conceptual model' *Proceedings of the Ecological Society of Australia* vol. 16 pp.201–13

Mountford, C.P. 1948 *Brown Men and Red Sand* Angus & Robertson: Sydney

Mountford, C.P. 1965 *Ayers Rock: Its People, Their Beliefs, and Their Art* Angus & Robertson: Sydney

Mulvaney, D.J. 1989 *Encounters in Place: Outsiders and Aboriginal Australians 1606–1985* University of Queensland Press: Queensland

Perry, R.A. (ed) 1962 *General Report on Lands of the Alice Springs Area, Northern Territory, 1956–57* Land Research Series No. 6, CSIRO: Melbourne

Pope, E.C. 1967 'When the rains come' in *A Treasury of Australian Wildlife* (ed. D.F. McMichael) Ure Smith: Sydney

Reid, J. and Fleming, M. 1992 'The conservation status of birds in arid Australia' *Rangelands Journal* vol. 14 no. 2 pp.65–91

Reid, J.R.W., Kerle, J.A. and Morton, S.R. 1993 *Uluru Fauna: The Distribution and Abundance of Vertebrate Fauna of Uluru (Ayers Rock–Mount Olga) National Park, NT* Kowari 4, ANPWS: Canberra

Russell, A. 1934 *A Tramp-royal in Wild Australia: 1928–1929* Jonathon Cape: London

Sattler, P.S. (ed) 1986 *The Mulga Lands* Proceedings of a symposium, published by the Royal Society of Queensland: Brisbane

Saxon, E.C. (ed) 1984 *Anticipating the Inevitable: A patch-burn Strategy for Fire Management at Uluru (Ayers Rock–Mt Olga) National Park* CSIRO: Melbourne

Schodde, R. and Tidemann, S.C. (eds) 1986 *Reader's Digest Complete Book of Australian Birds* 2nd edition, Reader's Digest Books: Sydney

Slater, P., Slater, P. and Slater, R. 1986 *The Slater Field Guide to Australian Birds* Rigby: Sydney

Smith, M.A. 1987 'Pleistocene occupation in arid Central Australia' *Nature* vol. 328 pp.710–11

Spencer, B. (ed) 1896 *Report on the Work of the Horn Scientific Expedition to Central Australia; Part I: Introduction, Narrative, Summary of Results and Supplement to Zoological Report* Melville, Mullen & Slade: Melbourne

Stevens, C. 1990 'Afghan cameleers' *Australian Geographic* vol. 20 pp.98–111

Strahan, R. (ed) 1983 *The Australian Museum Complete Book of Australian Mammals* Angus & Robertson: Sydney

Sweet, I.P. and Crick, I.H. 1992 *Uluru and Kata Tjuta: A Geological History* Australian Geological Survey Organisation: Canberra

Taylor, S.G. and Shurcliff, K.S. 1983 'Ecology and management of Central Australian mountain ranges' *Proceedings of the Ecological Society of Australia* vol. 12 pp.27–34

Terry, M. 1932 *Untold Miles: Three Gold-hunting Expeditions Among the Picturesque Borderland Ranges of Central Australia* Selwyn & Blount: London

Thompson, B.G. 1989 *A Field Guide to Bats of the Northern Territory* Conservation Commission of the Northern Territory: Darwin

Thompson, R.B. 1991 *A Guide to the Geology and Landforms of Central Australia* Northern Territory Geological Survey, NT Government Printer: Alice Springs

Tyler, M. 1985 *Frogs of the Northern Territory* Conservation Commission of the Northern Territory: Alice Springs

Uluru Kata Tjuta Board of Management and Australian National Parks and Wildlife Service 1986 *Uluru (Ayers Rock–Mount Olga) National Park plan of management* AGPS: Canberra

Urban, A. 1990 *Wildflowers and Plants of Central Australia* Southbank Editions: Melbourne

van Oosterzee, Penny 1991 *The Centre: A Natural History of Australia's Desert Regions* Reed: Sydney

van Oosterzee, P. and Morton, S.R. 1991 *Exploring Nature in the Deserts* Australian Museum Young Naturalist Series, Reed: Australia

Vickers-Rich, P. and Rich, T.H. 1993 *Wildlife of Gondwana* Reed: Sydney

Warner, L. 1986 *Stars and Planets of the Southern Hemisphere* Angus & Robertson: Sydney

Wilson, B.A., Brocklehurst, P.S., Clark, M.J. and Dickinson, K.J.M. 1990 *Vegetation Survey of the Northern Territory, Australia: Explanatory Notes to Accompany 1:1,000,000 Map Sheets* Technical Report No. 49, Conservation Commission of the Northern Territory

York Main, B. 1976 *Spiders* Australian Naturalist Library, Collins: Sydney

ENDNOTES

Chapter 1
1. J. R. W. Reid, J. A. Kerle and S. R. Morton 1993 *Uluru Fauna: The Distribution and Abundance of Vertebrate Fauna of Uluru (Ayers Rock–Mount Olga) National Park, NT* Kowari 4, ANPWS: Canberra, p.85
2. H. H. Finlayson, 1936 *The Red Centre: Man and Beast in the Heart of Australia* Angus & Robertson: Sydney. p.48
3. B. Spencer, 1896 *Report on the Work of the Horn Scientific Expedition to Central Australia; Part I: Introduction, Narrative, Summary of Results and Supplement to Zoological Report* Melville, Mullen & Slade. Melbourne, p.66
4. Alan Breaden in A. Russell, 1934 *A Tramp-royal in Wild Australia: 1928–1929* Jonathon Cape. London, p.142
5. W. C. Gosse in F. Gosse, 1981 *The Gosses: An Anglo Australian Family* Brian Clouston: Canberra, p.120
6. A. Groom, 1952 *I Saw a Strange Land* Angus & Robertson: Sydney, p.160
7. A. Groom, 1952 *see note 6 above*, p.173
8. E. Giles, 1889 *Australia Twice Traversed: The romance of exploration, being a narrative compiled from the journals of five exploring expeditions into and through Central South Australia and Western Australia from 1872 to 1876* Volumes I (320pp) and II (363pp), Sampson Low, Marston, Searle and Rivington: London, facsimile reprint, Macarthur Press: Sydney, p.100
9. E. Giles, 1889 *see note 8 above*, p.190
10. A. Groom, 1952 *see note 6 above*, p.171
11. A. Groom, 1952 *see note 6 above*, p.157
12. H. H. Finlayson, 1936 *see note 2 above*, p.42
13. A. Groom, 1952 *see note 6 above*, pp.132–3

Chapter 2
1. A. Groom, 1952 *see note 6 chapter 1*, p.164
2. H. H. Finlayson, 1936 *see note 2 chapter 1*, p.47
3. B. Spencer, 1896 *see note 3 chapter 1*, p.66

Chapter 3
1. W. E. Harney, 1990 *A Bushman's Life: An Autobiography* Viking O'Neil: Melbourne, p.184
2. W. E. Harney, 1963 *To Ayers Rock and Beyond* Robert Hale: London, p.55
3. Billy Marshall Stoneking, 1990 *Singing the Snake* Harper Collins: Sydney, p.53

Chapter 4
1. H. H. Finlayson, 1936 *see note 2 chapter 1*, p.31
2. B. Spencer, 1896 *see note 3 chapter 1*, p.84
3. C. Chewings, 1930 'A journey from Barrow Creek to Victoria River' *Geographical Journal* (London) vol. 76, p.317
4. H. H. Finlayson, 1936 *see note 2 chapter 1*, p.16
5. E. Giles, 1889 *see note 8 chapter 1*, p.113

Chapter 6
1. E. Giles, 1889 *see note 8 chapter 1*, p.97

APPENDIX 2
SPECIES LISTS & INDEX

For the animals except the invertebrates, all the species found in the park are listed here, in taxonomic order by common names. Alternative common names are given in brackets. Those species covered in this book have page numbers following. Scientific names are given for the animals except the birds, where space does not allow it.

For the invertebrates, common names only of those in the book are given within taxonomic groupings, and in most cases the names do not refer to actual species, since identification to species level is difficult, and many invertebrates are undescribed.

For the plants, space only allows a list of those covered in this book, in alphabetical order of common names within groups based on growth habit; scientific names follow.

Page numbers in bold type refer to illustrations. The letters U, W, E refer to species being present in Uluru-Kata Tjuta (U) and Watarrka (W), or now being extinct (E) in the parks.

The species are listed in this sequence:

Birds — below
Mammals — p.191
Frogs — p.192

Lizards — p.192
Snakes — p.193
Invertebrates — p.193

Plants — p.194

BIRDS

Emu U,W 22, 95, **97**, 100, 168, 174
Great-crested Grebe U
Hoary-headed Grebe U,W
Australasian Grebe U,W
Australian Pelican U
Darter U
Great Cormorant U,W
Pied Cormorant U
Little Black Cormorant U
Little Pied Cormorant U
White-necked Heron U,W 100
White-faced Heron U,W 100
Great Egret U,W
Little Egret U
Intermediate Egret U
Nankeen Night Heron U,W
Black Bittern U,W
Glossy Ibis U
Australian White Ibis U
Straw-necked Ibis U,W
Royal Spoonbill U,W
Yellow-billed Spoonbill U,W
Plumed Whistling Duck U
Black Swan U
Pacific Black Duck U,W 102

Grey Teal U,W 102
Pink-eared Duck U,W 102
Australian Wood Duck U,W
Black-shouldered Kite U,W
Letter-winged Kite U
Black Kite U,W 52, **100**
Square-tailed Kite U
Black-breasted Buzzard U,W
Whistling Kite U,W 100
Brown Goshawk U,W
Collared Sparrowhawk U
Wedge-tailed Eagle U,W 52, 56, 95, 99, 100, 102–103, **103**
Little Eagle U,W
Spotted Harrier U,W
Black Falcon U 158
Peregrine Falcon U,W 100, 101
Australian Hobby U,W 101
Grey Falcon U 101
Brown Falcon U,W 99, 100, 101
Nankeen Kestrel U,W 8, 100, 101, 178
Mallee Fowl U 99
Little Button-quail U,W

Black-tailed Native Hen U,W 100
Purple Swamphen U
Eurasian Coot U
Australian Bustard U,W 97, 103–104, **103**
Bush Stone-curlew U,W
Masked Lapwing U,W
Banded Lapwing U,W
Red-kneed Dotterel U 102
Oriental Plover U
Red-capped Plover U 102
Black-fronted Dotterel U,W 100, 102
Inland Dotterel U
Black-winged Stilt U 100
Banded Stilt U
Red-necked Avocet U
Wood Sandpiper U
Common Sandpiper U
Greenshank U
Marsh Sandpiper U
Great Knot U
Sharp-tailed Sandpiper U
Red-necked Stint U
Broad-billed Sandpiper U
Oriental Pratincole U

PLANTS

The plants are divided into groups in this sequence: grasses, herbs, shrubs, shrubs or trees, trees, vines and creepers, water plants, parasitic plants, ferns, and other.

GENERAL INDEX

Entries in bold refer to illustrations and maps. Individual species are covered in the preceding index, but groups of animals and plants are included here.